Forbidding Wrong in Islam
An Introduction

Michael Cook's massive study in Islamic ethics, *Commanding Right and Forbidding Wrong in Islamic Thought*, was published to much acclaim in 2001. It was described by one reviewer as a masterpiece. In that book, the author reflected on the Islamic injunction, incumbent on every Muslim, to forbid wrongdoing. The present book is a short, accessible survey of the same material. Using anecdotes and stories from Islamic sources to illustrate the argument, Cook unravels the complexities of the subject. Moving backwards and forwards through time, he demonstrates how the past informs the present. By the end of the book, the reader will be familiar with a colourful array of characters from Islamic history ranging from the celebrated scholar Ghazzālī, to the caliph Hārūn al-Rashīd, to the Āyatullāh Khumaynī. The book educates and entertains. At its heart, however, is an important message about the Islamic tradition, its values, and the relevance of those values today.

Michael Cook is Cleveland E. Dodge Professor of Near Eastern Studies, Department of Near Eastern Studies, Princeton University. His publications include *Early Muslim Dogma* (1981), *The Koran: A Very Short Introduction* (2000), and *Commanding Right and Forbidding Wrong in Islamic Thought* (2001).

THEMES IN ISLAMIC HISTORY comprises a range of titles exploring different aspects of Islamic history, society and culture by leading scholars in the field. Books are thematic in approach, offering a comprehensive and accessible overview of the subject. Generally, surveys treat Islamic history from its origins to the demise of the Ottoman empire, although some offer a more developed analysis of a particular period, or project into the present, depending on the subject-matter. All the books are written to interpret and illuminate the past, as gateways to a deeper understanding of Islamic civilization and its peoples.

Editorial adviser: Patricia Crone, Institute for Advanced Study, Princeton

Already published:
Chase F. Robinson, *Islamic Historiography*
0 521 62081 3 hardback
0 521 62936 5 paperback

Jonathan P. Berkey, *The Formation of Islam: Religion and Society in the Near East, 600–1800*
0 521 58214 8 hardback
0 521 58813 8 paperback

Forbidding Wrong in Islam

An Introduction

MICHAEL COOK
Princeton University

CAMBRIDGE
UNIVERSITY PRESS

CAMBRIDGE UNIVERSITY PRESS
Cambridge, New York, Melbourne, Madrid, Cape Town, Singapore, São Paulo

Cambridge University Press
The Edinburgh Building, Cambridge CB2 8RU, UK

Published in the United States of America by Cambridge University Press, New York

www.cambridge.org
Information on this title: www.cambridge.org/9780521536028

First published 2003
Reprinted 2007

Printed in the United Kingdom at the University Press, Cambridge

A catalogue record for this publication is available from the British Library

National Library of Australia Cataloguing in Publication data

Cook, M. A. (Michael Allan), 1940–.
Forbidding wrong in Islam: an introduction.
Bibliography
Includes index.
ISBN 0 521 82913 5 hardback
ISBN 0 521 53602 2 paperback
1. Islamic ethics. 2. Religious life – Shīʿah. 3. Religious life – Islam.
4. Islam – Doctrines. I. Title. 297.5

ISBN-13 978-0-521-82913-7 hardback
ISBN-13 978-0-521-53602-8 paperback

Contents

Preface		*page* xi
Map		xiii
1	**Introduction**	1
	1 Terminology	3
	2 Religious allegiances	5
	3 Sources	7
2	**The elements of the duty of forbidding wrong**	11
	1 Why?	11
	2 Who?	13
	3 To whom?	21
	4 About what?	22
3	**How is wrong to be forbidden?**	27
	1 With the tongue	28
	2 With the hand	29
	3 Recourse to the heart	35
	4 Are there other ways to forbid wrong?	38
	5 Concluding remarks	42
4	**When is one unable to forbid wrong?**	45
	1 The conditions of obligation	45
	2 The efficacy condition	48
	3 The side-effects condition	51
	4 The danger condition	53
5	**What about privacy?**	57
	1 The immunity of hidden wrongs	57
	2 Don't expose a respectable Muslim	61
	3 Concluding remarks	62

6 The state as an agent of forbidding wrong 65
1 The claims of the state to forbid wrong 65
2 The scholars on the role of the state: positive views 68
3 The scholars on the role of the state: negative views 70

7 The state as an agent of wrongdoing 73
1 The misdeeds of rulers 73
2 Rebuking rulers as forbidding wrong 74
3 Rebellion as forbidding wrong 79

8 Is anyone against forbidding wrong? 83
1 Does anyone deny the duty outright? 84
2 Has the future already arrived? 86
3 What do the Ṣūfīs have to say? 88
4 ᶜAbd al-Ghanī al-Nābulusī 91
5 Minding one's own business 93
6 Concluding remarks 95

9 What was forbidding wrong like in practice? 97
1 What wrongs do people commit? 98
2 Who actually forbids wrong? 102
3 Forbidding the wrongs of rulers 105
4 Forbidding wrong and rebellion 108
5 Concluding remarks 110

10 What has changed for the Sunnīs in modern times? 111
1 Religious allegiances in the modern Islamic world 111
2 The interaction with the West: attraction and repulsion 113
3 Living with the modern state: activism and quietism 118
4 Towards forbidding wrong in an Islamic state 122
5 Religious policing in Saudi Arabia 125
6 Forbidding wrong and privacy 129

11 What has changed for the Imāmīs in modern times? 131
1 Comparing Imāmīs and Sunnīs 131
2 The interaction with the West: attraction and repulsion 132
3 Living with the modern state: from quietism to activism 134
4 Towards forbidding wrong in an Islamic state 137
5 Forbidding wrong and privacy 141
6 Concluding remarks 144

12 Do non-Islamic cultures have similar values? 147
1 What are we looking for? 147
2 Pre-Islamic Arabia 149
3 Rabbinic Judaism 152
4 Medieval Catholicism 153
5 Non-monotheist parallels? 156
6 Forbidding wrong and monotheism 157
7 The distinctiveness of the Islamic case 159

13 Do we have a similar value? 163
1 Common ground 163
2 Rescue and forbidding wrong 165
3 Right and wrong 167
4 Concluding remarks 170

Index 173

Preface

In May 2000 the British police were searching the home of a suspected member of al-Qāᶜida in Manchester, and chanced on a terrorist manual written in Arabic. After the events of 11 September 2001, extracts from this manual were made available in an English translation. These extracts included instructions to be followed by undercover members of the organisation in order not to blow their cover; such a member should avoid manifesting his religiosity through his appearance or conduct. One point underlined in this connection was, in the wording of the translation, that he should 'not get involved in advocating good and denouncing evil in order not to attract attention to himself'. In the same way, a brother travelling on a special mission 'should not get involved in religious issues (advocating good and denouncing evil)'.[1]

The duty which the terrorist manual thereby set aside is a central, and in some ways distinctive, feature of Islamic ethics. As the celebrated Sunnī scholar Ghazzālī (d. 1111) put it, every Muslim has the duty of first setting himself to rights, and then, successively, his household, his neighbours, his quarter, his town, the surrounding countryside, the wilderness with its Beduin, Kurds, or whatever, and so on to the uttermost ends of the earth.[2] Of these demanding activities, all bar the first fall under the rubric of 'commanding right and forbidding wrong' (*al-amr biʾl-maᶜrūf waʾl-nahy ᶜan al-munkar*) – roughly speaking, the duty of one Muslim to intervene when another is acting wrongly.

This book is an epitome of a research monograph I recently published on this duty under the title *Commanding right and forbidding wrong in Islamic thought* (Cambridge 2001).

Note on footnotes: Unless otherwise indicated, all references are to my monograph *Commanding right and forbidding wrong in Islamic thought*, Cambridge 2001. Apart from cross-references and a few references to new sources, the purpose of these notes is to help any reader who wishes to do so to locate the relevant passage or passages in the monograph.

[1] *The New York Times*, 28 October 2001, B8. The passages are taken from pages 54 (item 11) and 40 (item 6) of the manual respectively.

[2] 445.

The original monograph was a detailed presentation of the results of some fifteen years of research. Its seven hundred pages were weighed down with several thousand footnotes and over fifty pages of bibliography. Moreover, the large-scale organisation of the material was according to the various sects and schools that make up the Muslim community, not by topic. In short, the monograph was written primarily for specialists. The text (as opposed to the footnotes) was not in principle inaccessible to non-specialists, but it would have taken considerable courage and persistence for anyone other than a specialist to read it from cover to cover.

The present epitome is designed specifically for the non-specialist. As can be seen from the table of contents, the material has been drastically rearranged to make the organisation thematic; only the last four chapters replicate the organisation of the monograph.

No one who has read the monograph need read this epitome. Except in a small number of cases readily identifiable from the notes, there is no new material here. I have often rearranged the data, and occasionally this leads to new and perhaps better ways of looking at things. But there is nothing here that would count as a novel theory.

At the same time, no non-specialist who reads this epitome has any need to go to the monograph. Everything that really matters about the subject is covered here. Perhaps the only exception would be someone with an interest in one particular sect or school; for such a purpose, the organisation of the monograph is more helpful.[3]

This epitome is subject to all the numerous debts set out in the 'Acknowledgements' and footnotes of the monograph. Some further information used here was kindly given to me by Şükrü Hanioğlu, Barbara von Schlegell, Matti Steinberg and Nenad Filipović. I have benefited considerably from the comments of Patricia Crone and Bob Moore on the typescript, and I regret that at the time I was working on this epitome, few reviews of the monograph had yet appeared. Finally, I would like to thank Janet Klein for preparing the index.

[3] I have written an even more succinct account of forbidding wrong that is to appear as the entry 'al-Nahy ^{c}an al-munkar' in the *Supplement* to the second edition of the *Encyclopaedia of Islam*. There is also an informative article by W. Madelung in the *Encyclopaedia Iranica* (London 1982–, art. 'Amr be ma^{c}rūf').

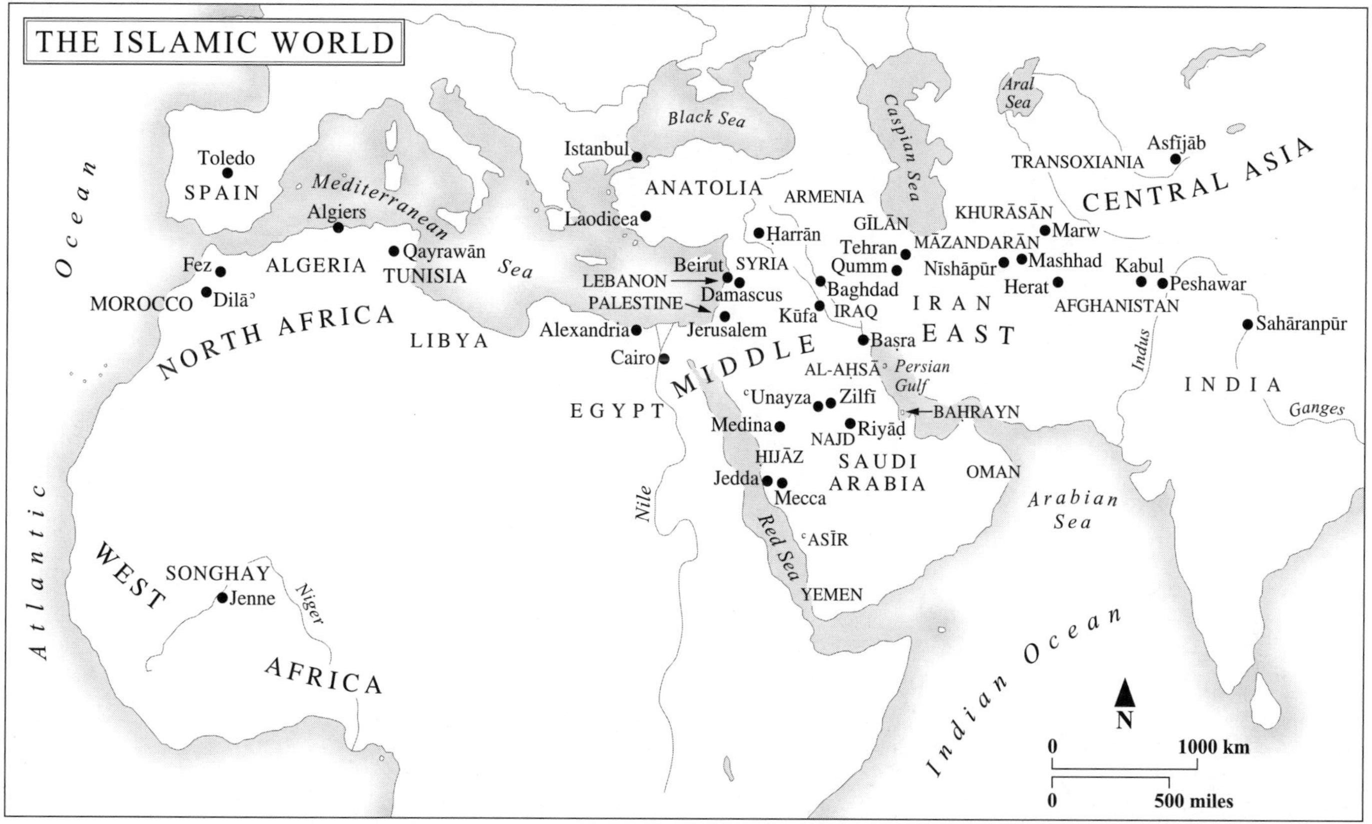

This map shows the location of places mentioned in the text, and contains information related to more than one period.

CHAPTER 1

Introduction

In the early evening of Thursday 22 September 1988, a woman was raped at a local train station in Chicago in the presence of several people.[1]

A brief account of the incident appeared that Sunday in the *New York Times*, based on what the police had said on the Friday. The salient feature of the incident in this account was that nobody had moved to help the victim, and her cries had gone unheeded – for all that the rape took place during the rush hour. As Detective Daisy Martin put it: 'Several people were looking and she asked them for help, and no one would help.'

A longer account which likewise appeared on the Sunday in the *Chicago Tribune* placed the matter in a very different light. Quoting what the police had said on the Saturday, the article began by stating that six bystanders were to be recommended for citizen's awards for their work in helping the police arrest and identify the suspect. The account which followed emphasised two features of the situation that did not emerge from the notice in the *Times*. The first was that the rape took place in a part of the station to which access was blocked by an exit-only turnstile. The second was that the bystanders were confused in their understanding of what was going on: the rapist had ordered his victim to smile, which she did. Although at one point she reportedly mouthed the word 'help', it was only after her assailant had run off that she screamed. Initially, at least, the bystanders took the woman to be engaged in voluntary sex. But one young bystander, Randy Kyles, took a second look and thought 'Man, this is strange'. Something seemed not to be right, so he did not get on his train when it came in. (Others on the platform, by contrast, remarked that what was happening was weird, but nevertheless boarded the train.) When the victim ran up the steps screaming that she had been raped, Kyles chased after the rapist, eventually flagging down a police car and getting him arrested. Kyles later explained his action as follows: 'I had to do something to help that woman. It just wasn't right. It could have been my mother, my aunt, one of my mother's friends.'

[1] ix–xi.

It is clear from these accounts that neither paper considered a rape at a local station in Chicago to be newsworthy in itself. The focus of journalistic attention – and the anticipated focus of the reader's interest – was the conduct of the bystanders. The account given in the *Times*, which went back to Detective Daisy Martin's statements on the Friday, placed their behaviour in a most unflattering light: though they greatly outnumbered the lone rapist, they had simply stood by and let it happen. The implication was that their conduct was shameful, and the reader reacts with appropriate indignation. How differently we would have behaved had we been there! Or at least, we hope we would have.

The account given in the *Tribune*, by contrast, suggests that at least some of the bystanders, and Kyles in particular, behaved commendably. They had two good excuses for not intervening during the rape itself – the physical layout of the station, and the appearance of consent created by the coerced smiles of the woman, even if these did not look quite right. Kyles himself behaved with energy and courage when the situation became clear. He felt that he had to do something to help the woman, just as we would have felt had we been there; and we hope that we would have acted as well as he did in the distinctly confusing circumstances of the case.

Underlying these two accounts, and the remarks of Martin and Kyles, is a broad moral consensus. One cannot just stand by and watch someone rape a woman, even a complete stranger, in a public place. Either one must do something about it, or one must have good and specific reasons for not doing anything. In other words, it seems, we have a clear conception that we have some kind of duty not just to behave decently ourselves, but to prevent others from doing things to their fellow humans that are outrageously wrong. Yet in everyday life we lack a name for the duty, still less a general formulation of the situations to which it applies and the circumstances that dispense us from it. The value is there, but it is not one that our culture has developed and systematised. 'It just wasn't right' is the bottom line in Kyles's explanation of what he did; the 'just' signals that, had he been pressed to explain himself further, he would have had nothing to say. We either understand or we don't. In fact, of course, we understand perfectly well, and some of us can on occasion wax quite eloquent on the subject; but our culture provides us with no ready-made articulation of our understanding.

In Islamic culture, by contrast, such a duty has a name, and it has been analysed repeatedly by the religious scholars whose writings make up the bulk of the literature of Islam. The main purpose of this book is to make this body of thought available in English in a concise and readable form. We can come back to the intriguing contrast between the treatment of the duty in Islamic and Western cultures at the end of the book.[2]

Before we delve into the thinking of the Muslim scholars, there are some preliminary matters that need attention: the terminology used by the Muslim scholars

[2] See below, ch. 13.

in referring to the duty; the religious allegiances of these scholars; and the main types of work in which they set out their ideas. The following sections address these themes, and are in the nature of road-maps.

1 Terminology

The phrase 'commanding right and forbidding wrong' has its source in Muslim scripture, that is to say in the Koran, which Islam considers to have been revealed by God to the Prophet Muḥammad (d. 632) through Gabriel. Thus in one verse, God is calling for unity among the believers, and addresses them thus: 'Let there be one community (*umma*) of you, calling to good, and commanding right and forbidding wrong; those are the prosperers' (Q3:104). In another verse He avers: 'You were the best community (*umma*) ever brought forth to men, commanding right and forbidding wrong' (Q3:110). And again: 'And the believers, the men and the women, are friends one of the other; they command right, and forbid wrong' (Q9:71) – a verse, incidentally, that is notable for its explicit mention of women in connection with the duty. As these examples show, the phrase is firmly rooted in the diction of the Koran.

But what goes for the phrase may not be true of the conception. There is no certainty that the Koranic phrase originally meant what the later Muslim scholars took it to mean. The Koranic uses of the phrase are vague and general, and give no indication of the concrete character of the duty, if any. Indeed, there was a trend in early Koranic exegesis that saw the duty as simply a matter of affirming the basic message of Islam: 'commanding right' was enjoining belief in the unity of God and the veracity of the Prophet, and 'forbidding wrong' was forbidding polytheism and the denial of the Prophet.[3] But whatever the Koranic phrase originally meant, the Muslim tradition overwhelmingly took it to refer to the duty we now understand by it.

Muslim scholars normally follow Koranic usage in referring to 'commanding right and forbidding wrong' in tandem. Occasionally they make scholastic distinctions between commanding right and forbidding wrong, but these are niceties we can leave aside.[4] For our purposes, they are two sides of the same coin, and in most contexts we can conveniently abbreviate the full phrase to 'forbidding wrong'.

Alongside the Koran, Islam possesses a second body of material at least some of which is accorded the status of revelation, namely tradition (*ḥadīth*). In early times, individual traditions were orally transmitted, but within a few centuries they had been reduced to writing and embodied in voluminous collections. In the Sunnī case, what the Muslim scholars consider to be authentic traditions from the Prophet form a body of material with a status comparable to that of the Koran. There are

[3] 22–4.
[4] xii n. 9; cf. below, 106.

numerous traditions that refer to forbidding wrong, often to encourage believers to perform the duty. However, the tradition that figures most prominently in the discussions of the later scholars, at least among the Sunnīs, is couched in different terms. Like many traditions in favour of forbidding wrong,[5] it is identifiable from its transmitters as stemming from the city of Kūfa in Iraq.

According to this tradition, Marwān, the governor of Medina, was presiding over the ritual prayer on a feast-day some time in the 660s or 670s. In this connection he did two things that were considered irregular: he brought out the pulpit despite the fact that it was a feast-day, and he delivered the sermon before conducting the prayer. In the face of these ritual infractions, a man got up and said: 'Marwān, you've gone against the normative practice (*sunna*)! You've brought out the pulpit on a feast-day, when it used not to be; and you've started with the sermon before the prayer!' At this point, one of the Companions of the Prophet commented that the man had done his duty, and proceeded to quote something he had heard the Prophet say: 'Whoever sees a wrong, and is able to put it right (*an yughayyirahu*) with his hand, let him do so; if he can't, then with his tongue; if he can't, then in his heart, and that is the bare minimum of faith.'[6]

This tradition, then, provides us with a clear example of a wrong that needs righting, and at the same time sets out a schema of modes in which a believer might respond to it; we will come back to these 'three modes' in a later chapter.[7] Yet in the payload of the tradition, the Prophet speaks not of 'forbidding' wrong but of 'righting' it, using a verb (*ghayyara*) whose primary sense is 'to change'.[8] From this the scholars derive the phrase 'righting wrong' (*taghyīr al-munkar*) – though because the phrase derives from a Sunnī tradition, it is less used by the Shīᶜites.[9] Despite the difference of language, the scholars take it for granted that 'forbidding wrong' and 'righting wrong' are the same thing, and we will follow them in this without further ado.

Both these ways of referring to the duty go back to early Islamic times. There is a third that is of later origin, and mainly an invention of Ghazzālī.[10] Following a precedent set by a somewhat earlier scholar, Māwardī (d. 1058), he adopted the word *ḥisba* as a general term for 'forbidding wrong'. He then developed a terminology based on the root behind this word (*ḥ-s-b*). Thus the person who forbids wrong is 'the one who performs *ḥisba*' (*al-muḥtasib*), the person who has committed the wrong is 'the one to whom *ḥisba* is done' (*al-muḥtasab ᶜalayhi*), and the wrong itself is 'that with regard to which *ḥisba* is done' (*al-muḥtasab fīhi*).

Because Ghazzālī was a very influential thinker, this terminology is frequently encountered in the works of later scholars.[11] But despite its systematic character,

[5] 45.
[6] 33f.
[7] See below, ch. 3.
[8] 34f.
[9] 258f.
[10] 429; 447–9.
[11] 21 n. 36; 296 and n. 298; 326 and n. 145; 371; 423 and n. 229; 452 n. 161; 455 and nn. 191f.

it led to a considerable amount of confusion. Long before the time of Ghazzālī, the word *ḥisba* had been applied to the office of a functionary I shall refer to as the censor (*muḥtasib*); his job was to oversee the markets and morals of the city in which he was appointed. This too was a form of 'commanding right', but distinct from the duty of the individual Muslim that is our primary concern in this book.[12]

2 Religious allegiances

As world religions go, Islam is relatively unified. It has nevertheless been shaped by a variety of cleavages, some deeper than others, with the result that Muslims have been divided into a large number of more or less distinct groups. These groups are relevant to us to the extent that they have constituted intellectual communities within which doctrines of forbidding wrong have been transmitted and discussed. In practice, of course, we are unlikely to know much of the views of a group unless it has survived into the present and preserved a significant literary heritage; so we shall have little occasion to refer to the numerous groups that died out at one time or another in the course of Islamic history.

By far the oldest and deepest cleavage is the sectarian division that separates Shīᶜites, Khārijites and the Sunnī mainstream. The main ground on which these sectarian allegiances were defined was the religious politics of the seventh century, above all the question who was the legitimate ruler of the Muslim community after the death of the Prophet. Both Shīᶜites and Khārijites were subject to further splits, generating numerous sects. On the Shīᶜite side, two of these sects will play significant roles in this book: the Imāmīs, who today constitute the predominant Shīᶜite group in Iran and elsewhere, and the Zaydīs, who survive only in northern Yemen. On the Khārijite side, only one sect survives today, namely the Ibāḍīs. Geographically speaking, the Ibāḍīs have long been confined to two widely separated regions: Arabia, where they make up the majority of the population of Oman, and North Africa, where they are found as minorities in Algeria, Tunisia and Libya. Each sect tended to have its own succession of imams, that is rulers whom it recognised as legitimate; those of the Imāmīs soon came to exercise no real political power, whereas those of the Zaydīs and Ibāḍīs did better. The various sects were likely to have distinct heritages of tradition (*ḥadīth*), and this was particularly pronounced in the Imāmī case. They also tended to regard each other, with some qualification, as infidels; truth was a zero-sum game, and only one sect could possess it. In modern times the Zaydīs and Ibāḍīs have shown a strong tendency to move towards the Sunnī mainstream, but the Imāmīs remain clearly distinct from it.

A later and less profound division separates the four surviving law-schools of Sunnī Islam: the Ḥanafīs, Mālikīs, Shāfiᶜites and Ḥanbalites. These are rival schools of thought in the field of religious law (*sharīᶜa*), and originate in the heritages of

[12] Cf. 475 n. 33.

founding figures of the eighth or ninth centuries: Abū Ḥanīfa (d. 767f.),[13] Mālik (d. 795), Shāfiʿī (d. 820) and Ibn Ḥanbal (d. 855). The law-schools differ on numerous legal questions, but they have tended to see their differences as in some sense legitimate; thus scholars of rival law-schools have not been given to calling each other infidels, or not at least on the basis of their legal views alone. It gradually became the norm for any Sunnī Muslim to belong to one or other of the four schools; thus both Māwardī and Ghazzālī were Shāfiʿites. But many early Sunnī scholars, and a few later ones, lacked such allegiances. An example is Ibn Ḥazm (d. 1064), a brilliant Spanish maverick. The law-schools were important as intellectual – and also social – communities, and as such they will play a significant part in this book; but in modern times they have tended to become less salient. Outside the Sunnī fold, the various sectarian groups likewise had their law-schools; but there will be less reason to refer to them, since in the sectarian environment the law-school is often (though not invariably) coterminous with the sect.

A third cleavage demarcates the various theological schools. The word 'theological' in this context is to be taken in a fairly broad sense, but it should be understood to exclude religious politics and law. The fundamental division here was between those who espoused the use of systematic reasoning in matters of theology and those who rejected it in favour of an exclusive reliance on Koran and tradition. By the ninth century the champions of systematic reasoning had split up into numerous schools, of which the only one that matters to us is the Muʿtazilites. They did not survive as an independent movement, but their views and works were to an extent adopted and transmitted by members of some of the sects and law-schools described above. The major role in this was played by the Shīʿite sects. Thus the Imāmīs adopted many Muʿtazilite views, though they did not preserve Muʿtazilite works written by non-Imāmīs. The Zaydī reception of Muʿtazilism went further, and included the preservation of a significant body of Muʿtazilite writing by a Shāfiʿite Muʿtazilite, ʿAbd al-Jabbār ibn Aḥmad al-Hamadhānī (d. 1025). On the Sunnī side, Muʿtazilism survived longest among the Ḥanafīs, but even they do not preserve a significant number of Muʿtazilite works. In addition to Muʿtazilism, two further theological schools of a somewhat later vintage will occasionally concern us. One was Ashʿarism, which became strongly associated with the Shāfiʿite and Mālikī law-schools; the other was Māturīdism, which came to prevail among the Ḥanafīs. Ranged against these schools were the enemies of systematic reasoning, whom we can call the traditionalists. We encounter them in a variety of contexts, but their greatest bastion was undoubtedly the Ḥanbalite law-school. In one way theological differences run deeper than legal differences: in theology, as in religious politics, truth tends to be seen as a zero-sum game, and those who find themselves in disagreement are prone to call each other infidels.

[13] Our sources tell us that Abū Ḥanīfa died at some point in the Muslim year 150, which began in February 767, and ended in January 768. So '767f.' means 'the parts of 767 and 768 corresponding to the Muslim year that began in 767 and ended in 768'.

But in another way the divisions run less deep: theological differences did not provide the basis for the formation of lasting social communities, but rather, as we have seen, rode piggyback on sectarian and legal groupings.

A fourth form of division, of great importance historically, is that between the numerous Ṣūfī brotherhoods that have come into existence over the centuries. But these brotherhoods will play very little part in this book. Some aspects of the heritage of Ṣūfī thought will occasionally concern us, as will the tensions between Ṣūfism and its enemies.

3 Sources

Islamic religious literature is vast and ramified, and references to forbidding wrong crop up in sources of very varied types and provenances. But the more sustained discussions of the duty tend to cluster in a limited number of genres.

As we have already seen, there is relevant material in both Koran and tradition. Scholastic cultures tend to invest heavily in commentary on their authoritative texts, and the Muslim scholars are no exception. Since the Koran is the most authoritative Muslim text, it is not surprising that it has been the subject of more commentaries than any other; these range in date from the eighth century to the present. What such commentaries have to say about the relevant verses thus provides us with a rich vein of material. There are likewise commentaries on the major collections of traditions, of which the most important from our point of view is that of Muslim (d. 875); but in general the commentaries on tradition have less to offer us than those on the Koran.

The most obvious type of source to go to for systematic and detailed accounts of the duties of Muslims is the vast legal literature of Islam. The study of law was the central activity of Muslim scholarship, and any topic that had a recognised place in the law-book was thus assured of continuing literary attention down the centuries, and wherever there were scholars to attend to it. The Sunnī law-schools, however, did not cover forbidding wrong in their law-books, with the result that their legal literature has only occasional and incidental remarks to offer on the subject. Fortunately the sectarian scholars – the Imāmīs, the Zaydīs, and the Ibāḍīs (at least in the east) – did not follow the Sunnī lead, and their law-books regularly included discussions of forbidding wrong. In the case of the Imāmīs the amount of material this yields is particularly large. In part this reflects the historical success of the Imāmīs over the centuries – they became far more numerous than the Zaydīs or Ibāḍīs, and thus supported many more scholars. But it is also a testimony to the impetus given by the Islamic revolution in Iran to the publication of Imāmī manuscripts; secularists would have left most of them to gather dust.

Another kind of work that may include a treatment of forbidding wrong is the theological handbook. This is particularly so with the Muᶜtazilites and their heirs, the Zaydīs and Imāmīs. The Muᶜtazilites, indeed, initiated by far the strongest tradition of systematic analysis of the duty to be found in Islam. By contrast, the Ashᶜarites possessed no such tradition, although they sometimes provided accounts of the duty in their treatises on theology. So too did the Ḥanbalites, to the extent that these traditionalists belatedly adopted the genre. The Māturīdites had no problem with the genre, but it was not their practice to include discussion of forbidding wrong in it.

Theological treatments of forbidding wrong tend to abstraction; more concrete and colourful material can sometimes be found in collections of responsa (*fatwās*). In such texts a scholar is responding to specific questions usually put to him by laymen, and these questions may include accounts of the actual circumstances that raised the issues. There is a rich collection of responsa of Ibn Ḥanbal on forbidding wrong that reflects the conditions in which Ḥanbalites lived in ninth-century Baghdad; Iran in the late twentieth century is represented in some responsa of Khumaynī (d. 1989).

From time to time scholars have devoted monographs to forbidding wrong. For example, there is a massive compilation on the subject by Zayn al-Dīn al-Ṣāliḥī (d. 1452), a Damascene Ḥanbalite who was also a Ṣūfī – indeed at one point he makes a specifically Ṣūfī contribution to the armoury of techniques for forbidding wrong. But Ṣāliḥī's work, in line with others of this genre, tends to be more interesting for the materials he transcribes from earlier sources than for any ideas of his own. In recent times monographic treatments of forbidding wrong have become significantly more common, among both Sunnīs and Imāmīs. Modern works of this kind are often of interest for the ways in which their authors seek to relate the heritage of forbidding wrong to modern conditions.

If there is one account of forbidding wrong that stands out from the rest, it is Ghazzālī's. This account forms part of a lengthy anatomy of piety to which he gave the famous – if not entirely modest – title *The revival of the religious sciences* (*Iḥyāʾ ᶜulūm al-dīn*).[14] In this work he devotes far more space to forbidding wrong than most earlier writers on the duty. But it is also the quality of his analysis that sets it apart. His account is a fine example of his talent for effective organisation – a talent explicitly recognised and appreciated by posterity.[15] It is also innovative, insightful, and rich in detail. Small wonder that the work in general, and its treatment of forbidding wrong in particular, achieved a wide currency in the Islamic world. A striking testimony to this was the appearance of reworkings of the *Revival* designed to render it compatible with milieux distinct from that of Ghazzālī himself. Such recensions were produced among the Mālikīs, Ḥanbalites, Ḥanafīs, Ibāḍīs, Zaydīs and Imāmīs; even the Monophysite Christians of Syria had their version.[16] At the same time numerous writers on forbidding wrong mined

[14] 427.
[15] 447; 450; cf. 449.
[16] 453–5; 600–3.

Ghazzālī's account of the duty.[17] The result of all this was to spread his ideas about forbidding wrong far and wide. Yet for one reason or another, certain features of his account tended to meet with resistance on the part of those who customised or borrowed from it;[18] monitoring their reactions can shed an interesting light on their attitudes to sensitive questions.

All these sources document the doctrines of forbidding wrong that were prevalent among the Muslim scholars. But it is only incidentally and unevenly that they reveal anything about the practice of the duty in real life – though responsa obviously have considerably more to tell us here than handbooks of theology. In addition to the kinds of source described above, however, we can have recourse to the large body of historical and biographical literature that the scholars have left behind them. The disadvantage of such anecdotal material is that it is scattered here and there in a random fashion. The advantage is that the works in which we find it do not have formal doctrinal agendas – which is not, of course, to say that they are innocent of doctrinal concerns and influences. Such material may not be the ideal source for reconstructing the practice of the duty, but it is the best we can hope to find for pre-modern times.

We are now ready to start looking at the doctrines of forbidding wrong put forward by the Muslim scholars.

[17] 452f.; 455.
[18] 140f.; 246; 295; 321f.; 372; 456–8.

CHAPTER 2

The elements of the duty of forbidding wrong

This chapter is mainly concerned to answer three basic questions about the duty of forbidding wrong: *who* has to do it, *to whom*, and *about what*? Once we have dealt with these elementary questions, we can go on in later chapters to more advanced issues, ranging from the techniques for forbidding wrong to the limits placed on them by considerations of privacy. But before we tackle our three basic questions, we have to start by briefly disposing of a more fundamental one: *why* should there be a duty to forbid wrong?

1 Why?

The reason this question will not detain us long is that the Muslim scholars had a simple and straightforward answer to it: God had imposed the duty, and had made His will known through explicit statements in both Koran and tradition. (Sometimes this is backed up by reference to consensus (*ijmāʿ*), but we can leave this aside.) A considerable range of Koranic verses and traditions were cited in this connection, but one particular verse, and, among the Sunnīs, one particular tradition, have pride of place. We have already met both.

The verse is Q3:104: 'Let there be one community (*umma*) of you, calling to good, and commanding right and forbidding wrong; those are the prosperers.' In the wider context of the passage, 'you' refers to 'those who believe' (Q3:102), so that it is natural to take God to be addressing the Muslims in general. At the same time the language – 'let there be' – is unambiguously prescriptive. So the obvious reading of the verse is indeed that God is imposing a duty on the Muslims, and this is how it was universally understood. The only thing that is a little obscure is the precise relationship between the 'community' God mentions here and the believers at large: are *all* Muslims to belong to this community that forbids wrong, or just some of them? We need not bother with this ambiguity here; but it attracted the attention of the scholars, and we will find ourselves coming back to it in the next section.

The tradition is the familiar saying of the Prophet with its three modes: 'Whoever sees a wrong, and is able to put it right with his hand, let him do so; if he can't, then with his tongue; if he can't, then in his heart, and that is the bare minimum of faith.' Again it is natural to take this to be addressed to all Muslims – we could even say, to each and every Muslim. And again, the language is manifestly prescriptive – 'let him do so'. There is, of course, the theoretical possibility that 'righting' wrong and 'forbidding' wrong could be distinct duties; but none of the Muslim scholars ever suggested this, and we have already agreed to follow their lead on the question. The only real issue might be whether the Prophet actually said the words attributed to him. The Sunnī scholars were agreed that he did. To show why they held this view would involve going into the technicalities of their assessment of the chain of authorities (*isnād*) by which the tradition is transmitted; for our purposes, it is enough to note that our tradition appears in one of the two most prestigious Sunnī collections of authentic traditions, that of Muslim.

Those who were not committed to the heritage of Sunnī tradition might, in principle, have grounded the duty in the Koran alone. But in practice they were not so parsimonious. Thus Muᶜtazilite authors – whether Sunnī or Shīᶜite – do not adduce the three-modes tradition, but quote others instead, one of them familiar to the Sunnī traditionists and one barely known to them.[1] The Imāmīs cited traditions from their imams, to whom they ascribed an authority comparable to that of the Prophet. But such variation did not affect the general agreement on the existence of the duty, and all parties accepted the authority of the Koran.

The one issue on which a pronounced disagreement arose was whether or not the duty was also grounded in reason. This was, in effect, a counterfactual question: suppose God had not imposed the duty through revelation, would it still be obligatory on purely rational grounds? The issue was accordingly academic, as one Imāmī scholar pointed out;[2] but academic questions are just what scholars like to argue about. This one seems to have arisen among the Muᶜtazilites. Many sources tell us that two leading Muᶜtazilite scholars, Abū ᶜAlī al-Jubbāʾī (d. 916) and his son Abū Hāshim al-Jubbāʾī (d. 933), were at odds on the question. The father held what we may call the rationalist view; the son held the revelationist view, making an exception only to the extent that the mental anguish suffered by a spectator of wrongdoing might give him a self-interested motive for intervening.[3] The underlying issue here is clearly the wider question whether there can be a rational basis for altruism. It was the revelationist view that became mainstream,[4] even among the Muᶜtazilites, but the rationalist view is occasionally found,[5] particularly among

[1] 206f. n. 67.
[2] 288.
[3] 199.
[4] 131; 202f.; 206; 270–2; 287f.; 349; cf. 212; 336 n. 206; 341; 344; 347; 401; 419f.
[5] 201; 206 n. 65.

the Imāmīs.[6] Ghazzālī did not speak of reason, but he did invoke common sense (*ishārāt al-ᶜuqūl al-salīma*).[7]

2 Who?

Who has to forbid wrong? We can think of the possible answers in terms of a spectrum. At one end – the inclusive end – we could imagine the duty being incumbent on everyone without exception; at the other – restrictive – end, we might envisage it being confined to a narrowly defined set of people. These are extremes, and in fact, as we shall see, the views of the Muslim scholars fall somewhere in between. The best way to present them is probably to start from the inclusive position, and to see how, and how far, the scholars depart from it. There are two very different ways in which they may do so. One is by excluding particular categories of people from the obligation to forbid wrong. The other will take more explaining, but it is essentially a response to the observation that it makes no sense to involve absolutely everybody in righting each individual wrong.

As to excluded categories, we should start by making explicit something so obvious that it is usually – but not always – taken for granted. Forbidding wrong is a duty of Muslims, not of unbelievers. One author who comments explicitly on this is Ghazzālī, who explains the exclusion of unbelievers with a rhetorical question: since the duty consists in coming to the aid of the faith, how could one of its enemies perform it? In another passage, he explains that the reason why we cannot have an infidel telling a Muslim not to commit adultery is that the infidel would be presuming to exercise an illegitimate authority over the Muslim, and would thus be humiliating him. Of course a Muslim adulterer richly deserves to be humiliated, but not by an infidel, who deserves it even more than the Muslim does.[8] For Ghazzālī, then, non-Muslims are not just excluded from obligation, they are not even permitted to engage in forbidding wrong to Muslims. Although we find occasional scholars suggesting that unbelievers could – and even should – play some role in forbidding wrong,[9] we can take Ghazzālī's view as standard.

Restricting ourselves to Muslim society, let us start by looking at what might be called the domestic order. Here a fundamental set of inequalities separated free adult males from children, slaves and women; a child, slave or woman was typically subject to the authority of a free adult male. So it would not surprise us were the scholars to exclude children, slaves and women from the obligation to forbid wrong. They did indeed exclude children; a child, like a lunatic, is not legally competent (*mukallaf*), and thus is not yet subject to the duties imposed by the law – though Ghazzālī took the view that a boy nearing puberty who understands what

[6] 270–2; 287f.
[7] 428.
[8] 429f.
[9] 222; 244 n. 111; 430 n. 19; cf. 415.

he is doing is *permitted* to forbid wrong.[10] But unlike children, slaves and women are legally competent, even if they lack the full set of rights possessed by a free adult male. Their case was accordingly less straightforward.

Whether slaves can or should forbid wrong is not a question that receives sustained attention from the scholars, but we do find sporadic references to it.[11] A pious slave whose master sends him on errands to a group of chess-players asks Ibn Ḥanbal whether he should greet them (playing chess being a sin in the view of most, but not all, of the law-schools). Ibn Ḥanbal replies that it is the duty of the slave to order them to desist.[12] The view that slaves are obligated is also held by Ibn Ḥazm, Ghazzālī and several other scholars, and we should probably take it to be standard.[13] But here and there dissentient voices are raised: a couple of Ḥanbalites, a Zaydī and an eastern Ibāḍī.[14] The latter is Khalīlī (d. 1871), who excludes slaves on the grounds that they lack the power to act, and that their business is the service of their masters.[15]

What of women?[16] As we have seen, God speaks of women forbidding wrong: 'And the believers, the men and the women, are friends one of the other; they command right, and forbid wrong' (Q9:71). So it is clearly at least admissible for women to engage in this activity. Yet in general women cannot be thought of as on a par with men, since God tells us that men are a step above them (Q2:228) and the managers of their affairs (Q4:34); moreover their place is felt to be in the home (cf. Q33:33), and they are said to lack judgement, a view that has the support of the Prophet.[17] We might accordingly expect the scholars to develop a doctrine of the role of women in forbidding wrong that would balance these antithetical considerations. In fact references to the question are relatively rare, if more frequent than in the case of slaves; and such references as we find tend to be rather laconic. It is a curious fact that much of what we have comes from the Ibāḍīs.

A few scholars exclude women outright. One eastern Ibāḍī in the ninth century takes it for granted that it would be absurd to suppose women to be obligated.[18] A much later one, Sālimī (d. 1914), justifies their exclusion by invoking the duty of women to keep their voices down.[19] The Zaydī Yaḥyā ibn Ḥamza (d. 1348f.) reaches the same conclusion on other grounds: one is the frivolity and weakness of women, the other the fact that the law does not even give them authority over themselves, let alone in so weighty a matter as forbidding wrong. The arguments are thus interestingly different: for the fourteenth-century Zaydī, women are intrinsically

[10] 429.
[11] 486.
[12] 94.
[13] 353 n. 108; 354 n. 122; 402; 429; 431f.; 486 and n. 137.
[14] 137; 247; 486.
[15] 423; 486.
[16] 482–6.
[17] 482f.
[18] 415.
[19] 422; 483.

incapable of forbidding wrong, whereas for the nineteenth-century Ibāḍī, what reins them in is an extrinsic legal restriction on their public behaviour.[20] Among the Sunnīs, views excluding women are very rare. There is an argument cited anonymously by Koran commentators according to which women and invalids are instances of categories of people incapable of forbidding wrong.[21] We are told that a ninth-century Ṣūfī was once speaking about forbidding wrong when a woman objected that her sex had been relieved of this obligation; but the rest of the anecdote, which we will come to shortly, indicates that in the opinion of the Ṣūfī her view was not quite right.[22]

The view that women are included in the obligation is again found among the Ibāḍīs, both eastern and western. Thus Ibn Baraka, an eastern Ibāḍī of the tenth century, wanted women to go forth to forbid wrong just as men do.[23] Among the Sunnīs, both Ibn Ḥazm and Ghazzālī explicitly included women;[24] Ghazzālī's statement was echoed by a fair number of subsequent Sunnī scholars.[25] With some reservations, we should probably think of this as the standard view.

This leaves the kind of compromise that we initially expected. An obvious way to articulate such a compromise was to make use of the three modes of the Prophetic tradition. This brings us back to the woman who interrupted the Ṣūfī: he responded by agreeing with her with regard to forbidding wrong by hand and tongue, but not with regard to 'the weapon of the heart'. We will be looking more closely at the three modes in the next chapter, but for the moment we need only remind ourselves that the heart – whether or not it is to count as a weapon – represents the minimal level of forbidding wrong.[26] For the rest, we have to go once more to the eastern Ibāḍīs for views of this kind. There our ninth-century scholar is also quoted, a little inconsistently, as saying that a woman should perform the duty in (or with) her heart;[27] so he sides with the Ṣūfī. A scholar active in the early seventeenth century held that women should forbid wrong with the tongue, though not with the hand.[28] A more complex view is that of the tenth-century Kudamī. Women are excused from speaking out, though they are permitted to do so provided this does not involve them in sexual self-display (*tabarruj*); given that they are excused, he does not like them to take upon themselves the hazards of going forth to forbid wrong, and feels that they should rather stay at home, as God has ordered them to do.[29] This brings into play the restrictions imposed on women by considerations of modesty, a line of thought most fully developed by

20 247; 483.
21 18.
22 483f.
23 415; cf. 396; 402; 422 n. 224.
24 429; 484; 485.
25 332 n. 184; 353 n. 108; 354; 484f.
26 483f.
27 415.
28 416.
29 415f.; 485.

Khalīlī at a later date. Khalīlī had no doubts about including women in the duty: invoking Q9:71, he took the view that God has made all believers partners (*sharrakahum*) in forbidding wrong. But how would this play out in practice? On the one hand, he said, a woman is the most suitable person to forbid wrong to other women, and she is likewise obligated with regard to males within her own immediate family (*dhawū ʾl-maḥārim*). Yet on the other hand, it clearly cannot be her duty to forbid wrong in a gathering of men of doubtful character, since for her to be there would be a wrong in itself. The significant thing about this restriction is that it in no way turns on a denial that women possess the mental qualities or legal authority needed to forbid wrong. In fact Khalīlī makes the point that if a woman is in a position to exercise power over wrongdoers, and no other Muslim is taking action against them, she has the duty of sending someone to forbid them – presumably a male whose presence at the scene of the wrongdoing would not be improper.[30]

In setting out the implications of the domestic order for the question who is to forbid wrong, I have treated what the scholars have to say about women in some detail. This is largely in deference to our current interest in such questions, though it is certainly true that the scholars themselves have more to say about women than about children or slaves. Altogether, we can conclude that while the views of the scholars may often embody an unspoken assumption that the forbidder of wrong is a free adult male, the explicit exclusion from the duty of slaves and women – as opposed to children – is relatively rare. Yet as we have seen, even scholars who included women might have reservations. Ghazzālī, in fact, has a discussion of what one might call the performance of the duty against the grain of authority, and he includes there the cases of the son against his father, the slave against his master, and the wife against her husband. What he does is to limit the level of forbidding wrong to which they should escalate; but he in no way goes back on the principle that they are obligated.[31]

It is time to move on from the domestic order to the social order above the domestic level. We could imagine the scholars restricting the duty, and even the right, to forbid wrong to a suitably qualified elite. Of course by now it does not seem very likely that they would do so: to the extent that they make only limited concessions to the inequalities of the domestic order, we would hardly expect them to change their tune when confronting the larger order of society. And in general they do not. Yet here too, there are some exceptions worth looking at. For example, an Imāmī tradition tells us the response of the imam Jaᶜfar al-Ṣādiq (d. 765) to the question whether forbidding wrong is incumbent on the whole community. His answer is that it is not; only a strong man who can expect obedience and knows right from wrong has the duty to forbid wrong.[32]

[30] 423f.; 485.
[31] 431f.
[32] 256f.

The most widespread idea of this kind is found in a saying that is usually quoted anonymously, though sometimes ascribed to Abū Ḥanīfa.[33] Here is a typical version: 'Putting things right (*taghyīr*) with the hand is for the political authorities (*umarāʾ*), with the tongue for the scholars (*ʿulamāʾ*), and in (or with) the heart for the common people (*ʿāmma*).'[34] This saying picks up the terminology of the three-modes tradition, but uses it to establish an explicitly elitist doctrine of forbidding wrong; we can refer to this conception as the tripartite division of labour. It was much cited among the Ḥanafīs,[35] which is perhaps no accident, inasmuch as this school achieved a degree of symbiosis with the Turkish dynasties that ruled so much of the central Islamic world from the eleventh century onwards.[36] But the saying also appears elsewhere – among the Mālikīs, Shāfiʿites, Ḥanbalites, and even the Ibāḍīs.[37] People tend to quote it rather unthinkingly as if they are comfortable with it, though one sixteenth-century Ḥanafī takes it literally enough to elaborate on it – thus he extends the category of scholars to include saints (*awliyāʾ*).[38] The scholars who quote it rarely focus on its incompatibility with the standard doctrine of forbidding wrong, though there are exceptions here and there.[39] If taken seriously, this saying excludes the common people from forbidding wrong either by deed or by word, even when they are able to do so. It limits the performance of the duty 'with the hand' to the military-political elite, something we will take up when we come to the political aspects of forbidding wrong. It likewise limits performance 'with the tongue' to scholars, and it is this view that we should pursue a little further here.

When we come in a later chapter to consider what forbidding wrong might have been like in the real world, we will find it hard to resist the conclusion that it was to a large extent an activity of scholars.[40] We would accordingly expect to find this linkage reflected in the doctrines of forbidding wrong that the scholars propounded, and occasionally it is.[41] Some exegetes take the view that in Q3:104 God commands that there be scholars in the community, and that the rest of the community should follow them.[42] One seventeenth-century Mālikī apparently held that the common people had no business forbidding wrong, and considered that it was not appropriate for a scholar to do so unless he was dressed like one.[43] In line with

33 309; 324; cf. 325 n. 139.
34 599.
35 312f. and n. 37; 318f.; 324 and n. 126; 325; 325f. and n. 143; 332 n. 183; 333 and n. 188; cf. 315 n. 49; 320.
36 333f.
37 137f.; 163; 356; 367f.; 399 n. 36; cf. 378 and n. 162.
38 318f.
39 163; 324; 326 n. 143; cf. 313.
40 See below, 102.
41 488f.
42 19 n. 23; 367.
43 356.

this is the occasional assertion that it is not for laymen to rebuke scholars.[44] Yet such views played only a marginal part in formal statements of the doctrine of forbidding wrong, even in communities such as the Imāmīs where the authority of the scholars was particularly salient.[45] In the end, perhaps the key ground on which the scholars could lay claim to a more prominent role than others in forbidding wrong was that they knew best – they were the experts on right and wrong. Ḥalīmī (d. 1012), a Shāfiᶜite scholar, accordingly placed much emphasis on the duty of the righteous scholar to forbid wrong. But he then considered as an afterthought whether a righteous Muslim who was not an outstanding scholar could do so, and conceded (but God knows best) that such a man might forbid an evil the status of which is apparent even to the common people.[46] Other scholars do not share Ḥalīmī's apparent reluctance in making this concession.[47] We certainly need the scholars for difficult cases, but as everyone knows, there are plenty of easy ones where ordinary people have no difficulty telling right from wrong. All in all, we can conclude that there did exist ideas of limiting the duty of forbidding wrong to one social group rather than another, but that they were not taken very far.

There was, however, another basis on which a category of people could be excluded, this time moral rather than social. The people in question were sinners. A sinner, it could be argued, lacked the standing to forbid wrong to others; were he to attempt it, he would be acting hypocritically, and in any case his chances of success would be reduced.[48] And yet why should a sinner be relieved of a duty that burdened the virtuous? This puzzle is a regular ingredient of accounts of forbidding wrong (though the Imāmīs rarely discuss it);[49] it is dramatised by Ghazzālī with a scenario in which a fastidious rapist reproves his victim for being unveiled while he ravishes her.[50] Occasionally the dilemma is resolved by limiting the duty to the virtuous. Thus Ḥalīmī, who has already restricted the duty – the ruler apart – to the *righteous* scholar, maintains his view when he comes to consider an unrighteous one: he would be better occupied reforming his own character, and lacks the requisite moral authority to forbid wrong to others. But this is highly unusual.[51] The standard answer is to deny the sinner an easy ride, and to consider him obligated.[52] Unlike his virtuous peer, he has two duties for which he is, so to speak, separately accountable: first, to set himself to rights, and second, to forbid wrong to others. After all, if only the sinless could undertake the duty, who would

[44] 326 n. 143; 367 n. 68; 464; 488f.
[45] 299 and n. 312; cf. 304; 403f.
[46] 342f.
[47] 132; 208 n. 70; 318 n. 79; 319; 345; 347; 350 n. 81, no. (2); 404 n. 79; 488; cf. 351 n. 91; 445.
[48] 363.
[49] 296.
[50] 430.
[51] 342; cf. 296 n. 295.
[52] 74 n. 212; 131f.; 137 n. 162; 324; 336 n. 206 (and source); 345; 350 n. 81, no. (2); 351 n. 91 (and source); 361; 366; 430; 488; cf. 363; 364; 419.

be able to perform it?[53] Once more, the scholars are on balance reluctant to restrict the range of those for whom forbidding wrong is a duty.

So much for the categories of people whom the scholars consider excluding from the duty. We now come to a quite different way in which they may seek to limit its incidence. In commonsense terms, we can pose the issue like this. Suppose that several of us are present at a scene of wrongdoing; you promptly intervene, with the result that the wrongdoer desists. Are we then to say that the rest of us failed to perform our duty? That seems forced, if not unfair. Should we say instead that, unlike you, we had no duty? But then on what ground would we claim to have been exempt?

The Muslim scholars approach this issue in terms of a conceptual distinction that applies across the whole range of religious duties. A duty may be incumbent on each and every legally competent Muslim, like prayer or fasting; in this case, it is an 'individual obligation' (*farḍ ᶜalā ᵓl-aᶜyān*). Or it may be incumbent on the community at large, like aggressive (as opposed to defensive) holy war; in this case it is a 'collective obligation' (*farḍ ᶜalā ᵓl-kifāya*). The key thing about a collective obligation is that once a sufficient number of Muslims undertake it, others cease to be obligated.

How did the scholars apply this distinction to forbidding wrong? Some held the duty to be individual, some held it to be collective – and a few spoke of it as both.[54] The standard view saw it as a collective obligation.[55] At the point at which we come upon the wrongdoing, or the wrongdoer starts his mischief, we are all obligated; but once you take care of the matter, the rest of us have no further obligation. This seems convincing enough. As the Muᶜtazilites argued, and after them the Imāmīs, the purpose of the duty is to get results; so if someone successfully discharges the duty, the object is attained, and it makes no sense for others to continue to be obligated.[56] Like the exclusions by category that we considered above, this view is also easy to square with Q3:104: all we have to do is to read the verse to mean that the 'community' designated to forbid wrong is to consist not of *all* the believers, but just of some of them.[57]

There are, however, those who prefer to see forbidding wrong as an individual obligation. This view has occasional supporters among the Mālikīs, led by the elder Ibn Rushd (d. 1126).[58] It is also present, and much more strongly, among the Imāmīs, where it may have a Muᶜtazilite origin[59] (though in general the Muᶜtazilites

[53] 74 n. 212; 132; 361; 430.

[54] 274; cf. 131 n. 122; 160 n. 112; 216 n. 101; 290 n. 256; 365.

[55] 152; 176; 201; 216 and n. 101; 243 n. 109; 273f.; 290f.; 313; 314; 317 n. 68; 324; 336 n. 206; 345 *bis*; 347 and n. 65; 350 n. 81, no. (5); 350 n. 83; 351 n. 91; 352; 365; 374; 375f.; 428; cf. 18; 377; 419.

[56] 275.

[57] Cf. 18.

[58] 364; 370 n. 88; 371 and n. 95; 375 and n. 132; cf. 377.

[59] 200f.

were collectivists).[60] In this milieu the view owed its relative success to its adoption by a major Imāmī scholar, Abū Jaᶜfar al-Ṭūsī (d. 1067); but in the long run the collective view prevailed even among the Imāmīs.[61] One sometimes suspects that the motivation for the individualist view is more rhetorical than conceptual – in other words, that what the individualists are trying to convey is that the duty is terribly important. That apart, what is at stake when they call the obligation an individual one?

The discussion of this question is far better developed among the Imāmīs than it is among the Mālikīs. Yet even among the Imāmīs, for some centuries after Ṭūsī it was by no means made clear what the disagreement amounted to.[62] The collectivists conceded the obvious point that the duty could, under some circumstances, become individual (consider a situation in which you are the only person present apart from the wrongdoer). At the same time, the individualists were not denying that the obligation ceases when someone else has successfully performed it (when there is no longer a wrong to right, how can there be a duty?). So what was the point at issue? Was the dispute merely verbal,[63] or was something substantive at stake?[64]

A lucid answer was provided by Bahāᵓ al-Dīn al-ᶜĀmilī (d. 1621) in an analysis that distinguishes three phases.[65] Imagine a town in which there is a wrongdoer, together with ten men each of whom thinks he might successfully right the wrong. The first phase is that in which the wrong is there, but no one has yet undertaken to put it right; here all are obligated, and if none steps forward, all are at fault. In this phase it makes no practical difference whether we call the duty individual or collective. Now skip to the third phase, in which the wrong has been put right; here, clearly, no one is obligated, and again it makes no difference how one categorises the duty. That leaves us with the second phase, in which someone has already undertaken to right the wrong, but has not yet achieved success; let us assume that he can be expected to succeed – and that he would not succeed any faster if others joined in. In this phase the individualist holds that the rest are obligated, whereas the collectivist holds that they are not. Only here, then, does it make any difference whether we call the duty individual or collective. Bahāᵓ al-Dīn was not the inventor of this analysis, merely an effective populariser; but in its mature form it is not older than the sixteenth century.[66]

All in all, what stands out from our discussion in this section is the reluctance of the scholars to limit the pool of potential forbidders of wrong in any very drastic way. Apart from those who lack legal competence, there is no domestic, social or

60 216 and n. 101.
61 216 n. 101; 275; 290.
62 275f.
63 290 n. 254.
64 292 n. 262.
65 291.
66 291f.

moral group whom they agree to exclude. And the categorisation of the duty as collective, though it takes us into deep scholastic waters, is at bottom mostly a matter of common sense.

3 To whom?

To whom are the people we have been discussing to forbid wrong? This question generates much less interest among the scholars, and they do not have very much to say about it. There are two issues that can be distinguished here.

The first is how to define the class of people whose behaviour may trigger the duty. One view is that the offender must be legally competent. Thus the mischief of children and lunatics is not a target of forbidding wrong; likewise excepted are the misdeeds of non-Muslim subjects of the Muslim state. This does not mean that such persons should be allowed to run wild – they must, of course, be restrained. The point is rather that such restraint is no part of forbidding wrong. A position of this kind is found in some Muᶜtazilite sources,[67] and it is echoed by Ghazzālī in an abbreviated Persian version of his account.[68] But in the fuller Arabic version that we normally rely on, he takes another view: the offender does not have to be legally competent, just human. When a boy or a madman drinks wine, for example, his lack of legal competence means that his action is not a sin; but it is still a wrong,[69] and as such in need of forbidding. By contrast, he says, when an animal misbehaves and causes damage to someone's property, the intervention this calls for is not a case of forbidding wrong; the point of the intervention is to safeguard the property of the owner, not to prevent wrongdoing.[70] Either way, it appears that from the point of view of our sources we are dealing with a rather marginal question. In general they seem to take it for granted that forbidding wrong is something done by and to fellow Muslims, who are assumed to be adult and sane. Of course one can argue about who exactly is to count as a Muslim. The Ibāḍīs, for example, reserve the term for themselves, and Ibāḍī sources occasionally mention a view that Ibāḍīs do not have to forbid the wrongs of non-Ibāḍīs whom others would call Muslims.[71]

The second issue is whether, within the class of people to whose misdeeds the duty applies, there are relationships that preclude forbidding wrong. Without doubt some relationships impose constraints on it. We have already noted this within the domestic order; here the scholars take the view that one should forbid the wrongs of one's parents, but they indicate in one way or another that harshness is not in

[67] 222.
[68] 437 n. 71.
[69] 437f.
[70] 438.
[71] 399f; cf. 410.

place.[72] Other instances can be found in the wider society. Thus according to Ghazzālī, the measures you can take are limited if the wrongdoer is your teacher or your ruler – though less so in the case of your teacher, since a scholar who does not practise his learning is owed no respect.[73] But scholars rarely go so far as to say that such relationships can override forbidding wrong altogether – which fits well with their general reluctance to marginalise the duty. The main exception is more apparent than real: there is a view that subjects should not forbid wrong to rulers. But as we will see in a later chapter,[74] this has more to do with the danger that delinquent rulers pose to those foolhardy enough to reprove them than it does with any respect due to rulers by virtue of their office. That apart, we find only stray exceptions, as with the idea that a layman should not rebuke a scholar.

4 About what?

What is to count as a wrong for the purposes of the duty? As we saw in the previous chapter, some early Koranic exegetes took a narrow view.[75] According to them, to command right was to command belief in the unity of God and the veracity of the Prophet, and to forbid wrong was to forbid polytheism and the denial of the Prophet.[76] But this is quite untypical. The great exegete Ṭabarī (d. 923) at one point expresses his disagreement with such a view: right refers rather to *all* that God and His Prophet have commanded, wrong to *all* that they have forbidden.[77] The Shāfiᶜite scholar Juwaynī (d. 1085) likewise says that the details of the duty are nothing less than 'the law from its beginning to its end'.[78] In practice, of course, some forms of wrongdoing were encountered more commonly than others; but that is something we can leave to a later chapter.[79] The complications we need to attend to here are more abstract in nature.

The first of these is a consequence of the fact that scholars are liable to disagree. A well-known manifestation of this phenomenon is the wealth of disagreements between the four Sunnī law-schools. For example, the Shāfiᶜites have a more lenient attitude to chess than the other schools; and they permit the eating of lizard, whereas the Ḥanafīs disapprove of it. What do such disagreements mean for the duty of forbidding wrong? The standard principle here is that you should not reprove anyone who is acting in a manner permitted by his own school; in other words, you have no business seeking to impose the requirements of your particular school on members

[72] 78; 93; 300; 361; 431f.; 437 n. 71; cf. 97 n. 110; 363 n. 36; 374 n. 118; 375 n. 124; 482.
[73] 431f.
[74] See below, ch. 7, section 2.
[75] See above, 3.
[76] 22–4.
[77] 24.
[78] 26 n. 56.
[79] See below, ch. 9, section 1.

of others.[80] Similar or related positions appear even outside the Sunnī fold. Thus there is a western Ibāḍī view that you are not obliged to rebuke non-Ibāḍīs for anything that is permitted in their law but not in yours.[81] The basic principle is also known to the Zaydīs, as it had been to the Muᶜtazilites, though the Imāmīs make little mention of it.[82] A finer point occasionally raised by the scholars is whether you may or should reprove someone whose conduct is wrong according to his own school, yet acceptable in yours. To take an example used by Ghazzālī, what should you do if you are a Shāfiᶜite eating a lizard, and are joined by a Ḥanafī? Ghazzālī says you should not forbid the Ḥanafī in such a case, though one Muᶜtazilite says the opposite.[83] Ghazzālī hastens to point out that tolerance in legal questions has no extension to theological differences.[84] Before leaving the matter of the disagreements of the law-schools, we should note that in one respect we are skating on rather thin ice. We are making the assumption that the points on which independent legal judgment is admissible (*masāʾil al-ijtihād*) include all those on which the law-schools are actually found to disagree (*masāʾil al-khilāf*); and this is not something self-evident. Thus there are those who say that temporary marriage (*mutᶜa*) is just wrong, irrespective of the view some early scholars held to the contrary.[85]

The second complication can already be discerned in the example with which Ghazzālī illustrates the first. Ghazzālī seems to assume that the Ḥanafīs prohibit eating lizard, whereas in fact they only regard it with disapproval. Does 'wrong' then include acts that are merely disapproved, and not actually forbidden? And in the same vein, does 'right' include acts that are merely commendable, and not actually obligatory? And if so, would it be obligatory to forbid something disapproved and to command something commendable, or would it only be commendable to do so?

There is a standard view on this question that is widely attested in Muᶜtazilite sources. According to this view, the category of 'right' does indeed include both obligatory and commendable acts; it is obligatory to command the obligatory, and commendable to command the commendable – the principle being that the command cannot be more obligatory than what is commanded. By contrast, *all* wrong must be forbidden, since the category of 'wrong' cannot be divided in an analogous fashion.[86] No explicit mention is made of what is merely 'disapproved'; we are left to infer that it is not part of the category. This position was widely adopted among the Imāmīs,[87] and it also appears elsewhere.[88]

80 65 n. 127; 133 n. 128; 136; 169 and n. 26; 214; 244; 296 and n. 296; 345; 350 n. 81, no. (4); 436f.; cf. 146 n. 2; 171; 315 n. 54; 351 n. 91.
81 400.
82 296.
83 214; 437.
84 437.
85 153 n. 69 (and source); cf. 159 n. 108 (and source).
86 213f.; 202; cf. 200.
87 272f.
88 419 n. 198.

The trouble with this view is, of course, that it is awkwardly asymmetrical. 'Right' is understood broadly, as including both the obligatory and the commendable; 'wrong', by contrast, is implicitly understood more narrowly, in a way that excludes the disapproved.[89] The bedrock on which this asymmetry rests is semantic: this just is what the words had come to mean for the scholars. But unsurprisingly, this did not prevent attempts to create conceptual symmetry. As one Imāmī scholar put it, the best course would be to apply the category 'wrong' broadly, despite the trivial semantic objections to such a usage.[90] We accordingly find brave souls here and there who are prepared to divide 'wrong' into the forbidden and the merely disapproved (nobody shows any interest in the alternative course of narrowing the usage of 'right').[91] The Shāfiᶜite Dawānī (d. 1502) formally does this,[92] as Ghazzālī had also done in an untidy afterthought to his account; it was thus commendable to prevent a disapproved wrong, and disapproved to remain silent about it.[93] A Zaydī scholar remarked that one may 'forbid' (though not in the literal sense) something that is not actually 'wrong', such as eating with the left hand.[94] But it was above all among the Imāmīs that this discussion flourished.[95] Here the desire for symmetry appears as early as the eleventh century, and finds formal expression in the twelfth.[96] In later centuries, symmetric positions predominated among the Imāmī scholars, though no consensus emerged on the way to ground such views.[97]

The third complication relates to time. We can best begin with the Muᶜtazilites, who as often offer us a sharp distinction. There are wrongs that have already happened, and there are wrongs that, unless something is done about them, are going to happen. Since the object of forbidding wrong is to prevent wrongs from happening, it follows that the duty can have no application to those that have already happened. This does not mean that the wrongdoers should get away with their misdeeds; they should be punished in accordance with the law. But such punishment is a matter of law-enforcement by the state, and can have no place in the forbidding of wrong by individuals. The kind of situation to which the duty applies is thus one in which you see whatever is needed for a drinking-party being assembled, or a man failing to prepare for prayer despite the fact that its appointed time is imminent, and you accordingly know that a wrong is in the making.[98] Another presumably Muᶜtazilite formulation, borrowed among both the Ḥanbalites and the Imāmīs, says that the offender must show signs of persistence;[99] a Ḥanbalite

[89] Cf. 281 n. 214.
[90] 289 n. 250.
[91] 289 n. 250.
[92] 350f.
[93] 442f.
[94] 273 n. 143.
[95] 272f.; 288–90.
[96] 273.
[97] 289.
[98] 208 and n. 71; 223 n. 152; cf. 277 n. 182; 279 n. 192.
[99] 133; 208 n. 71; 276 no. 2; 278 n. 186.

scholar who adopts this view remarks that, should the offender shows no signs of continuing his wrongdoing, what he has already done is beyond the scope of the duty.[100] There is, however, a point made by some Muᶜtazilite scholars that smudges the clear distinction between past and future: they allow that under the duty one might take action against past sins with the purpose of deterring future ones.[101]

Not everyone adopted anything as elaborate the Muᶜtazilite doctrine. But the view that punishment is to be inflicted only by the state, and not by individuals, is widespread,[102] if not quite universal.[103] Moreover, the full range of issues is considered by Ghazzālī, who comes up with a somewhat different view. Temporally he divides wrongs into three groups, not two: past, present and future.[104] As in the standard Muᶜtazilite doctrine, he removes past sins from the scope of the duty – they can only be punished, and this is reserved to the ruler. It is present sins that are the business of individuals engaged in forbidding wrong. Future sins are as much outside its scope as past ones: they require preventive measures, which again are reserved to rulers.[105] Thus unlike those Muᶜtazilites who speak of deterrence, Ghazzālī makes this a function of the state; individuals cannot go beyond counsel and exhortation in such cases (after all, there can be no certainty that the wrong in question will actually be perpetrated).[106] This position of Ghazzālī's is clear enough with regard to a prospective wrong that is not going to happen in the immediate future. But what does he make of the kind of situation referred to above, where someone is manifestly preparing to do something wrong (or not preparing to do something right)? His response is that such cases, on closer examination, will be seen to involve wrongdoing in the present. He has just given the example of young men who hang around the doors of women's bath-houses so that they can stare at the women as they enter and leave. Presumably he wants to say that just hanging around in such a location (or setting out wine-cups, or not washing when the time for prayer is fast approaching) is in itself a wrong.

If time is a problem, space should be one too. Are distant wrongs your responsibility in the same way as those committed nearby? Ghazzālī implies that they are, but that nearby wrongs take precedence.[107] The Zaydīs attend specifically to the question; one idea they mention is that the obligation is extinguished beyond a one-mile radius.[108] But the issue is rarely discussed.

We now know why there is a duty of forbidding wrong, who has to do it, to whom, and about what. But *how* is it to be done?

[100] 133.
[101] 208; 208 n. 71.
[102] 176 n. 73; 342; 343; 380; 413; 414 n. 159; cf. 415.
[103] 413.
[104] 435; cf. 436; 466.
[105] 440.
[106] 435.
[107] 445f.; see above, xi.
[108] 243 n. 105; cf. 251 n. 169.

CHAPTER 3

How is wrong to be forbidden?

By now we are sufficiently familiar with Muslim scholasticism not to expect simple answers to apparently simple questions. So when we ask how one is to forbid wrong, we can be sure that there will be no one way of doing it. In fact we have already met a key Prophetic tradition according to which there are three modes of forbidding wrong:[1] with the hand, with the tongue and in the heart – or, as some understand the usage, *with* the heart. This threefold division is a useful one. It is widely known, and frequently used by the scholars as a basic building block for their doctrines. Yet it has its limits.

For one thing, the schema was not employed by everyone. The Sunnīs, Ibāḍīs and Imāmīs made extensive use of it. But the Muᶜtazilites rarely did so,[2] and the Zaydīs only resorted to it in later centuries under Sunnī influence.[3] More surprisingly, Ghazzālī seems to have had no interest in it, though he must have been well acquainted with it (indeed he quotes the tradition together with its frame-story).[4] The schema is also a bit crude for many purposes. It does not, for example, distinguish between a delicate hint and a ruthless tongue-lashing, or between a restraining hand and recourse to arms. Finally, there is something rather peculiar about the sequence.[5] The tradition tells you to right a wrong with your hand, and failing that with your tongue, and failing that in your heart. This, then, is a de-escalatory sequence. But the Muslim scholars – with the balance of common sense surely on their side – regularly think in terms of an escalatory sequence: you start gently, and go only so far as is needed to right the wrong, and no further. Why brandish your sword when a polite suggestion would be enough?

In this chapter I will accordingly adopt the three modes of the tradition, but vary their order and introduce distinctions from other sources. In particular, I will draw on a widely quoted classification devised by Ghazzālī in which he distinguishes a considerably greater number of levels of response, arranged in an escalatory

[1] 33.
[2] 210 n. 76; 225 n. 165.
[3] 249; 250 *bis*.
[4] 431 n. 29 (and source).
[5] 263f.; 318.

sequence.[6] Since the tongue seems the natural instrument with which to forbid, I shall begin with it.

1 With the tongue

Despite the ordering found in the Prophetic tradition, we can think of the use of the tongue as the default mode of forbidding wrong. As we will see when we come to the practice of the duty, there are innumerable anecdotes about the verbal reproofs administered by pious Muslims to wrongdoers. The scholars, as might be expected, have a lot to say about the importance and variety of such reproofs. One Shāfiᶜite scholar tells us that to forbid wrong you must know how to talk to people of every social class (*ṭabaqa*) in a manner appropriate to each.[7] In fact the range of verbal responses to wrong is so broad that we can only handle it by introducing some distinctions.

The most obvious distinction relates to the degree of abrasiveness with which the wrongdoer is addressed. Here Ghazzālī in his classification has no less than three levels corresponding to the oral mode.[8]

The first is informing someone who is acting wrongly out of ignorance. The example he gives is a peasant performing the ritual prayer incorrectly; you know that this results from ignorance, since if the peasant did not wish to pray correctly, he would not be trying to do so at all. You should address yourself to such an offender with tact, and take care not to humiliate him; you stress that nobody is born knowing, and that we too did not know how to pray until those who knew better instructed us. Hurting a Muslim is as wrong as remaining silent in the face of his wrongdoing.

The second of Ghazzālī's oral levels is exhortation. This is for someone who, unlike the peasant, knows that what he is doing is wrong. Such exhortation may involve quoting traditions to him and telling him stories about pious Muslims of early times. But you should do this in a civil and sympathetic way, and without the self-satisfied arrogance to which scholars so easily fall victim.

The third level is harsh language. This is for someone who not only knows that he is doing wrong, but responds to a civil exhortation with obduracy and contempt. What you say to such a person should be fair comment, such as: 'You libertine! You fool! You ignoramus! Don't you fear God?' This level of response is naturally subject to more limitations than the previous ones. Thus Ghazzālī has reservations about recourse to it by a son against his father, a wife against her husband or a slave against his master; what he has to say about subjects administering harsh rebukes to rulers will occupy us in a later chapter.[9]

[6] 438–41.
[7] 343.
[8] 439f.
[9] See below, ch. 7, section 2.

All this is fairly standard. Thus there is nothing unusual about Ghazzālī's idea that forbidding wrong may take the form of informing people.[10] Similarly his distinction between civility (most often referred to as *rifq*) and harshness is taken for granted by the scholars.[11] Indeed one of the most common themes in accounts of forbidding wrong is the importance of doing so nicely.[12] The point is not lost on the scholars that making a man angry tends to be counterproductive;[13] they regularly indicate that harsh language should be employed only if a civil approach is of no avail.[14] Ghazzālī's view that the use of harsh language is restricted in certain relationships is likewise shared; thus an Imāmī scholar states that speaking gently to one's father is a duty, whereas speaking harshly is not,[15] and Ibn Ḥanbal in a responsum takes a similar view of reproving one's mother.[16]

The other distinction made by the scholars within the oral mode relates to the context in which the reproof is administered. It is one thing to admonish someone in private, and another to do so in public: according to an old saying, 'Whoever admonishes his brother in private (*sirran*) graces him (*zānahu*); whoever does so in public (*ʿalāniyatan*) disgraces him (*shānahu*).'[17] An eighth-century governor of Medina who was rebuked by a pietist at the Friday prayer subsequently complained that the man had gone out of his way to humiliate him by shouting at him in front of everyone. Had the pietist rebuked him in private, the governor lamented, he would have been happy to comply; instead he threw his verbal assailant into jail.[18] This governor may have been a wrongdoer, but in his preference for a private rebuke he had several Muslim scholars of later centuries on his side.[19]

2 With the hand

The best way into the issues here is again to start with Ghazzālī's classification; we can then see how other scholars view the types of action he describes. For our purposes three of Ghazzālī's levels are pertinent.[20]

The first is physical action that does not involve attacking people. There are two forms of this. One is destroying offending objects; examples are breaking musical instruments and pouring away wine. The other is removing someone from a place where he should not be; Ghazzālī gives the example of dragging a person in a state

[10] 93 n. 56; 254; 300 n. 315; 402.
[11] 96 n. 92; 211.
[12] 78f.; 96; 132 and n. 127; 153; 313; 329 n. 166; 359; 363; 366; 439 *bis*; 442; 489 and n. 168; cf. 97 n. 110; 170; 180; 191; 383; 387; 403 n. 70; 492 n. 194; 496.
[13] 78; 96.
[14] 96; 99; 211; 324; 363.
[15] 300.
[16] 93 n. 56.
[17] 79f.
[18] 62f.; 80.
[19] 137; 160; 170; 312; 343; 481.
[20] 440f.

of major ritual impurity out of a mosque. Within this level there are escalatory nuances. One should not, of course, be taking such measures at all if one can get the offender to perform the action himself. If they must be taken, one should stick to the minimum that is effective. If a musical instrument can be rendered non-functional by being broken, it should not be ripped to pieces; if wine can be poured away without breaking the vessels, they should be left intact; if all it needs to remove the man from the mosque is taking him by the arm, you should not drag him by the foot or pull him by the beard. Of course you may have no choice. If the wine is in bottles with narrow necks, pouring it away might expose you to danger – or it might simply waste too much of your time.

The second level is actual violence against the person of the offender. Here there are escalatory distinctions that are more than a matter of nuance. Before you even begin to inflict violence, you should where possible threaten it, as by telling the offender: 'Stop that, or I'll break your head!' (Ghazzālī in fact makes the threat of violence a level on its own, and allows a degree of exaggeration in it.) Once you do begin, you should try to limit yourself to punching and kicking, and perhaps the use of a stick. You can have recourse to arms only where it is necessary, and on condition that it does not lead to public disorder (*fitna*). He gives the example of someone on the other side of a river who has seized a woman or is playing a flute; you can take up your bow, and, after warning him, you can shoot – though not to kill.

The third level is collecting a band of armed men to assist you where you cannot accomplish the duty on your own. Of course the offender too may seek help, resulting in a pitched battle. Here for a moment Ghazzālī seems to hesitate. On the one hand, he reports the view that this cannot be done without the ruler's permission, and that individual subjects are not allowed to act in such a way because it would lead to anarchy. On the other hand, he cites the position that such permission is not needed, since once individuals are allowed to take action at the lower levels, there is no way to draw a line that precludes the formation of armed bands. But it is this latter view that Ghazzālī endorses as the more logical in the full version of his account – though in the Persian abridgement he sits on the fence at one point, and favours permission at another.[21] He does at least reassure us that it is unusual for matters to come to such a pass in forbidding wrong.

All these measures are, of course, considerably more drastic than even a harsh rebuke, and recruiting an armed band could well be thought extreme. We should therefore not expect Ghazzālī's account of these levels to reflect the consensus of the scholars to the same extent that his oral levels did. Let us take them one by one, and see what the wider world of Muslim scholarship had to say about them.

Ghazzālī, as we saw, identified two forms of physical action short of assaulting people. That which involved forcibly removing a person – as in the case of dragging

[21] 431 n. 28; 441 n. 91.

the man out of the mosque – is not generally discussed in other accounts of forbidding wrong. By contrast, attacks on offending objects are a ubiquitous theme. In principle there is a great variety of such objects. There are, for example, chessboards to overturn,[22] supposedly sacred trees to cut down[23] and decorative images to destroy or deface.[24] Ghazzālī at one point gives particular attention to the images that one finds at the entrances of bath-houses, or inside them; the problem is that they can be too high for one to reach.[25] But the targets that are mentioned again and again are liquor and musical instruments. They do, of course, go together: they are the necessary ingredients of a good party.

As Ghazzālī has already told us, the basic technique for dealing with liquor is to pour it away. This is standard.[26] An alternative occasionally mentioned is to spoil the wine by putting into it either salt (so Ibn Ḥanbal) or dung (so the Zaydīs).[27] Yet another measure, as mentioned by Ghazzālī, is to destroy the container – smash the bottle, break the jar, rip the skin.[28] But this is more drastic, since it destroys something that could be used for licit purposes. Hence the tendency is to see this measure as Ghazzālī did, that is to say as one to be taken only if it is not possible to pour the liquor away[29] – though one has the impression that for whatever reason the Ḥanbalites were more ready to have recourse to it than the Zaydīs.[30] There is also the risk that you could find yourself liable to pay compensation for the damage you have done.[31]

Unlike liquor, music cannot simply be poured away. The only course is thus to destroy the instrument itself (provided there is one – singing is a more intractable problem).[32] We thus hear of pouring away liquor and smashing musical instruments in the same breath, as things a pious man might do together.[33] Fortunately it is less problematic to deal with musical instruments in this fashion than it is to destroy vessels. For unlike a vessel, a musical instrument can scarcely he said to have an alternative and licit use (or at least, none that it is regularly used for); so the question of compensation hardly arises.[34] As a tenth-century Mālikī remarked somewhat acidly, the only known alternative use for musical instruments is as firewood.[35] Indeed the Saudis on entering Mecca in 1803 made a bonfire of stringed instruments (together with tobacco-pipes, offending objects unknown to the classical

22 97.
23 313 n. 38.
24 145 n. 2; cf. 115 n. 3; 329.
25 444.
26 97; 99; 230; 238f.; 245; 343; 414.
27 100; 238.
28 97; 230; 238f.; 309 n. 13; 380 n. 170.
29 230; 238f.
30 241.
31 238f.; 300; cf. 245.
32 Cf. 97; 244; 383; 384.
33 79; 118f.
34 133 n. 127; 238; cf. 309.
35 380 n. 170.

Muslim scholars).[36] We do not hear of individuals doing this; but for added drama, they could break the instrument over the head of its owner,[37] or throw it on the ground and stamp on it.[38] There was, however, a fastidious view according to which the fragments of the smashed instrument were to be returned to the owner,[39] though not if they could be reused to make a new instrument.[40]

We have taken it for granted in this exposition that *all* liquor and *all* musical instruments in the hands of Muslims were to be destroyed. This, however, is not quite right. Thus the Ḥanafīs had a category of licit liquor; under the doctrine that the duty had no application in matters over which the law-schools differed, this loophole had to be tolerated.[41] Likewise many scholars made an exception for the tambourine, especially at weddings, where it performed the useful function of publicising the marriage.[42] Others, however, were virulently opposed to tambourines, even at weddings.[43] For some reason the Ḥanbalites and the eastern Ibāḍīs were each riven by disagreement on the question. They also came up with occasional compromise views: a nineteenth-century Saudi scholar allowed tambourines at weddings during the day, but not at night,[44] while an Ibāḍī view held that it was in order to strike a tambourine once or twice to publicise a wedding, but not more.[45] We also find among the Ibāḍī scholars a certain partiality for a large and mournful pipe whose music was apt to focus one's thoughts on death and the afterlife;[46] and they are inclined to make concessions with regard to martial music.[47]

Despite the element of force inherent in this form of forbidding wrong with the hand, doubts about its appropriateness for individual Muslims are rare. Those who hold to the tripartite division of labour, of course, implicitly reserve such action to the organs of the state, and explicit statements to this effect are occasionally encountered. Thus an eastern Ibāḍī of the ninth century says that you have no right to break musical instruments, but should instead refer the matter to the authorities;[48] and a later Zaydī source states that objects that have a licit use may be broken only by the agents of the state.[49] But in general the duty of individuals to pour and break is not questioned.

Let us now move on to the next level, violence against the person of the offender. It is here that Ghazzālī's levels begin to be controversial. There is a widespread feeling that a line has to be drawn somewhere, and some would draw it hereabouts.

36 168 n. 18.
37 79.
38 100 n. 145.
39 238; 245; 414.
40 245 n. 124.
41 136; 214; cf. 92.
42 91 n. 22; 145 n. 2; 152 n. 52; 172; 380 n. 170; 412; cf. 343 n. 31.
43 68 n. 158; 119 n. 32; 412; 421; cf. 79; 149; 459.
44 176 n. 70.
45 412.
46 412.
47 410f.; 421.
48 415.
49 238 n. 78.

The saying about the tripartite division of labour implies that violence – all violence – is reserved to the state. Such views are not isolated. We find them among the eastern Ibāḍīs,[50] and within the Sunnī fold they are attested at different times for the Shāfiᶜites,[51] the Mālikīs[52] and the Ḥanafīs.[53] Some exception, however, may be made for emergencies.[54]

Another place to draw the line is between unarmed and armed conflict. For the most part armed conflict means the use of the sword; other weapons range from the sandal[55] to sticks[56] and whips[57] to the bow and arrow,[58] but these are rarely discussed. Views that allow violence but exclude recourse to arms are typically found among the Sunnīs.[59] Barbahārī (d. 941), a Ḥanbalite demagogue in early tenth-century Baghdad, held that forbidding wrong is to be performed with the hand, but without the use of the sword;[60] in this he was in agreement with Ibn Ḥanbal and later Ḥanbalites.[61] Juwaynī likewise allows individuals to take action only where this does not lead to armed conflict, which he reserves for the ruler.[62] The Mālikī scholar Abū Bakr ibn al-ᶜArabī (d. 1148) – not to be confused with the famous or infamous mystic – held the same view,[63] as did some other Mālikīs.[64] The Ottoman Ḥanafī Ṭāshköprīzāde (d. 1561), in the course of an account of forbidding wrong that plagiarises Ghazzālī's, interjects that the individual subject is never under any circumstances to take up arms.[65] A rather isolated Zaydī view reserves killing and fighting to the ruler.[66] One Imāmī scholar argues that killing can have no place in forbidding wrong since it is self-defeating: dead men cannot obey orders.[67]

There are also views that, while not excluding recourse to arms altogether, link it in one way or another to the state. The Muᶜtazilite Abū ᵓl-Qāsim al-Balkhī (d. 931) allowed subjects to have recourse to arms only in the absence of a ruler, or under conditions of overriding necessity;[68] other Muᶜtazilites took the view that the state is better placed to discharge the duty where fighting is involved.[69] One

[50] 414 and n. 159; 422; cf. 415.
[51] 343.
[52] 367.
[53] 326f.
[54] 326f.; 367.
[55] 336 n. 208; 491 n. 189.
[56] 244; 336 n. 208; 459; 491 n. 189.
[57] 230; 400; 473 n. 23.
[58] 441.
[59] Cf. also 198 n. 19.
[60] 128.
[61] 97; 135 n. 147; cf. 137 n. 165; 139.
[62] 346 *bis*; cf. 347.
[63] 367.
[64] 378.
[65] 322; cf. 457 n. 213.
[66] 248 n. 146.
[67] 286.
[68] 199; 269; cf. 413f.
[69] 222; cf. 215 n. 99.

Ḥanbalite scholar ruled out the use of the sword except where one was performing the duty together with the authorities.[70]

By far the most prominent position of this kind was developed among the Imāmīs. Here, despite some opposition, it became school doctrine that the use of violence – or some level of it – in forbidding wrong required the permission of the imam.[71] The exact level of violence deemed to require this permission is not very clear, but it is sometimes specified as killing and wounding, which would presumably involve the use of arms.[72] Very rarely we find Sunnī scholars adopting some version of this doctrine. Thus the Ḥanbalite Ibn al-Jawzī (d. 1201) holds such permission to be necessary for the use of blows,[73] and Ṭāshköprīzāde likewise requires it for violence against the person.[74] The path through which the Imāmī doctrine found its way to these authors is curious. Ghazzālī had explicitly rejected the Imāmī view, declaring the permission of the ruler unnecessary for any of his levels.[75] Ibn al-Jawzī and Ṭāshköprīzāde based their accounts of forbidding wrong on Ghazzālī's, but clearly found his views too alarming to endorse where violence was concerned. In negating them, such authors gave a place on the Sunnī side of the fence to the Imāmī view Ghazzālī had rejected.[76]

There were nevertheless a good many scholars who left individuals free to take up arms, and did so without evincing any such concern for the role of the state. This view is well attested among the Muᶜtazilites,[77] Zaydīs[78] and Ibāḍīs.[79] It is also by no means rare among the Sunnīs;[80] thus Abū Ḥanīfa is said to have held that forbidding wrong is obligatory by word and sword,[81] and Ibn Ḥazm gives strong support to recourse to arms where necessary.[82]

We can now turn to Ghazzālī's final level, the recruitment of armed bands.[83] Unlike those we have been concerned with so far, this one is peculiar to Ghazzālī. Not that the idea of taking up arms in forbidding wrong was an innovation in his time. Nor was there anything new about the idea that one might need helpers,[84] though earlier scholars had tended to mention it only in passing.[85] But it was Ghazzālī who put the two together, and made an issue of armed bands.[86] And as we

[70] 137 n. 165.
[71] 266–8; 285f.; 474 n. 26.
[72] 266f.; cf. 286.
[73] 140 no. 1.
[74] 322; cf. 457f. and n. 215.
[75] 430f.; 441.
[76] 140 no. 1; 322; 332; 457f.; 474 and n. 26.
[77] 198 *bis*; 201 *bis*; 204; 211 and n. 78; 224; 336; 337.
[78] 229 n. 15; 230; 238; 244 and n. 115; 248 and n. 145; cf. 251.
[79] 400; 413f.; cf. 402.
[80] 309; 323; 336; 337; 341; 347; 367; 390; cf. 308 n. 5.
[81] 309; 335.
[82] 390.
[83] 475.
[84] 74; 97f.; 312; 493 n. 201; 589; cf. 380 n. 169.
[85] Cf. 344; 345.
[86] 441.

have seen, he himself seems to have initiated the ensuing disagreement by saying one thing in Arabic and another in Persian.

Posterity had a variety of reactions. The western Ibāḍī Jayṭālī (d. 1349f.) strongly endorsed Ghazzālī's positive view.[87] The Damascene Zayn al-Dīn al-Ṣāliḥī, in drawing on Ghazzālī's account, carried over what he had to say about armed bands without comment.[88] ᶜIṣmat Allāh ibn Aᶜẓam (d. 1720f.), a resident of Sahāranpūr in northern India, followed suit; but he added the caveat that such a situation demanded careful consideration.[89] Many, however, found Ghazzālī's approval of armed bands downright unacceptable. These, they held, were not for individuals to form,[90] but rather for the ruler;[91] or at least, they were best left to him,[92] or needed his permission,[93] except in emergencies.[94]

In short, Ghazzālī in his discussion of forbidding wrong with the hand persists all the way from the destruction of objects to the formation of armed bands; but at each escalation he is deserted by more and more of his colleagues.

3 Recourse to the heart

The heart has no place in Ghazzālī's schema of levels. This, like his general disregard of the three modes, is surprising in a staunch Sunnī. It was even felt to be anomalous by some Imāmīs who drew on his account; they found a way to give recourse to the heart the status of a formal level.[95] But Ghazzālī himself mentions the heart only in passing, and so gives us no real assistance in fleshing out this third mode of the Prophetic tradition. We accordingly find ourselves on our own.

The main thing we need to confront here is the ambiguity of the role of the heart. The Arabic phrase *biʾl-qalb*, which is found in the tradition and becomes part of the standard usage of the scholars, can mean either '*in* the heart' or '*with* the heart'. (I use the awkward phrase 'recourse to the heart' where it seems desirable to leave the ambiguity unresolved.) On the first understanding, we are talking about an unobservable mental act that is without any impact on external reality; being in no position to change the world, we content ourselves with registering a protest that is perceptible only to God. This idea is perfectly intelligible; you may not be able to stop something, but you don't have to like it, and you can inwardly tell yourself (and God) so. But how could a mental reservation of this kind be

[87] 402; 458.
[88] 162 n. 119.
[89] 323.
[90] 246.
[91] 244.
[92] 372.
[93] 140 no. 2; 322; 372; 457.
[94] 372.
[95] 438 n. 75.

described as 'forbidding' or 'righting' a wrong in any real sense of the words? In this conception, then, there is no comparability between the role of the heart and those of the hand and tongue. On the second understanding, by contrast, we are clearly talking about a way of taking action against a wrong, one that uses the heart as its instrument – 'the weapon of the heart', as the Ṣūfī put it in his response to the woman's objection.[96] The roles of hand, tongue and heart are thus fully comparable. But just how does one put one's heart to work to prevent or protest against the wrongdoing of others?

Very occasionally we find a scholar who explicitly addresses these issues. Perhaps the first to put his finger on the problem was the Shāfiᶜite Nawawī (d. 1277) in commenting on the Prophetic tradition.[97] The objection could be made, he remarked, that disapproval in the heart does not right the wrong; in his response, however, he affirmed that the Prophet was indeed referring to a purely mental act. But it was the later Imāmī scholars who gave most attention to the problem. We can turn to al-Shahīd al-Thānī (d. 1557f.) for a lucid account.[98] He states that recourse to the heart (*al-inkār al-qalbī*) is used in two senses: one is a matter of inner belief and disapproval, whereas the other refers to turning away from the offender and showing him one's disapproval. The first, he says, can hardly be reckoned part of forbidding wrong, whereas the second can.

But the scholars never developed a clear consensus on this issue. Many of them seem not to have noticed the ambiguity, or if they did, they failed to address it. My sense is that more often than not they had in mind a performance confined to the heart, though I could not prove this.[99] Sometimes we can tell from the context of a passage which conception a scholar was thinking of, but we can hardly infer from this that he had a considered view of the matter.

Ghazzālī is a case in point. Though he gives the heart no place in his schema,[100] he does mention it on two occasions. In the first passage,[101] he says that someone who lacks the power to forbid wrong need do so only with recourse to his heart, since anyone who loves God dislikes and disapproves of sins committed against Him. This on its own is ambiguous. But fortunately Ghazzālī backs up what he has just said by quoting an old saying that encourages us to fight unbelievers, or failing that to frown in their faces. (Of course forbidding wrong in its usual sense is not directed at unbelievers, but if this did not bother Ghazzālī, it need not bother us.) In this first passage, then, he must surely be thinking of a performance *with* the heart, one whereby inner disapproval is manifested through facial expression. Now we turn to the second passage.[102] Here Ghazzālī considers the conditions under

[96] See above, 15.
[97] 33 n. 5 (and sources); cf. 320 n. 93.
[98] 284 and n. 224 (al-Shahīd al-Thānī, and source).
[99] Cf. 95f.
[100] 438 n. 75.
[101] 432 and n. 37 (and source).
[102] 440 and n. 82 (and source).

which you have a duty to respond to wrongdoing by silently manifesting your anger. If you cannot do more, and will not get yourself beaten up as a result of your scowling and frowning, it is your duty to display your anger in such a way; it is not enough for you to disapprove with recourse to your heart. Here, clearly, Ghazzālī is making a distinction between showing one's anger and performing a merely mental act, and he is identifying only the second with the heart. So this time he must mean *in* the heart. Uncharacteristically, Ghazzālī leaves us in confusion.

Some examples will serve to indicate the lie of the land. If we take the Imāmī scholars who were mentioned above for their insertion of the heart into Ghazzālī's schema of levels, we find that three of the four are clearly thinking of a narrowly mental act.[103] In one case, this reading is reinforced by the fact that the author in question is writing in Persian, a language in which the ambiguity of the Arabic phrase has to be resolved: he renders it as '*in* the heart' (*dar dil*).[104] In another case we find confirmation in the fact that the author adds the manifestation of disapproval and social avoidance to the schema as an independent level unrelated to the heart.[105] But the fourth author, Muḥsin al-Fayḍ (d. 1680), has a significantly different approach.[106] For him the level of the heart is made up of three sublevels: the first is indeed a purely mental act, but the second is the manifestation of disapproval, and the third is social avoidance and ostracism. It is easy to find earlier scholars, Imāmī and non-Imāmī, who regard recourse to the heart as no more than a mental act,[107] and others who see it as involving outward and visible signs.[108] Like Muḥsin al-Fayḍ, scholars who look for such signs tend to speak of a range of behaviour running from frowns to turning away from the offender to formally ostracising him (*hajr*).[109] But as we shall see in the next section, scholars often mention such measures without linking them to the heart.

A few scholars put forward an idea that transcends the distinction. The Ḥanafī ᶜAlī al-Qārī (d. 1606) speculates that performance with the heart could be a matter of mustering a kind of spiritual energy (*himma*) which, through divine intervention, may actually have an impact on the external world;[110] faith, as he points out, can move mountains.[111] This is a Ṣūfī view. The Egyptian Ṣūfī Ibrāhīm al-Matbūlī (d. 1472) held that performance with the heart was for the gnostics (*ᶜārifūn*), whose contempt for themselves precluded their actually forbidding anyone. Instead, the gnostic may turn to God in his heart to stop the wrongdoing, and in that way the offender will desist.[112] But again, there was no need to link this way

[103] 438 n. 75 (both Narāqīs and Qāḍī Saᶜīd).
[104] 438 n. 75 (Aḥmad al-Narāqī).
[105] 438 n. 75 (Qāḍī Saᶜīd al-Qummī).
[106] 438 n. 75 (Muḥsin al-Fayḍ).
[107] 250; 251 nn. 167, 169; 265 n. 81; 378 n. 162; 403; cf. 44; 255.
[108] 163 n. 122; 210 n. 76; 251 n. 167; 264; 265; 378 n. 162.
[109] 265 and n. 81.
[110] 318.
[111] 318 n. 85.
[112] 463.

of righting wrongs to the heart; the fullest account we have of it inserts it into Ghazzālī's schema as a level on its own, as we will see in the next section.

Sooner or later the notion of recourse to the heart seeped into the language of all significant sects and schools of Islam. But it is by no means universal as an element of formal doctrine. It is not a Muᶜtazilite concept,[113] and it makes only the rarest appearances in Muᶜtazilite works.[114] With equally scant exceptions,[115] it is not to be found among the Zaydīs,[116] or not until the emergence of a strong Sunnising trend in recent centuries.[117] It is also absent to a surprising degree among the Ashᶜarites;[118] thus neither Juwaynī nor Āmidī (d. 1233) mention it in their accounts of the duty.[119] In the case of the Muᶜtazilites and Zaydīs, it is hard to resist the suspicion that the virtual absence of a concept of recourse to the heart is linked to their disposition to political activism. But the Ibāḍīs, who were also activists, seem to have no problem with the concept.[120]

4 Are there other ways to forbid wrong?

If, as is generally the case, it is taken for granted that forbidding wrong is not confined to verbal rebukes, this invites the inclusion under its umbrella of a wide range of responses to wrongdoing. Are there any that do not fit into the three modes of the tradition?

As mentioned above, forms of behaviour that some scholars placed under the aegis of the heart are often discussed without any attempt at such linkage.

A case in point is Ṣāliḥī's account of the use of spiritual power by Ṣūfīs to right the wrongs they encounter.[121] He inserts this method into Ghazzālī's schema as a level on its own, giving it a designation that employs a technical term of Ṣūfism without making any mention of the heart: 'righting wrong through [spiritual] state' (*inkār al-munkar biʾl-ḥāl*). He quotes a saying of an earlier Ṣūfī: 'Inwardly righting a wrong through state is better than outwardly righting it through words.' He illustrates the procedure with a series of stories in which Ṣūfī saints right wrongs by bringing about supernatural intervention. Thus they turn wine into honey, vinegar or – in an elegant reversal of the miracle of Cana – water.[122] The Ṣūfī whose saying was just quoted was once asked to demonstrate the method. He had himself seated on a bench in the street (he was crippled), and waited till a mule went by

113 204; 211 n. 80; 226.
114 210 n. 76; 225 n. 165; 251 n. 167.
115 228; 248 n. 145; 251 n. 167.
116 247f.
117 249 *bis*; 250 *bis*.
118 346 n. 54; 347 n. 68.
119 346 n. 54; 350 n. 82.
120 400; 403; 415; 416.
121 162; 462–4.
122 162.

carrying jars of wine. He then pointed at the load and said: 'That's it!' The mule tripped, and the jars broke. After this had happened three times, he concluded: 'That's how to right wrongs!'[123] Another story tells how the ascetic Bishr al-Ḥāfī (d. 841f.) dealt with a brawny man who had seized a woman and was wielding a knife. To all appearances, he merely brushed shoulders with the man in passing, at which the would-be rapist collapsed. When asked what had come over him, the man revealed that the passing stranger had told him that God was watching him, whereupon his legs gave way under him; he took ill and died soon afterwards.[124] The attempt of some scholars to classify activity of this kind as a form of recourse to the heart makes a certain sense, but as Ṣāliḥī seems to have felt, it is by no means compelling.

Another such case is the manifestation of disapproval by a range of behaviour short of words or deeds. The Imāmīs quote a saying of ᶜAlī (d. 661) to the effect that the minimum response to sinners is to meet them with 'frowning faces'.[125] Likewise ostracism is quite often mentioned as a response to wrongdoing;[126] for example, two leading Saudi scholars of the nineteenth century held that those who visit the land of the polytheists for trade should be ostracised (these 'polytheists' are what we would call non-Wahhābī Muslims).[127] As we have seen, some scholars link such measures to the heart, and in this case Ṣāliḥī is one of them.[128] But again, there is no consensus here,[129] nor is it obvious that there should be. Thus if we go back to the older Imāmī scholars, it seems that such responses may be linked to each of the three modes. In addition to those who tie them to the heart, two scholars regard them as 'a kind of action' (*ḍarb min al-fiᶜl*), which would suggest the hand, while two see them as actions taking the place of verbal rebukes, so pointing to the tongue.[130]

A quite different response to wrongdoing, or the prospect of it, is not to be present. This means that you either avoid a scene of wrongdoing altogether, or, if you are already there, you leave. This is usually presented as a course to be taken only where you are not in a position to speak out or take action against the wrong.[131]

The most drastic form of this idea is the principle that, if you have the misfortune to live in a land where wrongdoing prevails, and there is no possibility of righting the wrongs, then it is your duty to emigrate. This sweeping view is espoused by some scholars, and ascribed to Abū Ḥanīfa and Mālik;[132] it is, however,

[123] 463.
[124] 463.
[125] 255; cf. 413.
[126] 37 n. 22; 96 n. 82; 248 n. 145; 255 n. 22; 265; 324; 336 n. 206; 338; 341; 361; 366; 403; 421.
[127] 176.
[128] 163 n. 122.
[129] 96 n. 82; 211 and n. 80; 248 n. 145; 403; cf. 176 n. 73.
[130] 265.
[131] E.g. 363.
[132] 75 and n. 218; 229 n. 15; 309; 341; 361f.; 374 n. 118; 380 n. 169; cf. 384.

rejected by others (though they may consider such emigration to be meritorious).[133] Thus Ghazzālī says that there is no need to emigrate in the face of intractable wrongdoing; or at least, you are not obliged to emigrate provided you are not being forced to participate in the wrongdoing, as by rendering assistance to unjust rulers.[134]

A less harsh view does not go so far as to oblige you to abandon your homeland, but does require you to absent yourself from the wrongdoing, staying at home as much as you can. This, in fact, is Ghazzālī's position.[135] Similarly the Ḥanbalite Abū Yaᶜlā ibn al-Farrāᵓ (d. 1066) says that you should only go to a party where there will be liquor and music if you are able to put a stop to these wrongs; otherwise you risk appearing to condone them.[136] It may, of course, happen that you arrive at the party in pious good faith, and are taken unawares by what you find there; here the Ḥanbalite jurist Ibn Qudāma (d. 1223) says that, if you cannot right the wrong, it is your duty to leave.[137] (The Ḥanafīs tend to be more accommodating: for example, one says that you can enjoy the food while not listening to the music.[138]) Parties are not, of course, the only such occasions. Someone asks Ibn Ḥanbal: 'Say I'm called to wash a corpse, and I hear the sound of a drum.' His answer is that one should break the drum if possible, and otherwise leave.[139] Likewise if your parents grow vines to make wine, and ignore what you say to them, you should move out.[140] As one tradition has the Prophet say: 'No eye which sees God disobeyed should blink before righting the wrong or departing the scene.'[141]

Sometimes the scholars go beyond the simple injunction to avoid or leave a scene of wrongdoing, and suggest that you are free to arrange your life in such a way as to minimise your obligation to forbid wrong. The Imāmī Ibn Ṭāwūs (d. 1266) writes in such terms to his son.[142] But there is nothing specifically Shīᶜite about such ideas. On the Sunnī side, we are told that no less an authority than Mālik went so far as to absent himself from the Friday prayers in Medina for a quarter of a century because he feared that he would see a wrong and be obliged to take action against it.[143] Likewise Sufyān al-Thawrī (d. 778), for whom markets are dens of iniquity in which one sees nothing but wrongs,[144] advises a man to be sparing in his visits to them, since once there he would have a duty to command and forbid.[145] This is in sharp contrast to Ghazzālī's view that if you know of an

[133] 171; 313; cf. 173.
[134] 432.
[135] 432; cf. 363.
[136] 136 n. 156; cf. 145 n. 2; 410 n. 120.
[137] 145 n. 2; cf. 75; 444.
[138] 314 n. 48.
[139] 97.
[140] 93.
[141] 206.
[142] 278 n. 191.
[143] 382; cf. 364.
[144] 69.
[145] 75.

evil in the market-place, and are capable of putting a stop to it, then it is your duty not to sit at home, but rather to sally forth to confront the evil.[146] This, in fact, is part of a purple passage in which Ghazzālī strongly condemns staying at home in general, and insists on the duty to go forth and right wrongs to the uttermost ends of the earth.[147] Yet Ghazzālī himself, in another part of his *Revival*, extols the virtues of a solitary life (*ᶜuzla*); one of them is that the solitary is not exposed to situations in which he would incur the burdensome duty of forbidding wrong.[148] In any case, you do not have to go out of your way to find wrongs to right.[149]

Finally, for all that forbidding wrong is a duty that falls upon individuals, it may make sense in some situations to enlist a few people to help you. One might have thought that the scholars would give close attention to such activity and surround it with their usual ifs and buts. Yet as we have seen,[150] it is only when such a group engages in armed conflict that they take much notice, responding to the rather extreme position staked out by Ghazzālī. Otherwise they simply take it for granted that it is good to have helpers.[151] Occasionally they affirm that people have a duty to come to the aid of those seeking it.[152] Māwardī, however, is perhaps the most intriguing exception to the general pattern. In one work, he presents – and appears to share – the view that, in cases where the offence is the work of a group (and not of isolated individuals), it is necessary to have capable helpers; without them one risks being killed without attaining the goal, a course that reason condemns.[153] This is likely to have come from a Muᶜtazilite source, though not one we still possess. But in another work, he provides a list of the differences between the individual forbidder of wrong and the official censor (*muḥtasib*). One such difference is that the censor has the right to engage helpers, whereas the individual does not.[154] What we should make of this apparent contradiction is unclear. In fact, as we shall see in a later chapter,[155] the most interesting material regarding such groups is not doctrinal but anecdotal.

By now we have looked at all ways of forbidding wrong that figure prominently in the literature. But this coverage is not intended to be exhaustive. Thus among the Imāmīs of later centuries, we read of twisting ears as a means of forbidding wrong.[156]

[146] 139f.; 140 n. 178, no. (2).
[147] 445f.; see above, xi.
[148] 603.
[149] 364.
[150] See above, 35.
[151] 97f.; 137; 171; 312; 364; 380 n. 169; 431; 493 n. 201.
[152] 413; 493 n. 201; cf. 336 n. 206.
[153] 344.
[154] 345.
[155] See below, 103f.
[156] 284.

5 Concluding remarks

It will be evident by now that the fundamental principle running through the bulk of the material presented in this chapter is that of minimal escalation. Sometimes this principle is left implicit, but this is not always so. Some scholars employ a technical term for the notion of 'escalation' (they may speak of *irtiqāʾ*, *tadrīj* or *tadarruj*).[157] The principle itself is clearly and explicitly formulated by the Muᶜtazilites. The Zaydī Muᶜtazilite Mānkdīm (d. 1034), for example, puts it as follows:[158] since the purpose of the duty is simply to bring about good and put a stop to evil, one may not have recourse to drastic measures where the purpose is achieved by gentle ones. He goes on to defend this principle on the basis of both reason and revelation. As to reason, when someone has a purpose, it is impermissible for him to take a difficult course where an easy one would do just as well. As to revelation, God in Q49:9 first commands us to try to put things right between groups of believers who are fighting one another, and only then does He go on to tell us to fight the group that is in the wrong – thus prescribing a process of escalation. Other scholars, especially Muᶜtazilites, articulate the same basic idea.[159]

The complication, as we noted at the beginning of this chapter, is that in the Prophetic tradition the three modes are presented in a de-escalatory sequence. This does not seem to have bothered the Sunnīs much; but it did bother the Imāmīs,[160] who like the Sunnīs adopted the schema as a basic building block of their doctrines of forbidding wrong. Among the earlier Imāmī scholars we find both sequences, but it is only with al-ᶜAllāma al-Ḥillī (d. 1325) that we find the problem brought out into the open in his monumental work on the disagreements among the Imāmī jurists. He considers the dispute to be verbal rather than substantive.[161] He was later criticised for this,[162] but there was something to be said for his view. The de-escalatory sequence makes sense as a statement that one does as much as one can; the escalatory sequence says that one does no more than is necessary.[163] Or, as al-Shahīd al-Awwal (d. 1384) puts it, the de-escalatory sequence is ordered with regard to strength (*qudra*), and the escalatory sequence with regard to efficacy (*taʾthīr*).[164]

As might be expected, the scholars sometimes show an awareness that the principle of minimal escalation cannot always be applied mechanically. It may not always make sense to begin at the beginning; as the Ḥanafī Muᶜtazilite Jaṣṣāṣ (d. 981) indicates in a discussion of the duty of Muslims to kill collectors of illegal

[157] 201; 283 n. 219; 441.
[158] 210.
[159] 132; 202; 210 n. 76; 238; 244; 264 n. 78; 283; 317 n. 68; 336 n. 206; 438–41; cf. 314f.
[160] 263f.; 283f.
[161] 264.
[162] 284 n. 221.
[163] 264.
[164] 284 n. 221.

taxes, one may find oneself having to resort to arms without prior warning, if such warning would defeat the purpose of the action.[165] The Zaydī imam al-Manṣūr al-Qāsim ibn Muḥammad (d. 1620) raises the further question what you should do if, by the time you have worked out just where in the escalatory sequence to pitch your intervention, the wrong will already have been committed; his answer is that in such a case you should act without reflection.[166]

Sometimes more intellectually dissident ideas appear. It is not surprising to find them among the later Imāmī scholars, who combined cleverness with a certain delight in picking holes in the arguments of their predecessors.[167] Thus Muqaddas al-Ardabīlī (d. 1585) seems to have been the first to subvert the ordering of the modes by making the point that performance with the heart may in fact be more drastic than performance with the tongue: cutting someone dead is harsher than a gentle rebuke.[168] He also observed that, were it not for the consensus on the point, the permissibility of any kind of violence in performing the duty would be problematic.[169] In the same vein, Bahāʾ al-Dīn al-ʿĀmilī suggested in passing that it did not really make sense to speak of 'commanding' and 'forbidding' except in relation to some kinds of verbal performance, though he accepted that it was a convention of legal usage to do so.[170] This extended an argument that was by then a couple of centuries old: that performance in, or even with, the heart does not properly speaking fall under forbidding wrong, since it does not involve commanding or forbidding.[171] But these scholars were content to raise difficulties; they did not seek to demolish and replace the framework of ideas erected by the older Imāmī scholars.

[165] 337.
[166] 248 n. 148.
[167] 298.
[168] 284.
[169] 285; cf. 286f.
[170] 285.
[171] 284 and n. 224.

CHAPTER 4

When is one unable to forbid wrong?

According to the Prophetic tradition about the three modes, anyone confronted with a wrong should right it with his hand if he is 'able'; but if he 'can't', he defaults to his tongue, and if again he 'can't', to his heart. The scholars frequently talk in the same vein.[1] This usage comes easily enough, but if we are looking for precision it may be inconveniently vague. How can we be more specific about the circumstances that render someone 'able' or 'unable' to forbid wrong?

1 The conditions of obligation

The question just asked brings us face to face with a standard component of the scholarly discussion of forbidding wrong that we have not so far encountered. A systematic account of the duty normally includes a schematic presentation of a set of conditions of obligation. What is involved here can best be seen in the first instance from an example. Let us take the account of the Zaydī Muᶜtazilite Mānkdīm, itself based on a work of his Muᶜtazilite teacher ᶜAbd al-Jabbār.[2]

Mānkdīm begins by saying that forbidding wrong has conditions (*sharāʾiṭ*), being obligatory only when they are satisfied. These conditions are as follows:

(1) *Knowledge of law.* One must know that what one commands is indeed right and what one forbids wrong. If this condition is not satisfied, one risks commanding what is wrong and forbidding what is right, which is obviously not permissible.

(2) *Knowledge of fact.* One must know that the wrong one proposes to forbid is actually in the making (*ḥāḍir*). For example, one might see the wherewithal for drinking or making music being assembled.

(3) *Absence of worse side-effects.* One must know that taking action against the wrong will not lead to a yet greater evil (*maḍarra*). Thus if one knows that

[1] 134 and n. 136; 153; 155; 171; 176 n. 70; 180; 197f.; 198; 201; 202; 230; 238; 248 n. 145; 259; 263; 275 nn. 164f.; 278f. and nn. 191, 194; 284 n. 221; 304; 312; 324; 344; 387 n. 228; 398; 400; 412; 416; 429; 432f.; 459 n. 226; 478 n. 71.

[2] 207–9.

telling off wine-drinkers will lead to the killing of Muslims or the burning of a quarter of a town, then the condition is not satisfied and there is no obligation to proceed.

(4) *Efficacy.* One must know that speaking out [or taking action] will have an effect (*taʾthīr*).

(5) *Absence of danger to oneself.* One must know that one's action will not bring harm to one's person or property.

Mānkdīm has more to say about these conditions than appears in this summary, but there is only one qualification that we need to mention here. With regard to all but the first condition, Mānkdīm adds that it is enough to have good reason to believe (*ghalabat al-ẓann*) that the condition is satisfied. In the case of the first condition, however, you have to have actual knowledge of the point in question; just having good reason to believe that something is right or wrong is not enough.

Most of the schemas of conditions found in the works of the scholars bear a marked family resemblance to Mānkdīm's, but there are numerous variations.

The use of such a schema is standard among the Muᶜtazilites,[3] from whom it was acquired by the Zaydīs,[4] the Imāmīs[5] and – more surprisingly – the Ḥanbalites.[6] Some scholars adopted a rather distinctive way of handling the conditions that goes back to the Ḥanafī Muᶜtazilite Abū ʾl-Ḥusayn al-Baṣrī (d. 1044).[7] Here the conditions are divided into two sets: a first set of five conditions has to be satisfied for it to be *good* to proceed, and an additional set of three for it to be *obligatory*. But in general the scholars were content to operate with a single set of conditions of obligation. Among the Imāmīs, where accounts of forbidding wrong are particularly plentiful, the single-set schema has a complex history in which conditions are amalgamated, dropped and added. Thus the Imāmī Muᶜtazilite al-Sharīf al-Murtaḍā (d. 1044) set out six conditions that were essentially the same as Mānkdīm's five – Murtaḍā chose to divide danger to life and property between two separate conditions.[8] Thereafter this set of six was sometimes repeated,[9] but the most common Imāmī format came to be a set of four conditions, and even these might be pared down to three[10] (or, in one bizarre instance, inflated to fourteen).[11] Yet no significant issues are at stake in this variation.

Another family, or perhaps rather a sub-family, of such schemas is loosely associated with the Ashᶜarites. On the Mālikī side, a three-condition schema was used by Bājī (d. 1081) and the elder Ibn Rushd;[12] in the formulation of Ibn Rushd,

[3] 207 n. 69.
[4] 243 and n. 110.
[5] 276–81; 292–6.
[6] 133–6.
[7] 222f.
[8] 276 nos. 4f.
[9] 276.
[10] 276–9; 292f.
[11] 293.
[12] 363f.

this triad had a long future ahead of it.[13] It has a structure reminiscent of Abū ʾl-Ḥusayn's schema: there are two conditions for it to be good to proceed, and an additional one for it to be obligatory. A single-set triad made a somewhat belated appearance among the Shāfiʿites,[14] although at an earlier date Āmidī had set out a seven-condition schema.[15] Ghazzālī has nothing quite comparable; he handles efficacy and danger under the rubric of being able to perform the duty.[16] The later scholastic tradition among the Mālikīs and Shāfiʿites is much less interesting than that of the Imāmīs, but two late Mālikī commentators argue one condition of their triad to be redundant: efficacy, they say, entails the absence of worse side-effects.[17]

In some works, and indeed in some scholarly communities, no such schema of conditions is to be found. This is the case among the early Ḥanbalites,[18] as also among the eastern Ibāḍīs.[19]

Let us nevertheless take Mānkdīm's schema as our point of reference. If we look it over once more, we see that its five conditions fall into two groups, the first two forming one group and the last three the other. The conditions of the first group are in an obvious way more fundamental. If you do not know that a certain action is wrong, or do not have good reason to believe that someone is going to perform it, then you have no assurance that there is a wrong there for you to forbid. Once these two conditions are satisfied, however, you have what we might call a presumptive obligation to forbid wrong. This is where the second group of conditions becomes relevant. What these conditions do is to direct your attention to the probable consequences of forbidding a wrong, and to help you to identify situations in which your presumptive duty is overridden by the undesirability of the likely outcome. This distinction is not made by the scholars, but it will stand us in good stead.

The first two conditions take us back to some questions already considered in an earlier chapter. The first could be seen as underlying the discussion of the respective roles of scholars and laymen in forbidding wrong,[20] while the second is connected with the issue of past and future wrongs.[21] There is not much that needs to be added here regarding either condition. With regard to knowledge of law, we should perhaps note that actual knowledge is almost universally regarded as essential,[22] although some Imāmī scholars have their doubts.[23] Thus they consider an ingenious scenario in which you know (say from reliable and presumably expert witnesses) that someone is acting wrongly, but you do not yourself know exactly

[13] 374f.
[14] 351.
[15] 349f. and n. 81.
[16] 433f.
[17] 375 n. 127.
[18] Cf. 98.
[19] 416f.
[20] See above, 17f.
[21] See above, 24f.
[22] 133; 153; 207f.; 276 no. 1; 314f.; 317 n. 68; 350 n. 81, no. (2); 351; 363; 363f.
[23] 295 and n. 288; cf. also 244 n. 112.

what it is that is wrong about his conduct; might it not be said that you are still obligated, but now have the added duty of finding out just what it is that is wrong? Turning to knowledge of fact, which is likewise generally accepted,[24] there is an analogous disagreement. Here Mānkdīm's view – that it is enough to have good reason to believe – is typical, and the Ḥanbalite Abū Yaᶜlā is unusual in insisting on actual knowledge.[25] Another point that calls for comment regarding this condition is Mānkdīm's requirement that the wrong be 'in the making'. This is in line with our earlier discussion of past and future wrongs, it being widely accepted that the past is beyond forbidding. Yet there is surely every reason to forbid a wrong that began in the past if it looks like continuing in the future. Thus where Mānkdīm refers to a wrong in the making as if it had not yet started, an Imāmī Muᶜtazilite speaks rather of indications that the wrongdoer will persist (*amārat al-istimrār*).[26] It would probably be a mistake to see a substantive difference of doctrine here.

Unlike the first two conditions, the three consequential conditions – if we may call them that – take us into new terrain, and it is to them that the bulk of this chapter is devoted. Let us begin by taking a closer look at the efficacy condition.

2 The efficacy condition

The efficacy condition says that you are not obliged to forbid wrong if it won't work. This sounds like good sense; what then is left for the scholars to argue about? Let us start by assuming that we do indeed accept the condition, as most scholars who discuss the matter do.[27]

An obvious question of fine-tuning arises here: just how good does the prospect of success have to be to satisfy the condition? For Mānkdīm, as we saw, it is enough that you have good reason to believe that you will succeed. It would certainly seem unreasonable to ask for *more* than this, and no scholar insists that you have to be certain. We are, after all, talking about the future, and we are not prophets; thus when Mālik is asked about a case in which a man knows that the offender will not obey him, his reply turns on the consideration that in the event God might nevertheless bestow success on his effort.[28]

But might the condition be satisfied by *less* than having good reason to believe? Could a mere possibility of success be enough? The scholars do not often address the issue explicitly. One of the exceptions is Ghazzālī.[29] He begins with a clear statement that having good reason to believe generally suffices. He then goes on to

[24] 133; 208 and n. 71; 243 n. 110; 276 no. 2; 279 n. 192.
[25] 133.
[26] 276 no. 2; cf. 133; 208 n. 71; 223 n. 153; 278 n. 186; 350 n. 81.
[27] 202; 209 and n. 73; 222f.; 336 n. 206; 350 n. 81, no. (6); 350 n. 84; 351; 352; 353 n. 109; 363; 363f.; cf. 77f.; 99; 313; 314; 380 nn. 169, 175; 432f.; 498.
[28] 359; cf. 134 no. 4.
[29] 434 no. (1).

consider the grey area in which it is unlikely that proceeding against a wrong would work, but it just might; here, he says, there is dispute, but the better view is that in such a case the condition is satisfied. Abū Yaᶜlā takes a rather similar line.[30] He too presents the area as a grey one. In defence of the view that there is a duty even where success is unlikely, he brings up the argument that the unlikely is not impossible – much as Mālik had pointed out, the offender may experience a change of heart. In defence of the view that proceeding against the wrong must be likely to succeed, however, he adduces the axiom that the point of the duty is to get results.[31] Like Ghazzālī, he seems to come out in favour of the position that having good reason to expect success is not a condition for obligation.[32] Other scholars, particularly among the Imāmīs, formulate the condition in terms of deeming it possible (*tajwīz*) that the outcome will be successful.[33] Does this mean that they side with Ghazzālī and Abū Yaᶜlā? Murtaḍā for one distinguishes such deeming possible from having good reason to believe;[34] but a later Imāmī scholar of great authority, al-Muḥaqqiq al-Ḥillī (d. 1277), seems rather to equate them.[35] With exceptions, later Imāmī scholars tend to the less restrictive view, so rendering the condition more easily satisfied.[36] Overall, however, my sense is that the scholars tend to think in terms of a good prospect of success.

If it is an option to dilute having good reason to believe into merely deeming possible, could we not go further and discard the condition altogether? To spell out the obvious, this would mean that the prospect of success would have no bearing at all on the question whether or not one has an obligation to forbid a given wrong.

The most significant scholar to take this position was the Shāfiᶜite Nawawī, whom we have already met thanks to his role as a commentator on the three-modes tradition. With implicit approval, he gives it as the view of the scholars (whom he does not further identify) that the duty is not voided if one thinks that one will not be successful; and he says in his own voice that someone who is able to perform the duty verbally must do so even if he will not be listened to.[37] His view was to prove mildly infectious. Later Shāfiᶜite commentators on the tradition tend to repeat or take note of his position, and it also makes appearances in other Shāfiᶜite works.[38] Non-Shāfiᶜites are less receptive to it,[39] but it is picked up by several Mālikīs,[40] a Ḥanbalite[41] and probably a Zaydī.[42] Some writers seem

[30] 134 no. 4.
[31] Cf. 210; 352.
[32] 134 n. 139.
[33] 276 no. 3; cf. 351.
[34] 276 n. 175.
[35] 277 n. 181.
[36] 293 and n. 273.
[37] 352f.
[38] 353.
[39] 353 n. 110.
[40] 377.
[41] 353 n. 110.
[42] 248 n. 148.

unconscious of the difference between Nawawī's position and the standard view, but others are well aware of it.[43]

Nawawī is not, however, the sole source of the deviant view. Mazātī (d. 1078f.), a western Ibāḍī, holds that even where one is unable to put a stop to a wrong, one has a duty to forbid it with one's tongue,[44] and such a position had likewise been espoused by some eastern Ibāḍīs long before Nawawī.[45] The notion that it is obligatory to proceed verbally even where it will not work is also found in the Persian version of Ghazzālī's account of forbidding wrong.[46] But such views appear rarely if at all among the Ḥanafīs, the Ḥanbalites, the Muᶜtazilites or their Zaydī and Imāmī heirs.

What is the idea behind this rejection of the efficacy condition? Nawawī says that one's duty is to command and forbid, not that the offender should comply.[47] This suggests that in some sense one does it for the record,[48] and that the consequences are irrelevant. However, one of the Koranic verses quoted by Nawawī in support of his position states that 'the reminder profits the believers' (Q51:55), which would suggest that speaking out does in fact achieve something.[49] How we should resolve this ambiguity is unclear.

It is also possible to find a compromise between affirming and rejecting the efficacy condition. Among the eastern Ibāḍīs we encounter the principle that, where you have no expectation that your rebuke will be accepted, it is your duty to reprove the offender only once; anything more is supererogatory.[50] The idea that you should tell off offenders a limited number of times and then leave off is also found elsewhere, as among the Ḥanbalites and Imāmīs.[51] Thus Ibn Ḥanbal says that if your neighbour is an offender, you make up to three attempts; if he accepts your rebuke, well and good, but if not, you leave off.[52]

This leaves one last issue to be addressed in this section. Let us assume that we hold by the condition, and thus believe that we have no obligation to proceed in a case where there is no prospect of success. The question remains open whether, in such a case, it would still be *good* to proceed. A fair number of scholars maintain that it is.[53] The reason they tend to give is that it is a public affirmation of the norms of Islam (*iẓhār shaᶜāʾir al-Islām* or the like).[54] But not everybody holds this view. Some later Imāmīs say only that if the condition is not satisfied, you are still free

43 377f.
44 400.
45 417; cf. 420.
46 433 n. 41.
47 352.
48 Cf. 59; 134 n. 138; 360; 363 n. 34.
49 352 n. 106.
50 417 and n. 181.
51 99; 257f.; cf. 78.
52 99 and n. 132 (source).
53 209 n. 73; 294 n. 276; 313; 350 n. 81, no. (6); 350 n. 84; 352 n. 104; 353 n. 109; 433 no. 3; cf. 59.
54 350 n. 81, no. (6); 350 n. 84; 353 n. 109; 433 no. 3.

to proceed.[55] Among the Muᶜtazilites, Mānkdīm notes disagreement, and mentions the basis of the rival views: that it is good to proceed because it is tantamount to calling others to the faith, and that it is bad because futile (*ᶜabath*). He does not take up a position himself,[56] and contradictory views are cited from his teacher ᶜAbd al-Jabbār.[57] The argument from futility is used by the Muᶜtazilite Koran commentator Zamakhsharī (d. 1144) to pour scorn on the idea of seeking to rebuke or restrain collectors of illegal taxes; this, he suggests, is a case where not to proceed is a duty.[58] Likewise for Muᶜtazilites in the tradition of Abū ʾl-Ḥusayn al-Baṣrī, efficacy is a condition even for it to be good to proceed.[59]

One question we have not had occasion to discuss in this section is just what degree of success is needed to satisfy the condition. Ghazzālī at one point speaks incidentally of a situation in which forbidding wrong might have an effect by putting a stop to the wrong, or discrediting the wrongdoer, or encouraging the faithful.[60] These are by no means the same thing. Yet in formulating the efficacy condition, the scholars make no reference to such gradations; the only outcomes they seem to envisage are unqualified success and failure.

3 The side-effects condition

Even if forbidding wrong works, it may have costs; indeed its costs may outweigh its benefits. It is therefore no surprise to find that the scholars regularly void the obligation where such is the case. Sometimes they are content to use a single condition to cover all relevant costs. This is the absence of (worse) side-effects condition – let us call it the side-effects condition for short – in its broad sense, as we find it among the Imāmīs, Shāfiᶜites and Mālikīs.[61] But often the scholars carve out one particular set of costs, those incurred by the person who forbids the wrong, and cover them separately; as we will see in the next section, it is these costs that get the lion's share of scholastic attention. Our side-effects condition then has the residual function of covering all other relevant costs; we can now call it the side-effects condition in its narrow sense. Since this narrow sense is something of a poor relation, we will not have to devote much space to it.

As we saw, Mānkdīm formulates the condition in terms of knowing (or having good reason to believe) that taking action against a wrong will not lead to a yet greater evil. Thus if you know that telling off wine-drinkers will lead to the killing

[55] 294 and n. 276.
[56] 209 no. 4; 213.
[57] 209 n. 73.
[58] 279 n. 192 (source); 337 n. 216.
[59] 222f. and n. 151.
[60] 433.
[61] 277 and n. 178; 351; 363; 363f.

of Muslims or the burning of a quarter in a town, then you have no obligation to proceed, nor is it good to do so.[62]

The basic principle we see here, that there is no obligation where the result would be an evil,[63] or a greater evil,[64] is generally accepted by those who deal in sets of conditions. It is likewise echoed or invoked in less formal contexts.[65] Often the evil envisaged is the outbreak of disorder (*fitna*);[66] as we will see in a later chapter,[67] it is on such a basis that rebellion against unjust rule is sometimes condemned.[68] At the same time it is generally agreed that, where adverse side-effects predominate, one ought not to proceed.[69] All this is pretty standard.

There are nevertheless dissonant notes. Some of these would favour a more active stance in forbidding wrong. Thus a Zaydī scholar mentions a view to the effect that if the offender reacts by doing something worse, the entire responsibility is his.[70] Ghazzālī (who lacks a formal account of the side-effects condition)[71] refers to a similar view; he says that some have actually held it, and that it is not to be dismissed out of hand.[72] But the only scholar I know who champions such a position in his own voice is the western Ibāḍī Jayṭālī. The passage comes in his recension of Ghazzālī's *Revival*.[73] At one point Ghazzālī considers the question whether it is virtuous to be rude when forbidding wrong to rulers. In response he makes a distinction with regard to the prospective backlash: if you fear only for yourself, it is commendable, but if others will be harmed, it is not permitted. Jayṭālī disagrees.[74] His view is that provided one's sole purpose is to right the wrong and proclaim the truth, it makes no difference who is harmed. He points out that Ibāḍīs in the past had suffered greatly as a consequence of the rebellions of their co-religionists, yet this had never been taken as a reason not to rebel.

Such reckless disregard of consequences is unusual in the thinking of the scholars. In this respect there is a sharp contrast between Jayṭālī and his Damascene contemporary Ibn Taymiyya (d. 1328). For Ibn Taymiyya it is a general rule that when a course of action carries both costs and benefits, what matters is which is preponderant.[75] Thus the benefit (*maṣlaḥa*) secured by forbidding wrong must outweigh any undesirable consequences (*mafsada*).[76] A nice example is provided

[62] 208f. no. 3.
[63] 276 no. 6; 351; cf. 350 n. 84.
[64] 133 no. 3; 202; 208f. no. 3; 209 n. 72; 222 n. 151; 243; 363; 363f.; cf. 367.
[65] 287 n. 238; 386; 433; 446.
[66] 350 n. 84; 367; 446; cf. 441.
[67] See below, 81f.
[68] 8; 52f.; 153; 160 n. 108; 308f.; 394; 394f. n. 7.
[69] 202; 208f. no. 3; 213; 222 n. 151; 433; 446.
[70] 243 n. 110.
[71] 433 n. 48.
[72] 433.
[73] 401–3.
[74] 402f.
[75] 154.
[76] 153; cf. 171; 180.

by a story told of his visit to the enemy camp during one of the Mongol invasions of Syria. The Mongols, as usual, were drunk; but when one of his companions wanted to reprove them for their drinking habits, Ibn Taymiyya restrained him on the grounds that the Muslims stood to suffer more if the Mongols renounced their liquor.[77] He is more aggressively utilitarian than the scholars at large,[78] but in general they are closer to his way of thinking than to Jayṭālī's.

There is also a divergence that would further limit activity in forbidding wrong. Mānkdīm, as we saw, holds the condition to be voided only where the undesirable consequence is *worse* than the wrong to be righted. But a good many scholars word the condition without this element of comparison. Presumably it would be their view that *any* undesirable consequence suffices to override the duty; but if there is a substantive disagreement here, the scholars do not bring it out into the open. Most, though not all, non-Imāmī scholars use a comparative wording, while most, though not all, Imāmī ones do not.[79] Whether this means that the Imāmīs tend to consider the condition more easily voided than do the non-Imāmīs is not really clear to me.

4 The danger condition

If forbidding wrong carries costs, it is in practice the person doing the forbidding who is most likely to incur them. One young man complains to Mālik that there are people who make him suffer if he commands them: the poets lampoon him, the reprobate beat him up and imprison him.[80] So it makes sense that the risks he runs should receive more attention from the scholars than the dangers his action may pose for others. But there is also a more specific reason for this apparent imbalance. The confrontations that arise from forbidding wrong tend to be particularly dramatic and dangerous in cases where the wrongdoer wields political power. There is therefore an abiding scholarly fascination, both doctrinal and anecdotal, with situations in which the pious take it upon themselves to rebuke rulers for their misdeeds. We will come to the role of the state as both a subject and an object of forbidding wrong in later chapters, so we can defer till then the discussion of these bruising encounters between piety and power, as also of rebellion.[81] What concerns us here is the broad outlines of what the scholars have to say about the absence-of-danger condition (or conditions) – or, as I shall call it for short, the danger condition.

This condition is generally accepted. There are numerous formal statements to the effect that the prospect of coming to harm – or some degree of it – voids the

[77] 154f.
[78] Cf. 435.
[79] Cf. 209 n. 72; 277 n. 180 (and sources).
[80] 360.
[81] See below, ch. 7, sections 2 and 3.

obligation.[82] As with the efficacy condition, the idea is also commonplace in less formal contexts.[83] But in contrast to the efficacy condition, there is no school of thought that rejects the danger condition in a clear and explicit fashion. It is possible to find occasional passages that, strictly construed, would imply such a rejection.[84] Thus there is a long activist tradition transmitted by the Imāmīs from their imam Muḥammad al-Bāqir (d. *c.* 736).[85] In harsh rhetorical language, he foretells that in the last days there will be people who, despite their pious observances, do not consider forbidding wrong to be obligatory unless they are safe from harm, thereby brushing aside the noblest of duties. But statements of this kind tend to look like products of rhetoric, enthusiasm or inadvertence, rather than expressions of a settled doctrinal position.

Just as with the efficacy condition, a question of fine-tuning arises. But in this instance the issue discussed by the scholars is not how probable the harm must be for the condition to be satisfied, but how severe. Harm, after all, comes in many shapes and sizes. As we have already seen, the scholars may show concern not just for the person of the forbidder of wrong, but also for his property,[86] and occasionally they extend this to things as intangible as his honour (*ʿirḍ*)[87] or social standing (*jāh*).[88] Moreover, their intention can hardly be to void the duty at the slightest inconvenience. As Ghazzālī points out, some degree of unpleasantness is only to be expected when one forbids wrong.[89] Indeed there is warrant for enduring such unpleasantness in the Koran; in Q31:17, the sage Luqmān tells his son to 'perform the prayer, and command right and forbid wrong, and bear patiently whatever may befall thee'. The exegetes usually identify 'whatever may befall thee' as the adverse consequences of forbidding wrong;[90] thus the verse is often quoted to establish the need for perseverance (*ṣabr*) in performing the duty.[91]

How then are we to establish a level above which harm will void the duty? The scholars have nothing very precise to say about this, but they do come up with a couple of approaches to the problem. One is relative: as in the mainstream version of the side-effects condition, you compare the prospective harm with the wrong you are seeking to right, and act accordingly.[92] The other seeks to make absolute distinctions between mild and severe forms of harm. Here losing one's life will obviously count as severe, whereas insults, blows and the like may count as mild.[93]

[82] 77; 134 no. 5; 202; 209 no. 5; 209f. n. 74 *ter*; 223 n. 152; 244 n. 112; 259; 276 nos. 4f.; 280f.; 294; 324; 344; 363; 363f.; 366f. *bis*; 369f.; 416; 417; 432f. nos. 1 and 4; 476; cf. 380 n. 169.
[83] 77; 98f.; 128; 229; 336 n. 206; 337f.; cf. 54; 254; 313; 400 *bis*; 416 n. 175.
[84] 59 *bis*; 73; 135; 172; 313; 314; 350 n. 81.
[85] 256; cf. 294f. and n. 282.
[86] 134 n. 141; 202; 209 no. 5; 223 n. 152; 276 no. 5; 281; 366 n. 58.
[87] 293.
[88] 434f.; cf. 209 no. 5.
[89] 434 no. (3).
[90] 28f.
[91] 72; 137 (and source); 153 (and source); 313 (and source); 442 (and source); 492.
[92] 43; 210 n. 74; 294 n. 279.
[93] 98; 281 n. 211; cf. 340 n. 5.

It is Ghazzālī who provides the most elaborate account of degrees of harm.[94] Thus with regard to social standing, he points out that it is one thing to have to walk on foot rather than ride a horse, and quite another to be paraded around the town bareheaded and barefooted. But as he sensibly observes, there are bound to be grey areas in which one has to use one's judgement.

There is also the matter of differences between people. Mānkdīm points out that one man might not be much affected by insults and blows, whereas another might suffer and lose standing, and this is clearly relevant to determining whether each is obligated.[95] What is not relevant, Ghazzālī says, is the difference of temperament between the timid, for whom even distant eventualities loom terrifyingly close, and the foolhardy, who recognise disaster only when it has already struck; instead we should take as our standard a balanced and sensible personality.[96]

But let us set aside these teasing issues and take the danger condition as given. Just as in the case of the efficacy condition, the question for us now is whether in the absence of obligation it is still *good* to proceed. The standard answer is that it is;[97] if you are willing to take risks in God's cause, you will be rewarded.[98] In the limit, this means endorsing the view that someone who is killed forbidding wrong dies the death of a martyr (*shahīd*), and many scholars have no problem with this.[99]

Others prefer to make distinctions. In one view, often found among the Muʿtazilites and their Zaydī heirs, the criterion is the prestige of Islam. As Mānkdīm tells us, proceeding in the face of danger may serve the purpose of elevating the dignity of the faith (*iʿzāz al-dīn*), or it may not; it is good to proceed in the first case, but not in the second.[100] In a variant of this view, it depends on whether or not one is a religious role model.[101] For other scholars the distinction may turn on the degree of prospective harm.[102] Thus an eleventh-century Imāmī scholar allows that there are cases not involving mortal danger where suffering is rewarded, as when one is subjected to abusive language or the loss of a part of one's property.[103] Likewise the later Imāmī scholars occasionally take the view that it is permissible to proceed in the face of bearable loss, especially where property is concerned.[104]

As this suggests, not everyone is comfortable with heroism. Occasionally we find that though recognised, it is tacitly or explicitly relegated to the past.[105] It may

94 434f. no. (3).
95 209 no. 5; cf. 54.
96 434 no. (2).
97 129; 134f.; 202; 210 n. 74; 223; 244 n. 112; 318; 366f.; 378; 423 n. 227; 432 n. 40; 433 no. 4; 476; cf. 139; 201; 314; 378 n. 158; 402; 582.
98 318; 366f.; 432 n. 40.
99 128; 228; 251; 320; 324 and n. 137; 441; 446; 476; cf. 105; 137; 309; 318.
100 209 no. 5; 209f. n. 74; 224; 226; 244 n. 112; cf. 352 n. 104.
101 209f. n. 74.
102 Cf. 313.
103 280f.
104 294.
105 53 n. 47; 98f.; 210 n. 74; 476f.; cf. 327.

also be rejected outright, particularly where the danger is mortal.[106] Abū Yaᶜlā, who is pulled in different directions by his Ḥanbalite heritage and his openness to Muᶜtazilite methods, tells us in the usual way that in the face of danger the more virtuous course is to proceed;[107] yet he also argues that if you are killed, the result is the humiliation of the faith (*idhlāl al-dīn*) rather than its elevation.[108] Such views are also found among the Mālikīs,[109] and they are standard doctrine among the Imāmīs until modern times.[110] Indeed a tenth-century Imāmī secretary condemned heroism in forbidding wrong as stupidity tantamount to provoking a wild beast.[111] The Imāmī religious scholars were more restrained in their language, but Murtaḍā, for example, denies that courting death can be justified even in terms of the elevation of the faith.[112] The argument that getting oneself killed amounts to suicide is known to both Sunnīs and Shīᶜites;[113] Sunnī scholars occasionally refute it.[114]

As indicated above, we will come back to some of these themes in a later chapter in connection with rulers. For the moment, we have said enough about what the forbidder of wrong owes to himself; we come now to something he owes to the wrongdoer.

[106] 476; cf. 42f.; 344; 416 n. 175; 432 no. 1.
[107] 134.
[108] 135f.
[109] 363; 363f.; 369f.; 378; cf. 366 n. 60.
[110] 223 n. 153; 280f.; 282; 294; 295.
[111] 280 n. 207.
[112] 281.
[113] 7f.; 134; 295 n. 286.
[114] 366 n. 59; 433 no. 4.

CHAPTER 5

What about privacy?

Underlying the problems considered in this chapter is a straightforward clash of two values: it is a good thing to stop wrongdoing, but a bad thing to violate privacy. As the Mālikī Ibn al-Rabīᶜ al-Khashshāb (d. 956f.) put it, the believer's home (*bayt al-muʾmin*) is his castle (*ḥirz*) – or at least it may be (a qualification we will come to).[1] How then do the scholars seek to reconcile the conflicting demands of the two values?[2]

Two things make it harder to answer this question. One is that the scholars do not possess any single concept equivalent to our notion of privacy; what they have is rather a cluster of related concerns. The other is that in their discussions of forbidding wrong they do not give their thinking on these concerns any very systematic shape – we look in vain for an equivalent of the simple schemas that provided backbone for previous chapters. Perhaps related to this, we do not encounter any dramatic polarisations of scholarly opinion at the intersection of privacy and forbidding wrong. But the material is nevertheless quite rich, and it articulates real tensions.

1 The immunity of hidden wrongs

It is a basic principle that, to be a valid target of the duty, a wrong must in some way be public knowledge. If a wrong is private in the sense that we do not know about it, it is beyond the scope of the duty.[3] Such wrongdoing, as is pointed out in a Prophetic tradition, harms only the wrongdoer.[4] Ibn Taymiyya puts it like this: 'Manifest wrongs must be acted against, in contrast to hidden ones, the punishment of which afflicts only the perpetrator';[5] the punishment he refers to is God's. As Ibn al-Rabīᶜ indicates, when offenders gather to drink liquor, or to sell it, or to

1 380.
2 479–82.
3 Cf. 383 n. 202.
4 43 n. 60; cf. 172.
5 480 n. 84.

make music that is audible to the Muslims in their homes and streets, this amounts to holding the faithful in contempt; but wrongdoing that is between the offenders and God is another matter.[6]

Of course, if we do not know about a wrong, the question of forbidding it does not in practice arise. What gives substance to the immunity of hidden wrongs is the fact that we are forbidden to go on fishing expeditions for the purpose of uncovering them. We may not spy on people, nor may we enter a home on the off-chance of discovering wrongdoing in it.[7] Thus in the responsa of Ibn Ḥanbal, there is a presumption against resorting to investigation (*taftīsh*) to discover or confirm offences. If you hear the sound of music, but do not know where it is coming from, it is not your duty to proceed: 'Do not investigate what is not out in the open (*mā ghāba*).'[8]

This reluctance to pry is not simply an expression of a human value widely shared by the world's cultures. It is also rooted in scripture. There is a famous story told about ᶜUmar ibn al-Khaṭṭāb (r. 634–44), a caliph who in Sunnī sources has the image of a man with his heart in the right place, but a tendency to go too far. On this occasion he entered a man's home by climbing over the wall, and caught him engaged in wrongdoing. But the man retorted that, while he had indeed sinned in one respect, ᶜUmar had sinned in three. He had spied, whereas God has prohibited this (Q49:12). He had entered through the roof, whereas God has commanded us to enter houses by their doors (Q2:189). And he had entered without pronouncing a greeting, whereas God has forbidden us to enter a house without first greeting those who dwell in it (Q24:27). ᶜUmar let the man be, merely stipulating that he should repent.[9] What this comes down to is two things that the scholars endorse: the prohibition of spying (*tajassus*),[10] and the sanctity of the home.

While the principle of the immunity of hidden wrongs is simple enough to grasp, it may not always be easy to apply. Just what is to count as hidden? There is a considerable grey area here, a domain that invites inference and suspicion. Some examples will convey a sense of the kinds of case that bother the scholars.

Suppose you discern under someone's robe a shape that looks uncommonly like a bottle of liquor or a lute. Ibn Ḥanbal considers cases of this kind in his responsa; but as the later Ḥanbalite tradition was well aware, his various pronouncements are not entirely consistent.[11] The basic distinction he makes is between an object that is out in the open (*makshūf*) and one that is under cover (*mughaṭṭā*). If the offending object is out in the open, then other things being equal you ought to destroy it; here there is no problem. But what if it is concealed? As might be expected, Ibn Ḥanbal tends to say that one should leave it alone; for example, an instrument

[6] 380; 381.
[7] Cf. 117; 119; 178 n. 90.
[8] 100; cf. 80; 245.
[9] 81f.; cf. 480 n. 85.
[10] 245; 346; 350 n. 81, no. (7); 350 n. 84; 403; 436; 438.
[11] 100 and n. 147.

concealed by a garment is not to be broken, even if it is clear what it is. But he also says that, if you catch sight of a concealed musical instrument, and it is clear to you what it is, you should break it, just as you should break a concealed liquor container if you know it to contain liquor. On the other hand, if chess-players cover the board, or move it behind them, you should take no action. What Ghazzālī has to say on such questions is more straightforward.[12] In brief, you may not challenge a sinner who has something concealed under his robe unless there is some special reason to suspect him. The object he is concealing could well be a bottle of wine, but then again it might be vinegar – a sinner needs his vinegar like anyone else, and people have all sorts of reasons for concealing things. But if the garment is thin enough to reveal the outlines of a musical instrument, it counts as out in the open.

What if you see a suspicious jar, one that might or might not contain liquor? Again, Ibn Ḥanbal's views do not hold together well.[13] We learn that if you see a jar that you merely suspect to contain liquor, you should leave it alone and not investigate. Yet when a man told Ibn Ḥanbal that he had opened a jar in a home to which he had been called and found it to contain liquor, the response was that he should have put salt in it to spoil the liquor. (Perhaps this obligation arose once the man had opened the jar, irrespective of whether he should have done so.) A Zaydī scholar of the early eleventh century says that if you do not know for sure that there is wine in the jar, but have good reason to think so, you must proceed; the catch is that if it turns out that you were wrong, you are liable to pay compensation.[14] A later scholar requires actual knowledge.[15]

What if you encounter a couple walking in the street looking as if they might be unmarried? Mālik is asked about a Muslim who walks with a young woman to whom he chats; when challenged he claims that she is his freedwoman (*hiya mawlātī*). Should one not step out, asks the questioner, and do something to stop this kind of thing? Mālik replies that he thoroughly approves of such action.[16] Unfortunately later scholars do not take up this question, but history relates that in early tenth-century Baghdad the Ḥanbalites would challenge men and women seen walking together in public; if they did not get a satisfactory answer, they would beat the offender and hand him over to the chief of police.[17] Against this we can pit an anecdote in which the caliph al-Maʾmūn (r. 813–33), on campaign against the infidel in Anatolia, faces down a shrouded zealot who has come to command and forbid him in the expectation of being killed for it.[18] What, the caliph asks the zealot, would he do if he came upon a young couple talking amorously with each other here in this mountain pass?

[12] 436 (and source).
[13] 99f.
[14] 239 no. 2.
[15] 245 n. 120.
[16] 359.
[17] 117.
[18] 10f.

The zealot: I would ask them who they were.
The caliph: You'd ask the man, and he'd tell you she was his wife. And you'd ask the woman, and she'd say he was her husband. So what would you do with them?
The zealot: I'd separate them and imprison them.
The caliph: Till when?
The zealot: Till I'd asked about them.
The caliph: And who would you ask?
The zealot: [First] I'd ask them where they were from.
The caliph: Fine. You've asked the man where he's from, and he says he's from Asfījāb [far away on the frontiers of Transoxania]. The woman too says she's from Asfījāb – that he's her cousin, they got married and came here. Well, are you going to keep them in prison on the basis of your vile suspicions and false imaginings until your messenger comes back from Asfījāb? Say the messenger dies, or they die before he gets back?
The zealot: I would ask here in your camp.
The caliph: What if you could only find one or two people from Asfījāb in my camp, and they told you they didn't know them? Is that what you've put on your shroud for?

Incidentally, this is not the last we will hear of the caliph and the zealot.

A final example: should you enter a home from which you hear the sound of music? The usual answer is that you should.[19] Our eleventh-century Zaydī tells us that if you hear singing or the noise of musical instruments coming from inside a home, and recognise (the signs of) wine-drinking, it is your duty to enter. In the same way, he says that if you know – or just have good reason to think – that there is wine there, then you must go in and pour it out.[20] But as usual, nothing is simple, and there are finer points to be considered. We have already met the case where you hear the sound of music, yet do not know where it is coming from;[21] compare the delicate issue that arises where others can hear the noise of wrongdoing, but you can't.[22] There is also the question how sure you have to be about the wrongdoing before entering a home: some require only that you have good reason to believe,[23] but others may require actual knowledge.[24] There is even a view, quoted but not held by the eastern Ibāḍī authors, to the effect that in such cases you should not enter a home at all if refused leave to enter.[25] But one of them goes on to say that you may climb over the wall if denied leave, though you must not damage it.[26]

[19] 309 n. 14; 381; 414; 436.
[20] 239 no. 3; cf. 240 nos. 8f.; 383.
[21] See above, 58.
[22] 418 n. 189.
[23] 230; 239 no. 3; 245; cf. 418.
[24] 200; cf. 245 n. 118; 418.
[25] 414; 417.
[26] 414.

With that we may contrast the response of Sufyān al-Thawrī to a certain Ṣūfī who described how he and his companions would enter the homes of evildoers by clambering over the walls: 'Don't they have doors?'[27]

These four examples are enough to convey the flavour of the thinking of the scholars with regard to the immunity of hidden wrongs. The basic point is clear enough. As Ghazzālī tells us, one may learn of a wrong through coming upon indirect evidence of it, but one has no right to go looking for such signs – eavesdropping for the sound of music, sniffing to detect the aroma of wine, feeling a garment in search of the shape of a lute, or collecting gossip from a man's neighbours.[28] A more systematic account of the concerns of the scholars would be possible only against the background of a broader and deeper study of their notions of privacy.

2 Don't expose a respectable Muslim

If I understand the thinking of the scholars correctly, a wrong that we have come to know about is no longer hidden, and its immunity is thereby lifted. At this point, then, we confront a forbiddable wrong. Yet privacy can still do something for the wrongdoer. The manner of our response to the wrong, or indeed whether we respond to it at all, may be shaped by the principle that we should not expose the private life of an outwardly respectable Muslim to public shame.

Though not found in the Koran, this principle is enshrined in a much-quoted tradition. Here the Prophet avers that whoever keeps concealed something that would dishonour a Muslim (*man satara Musliman*) will receive the same consideration from God.[29] A less common but more vivid version of the tradition makes reference to the pre-Islamic Arab practice of female infanticide: whoever covers up (*satara*) the shame of a believer is as one who brings to life a buried infant from her grave.[30]

Like the three-modes tradition, this saying of the Prophet is also found embedded in a frame-story, and this anecdote provides an indication of what is at stake in such covering up (*satr*).[31] A certain Companion of the Prophet, ᶜUqba ibn ᶜĀmir (d. 677f.), had settled in Egypt, where he served as governor in 665–7. His secretary once complained to him that he had neighbours who drank wine, and proposed to summon the police to arrest them. ᶜUqba told him not to do this, but rather to counsel and threaten them. He did so, but to no effect; so again he proposed to call in the police. ᶜUqba once more told him not to do so, and this time quoted what he had heard the Prophet say, in the version with the buried infant.

27 81.
28 436; 438.
29 44.
30 44 n. 61.
31 80f.

The idea that one should not expose the private sins of a Muslim even when one knows about them is accordingly part of the heritage of the scholars. Thus Abū Yaᶜlā says that neither a scholar nor a layman has a duty to expose a wrong that is covered up (*qad sutira*); he quotes yet another Prophetic tradition to the effect that no one who comes upon something shameful should reveal it.[32] As in the frame-story, there may be a link between covering up a scandal and warding off the attentions of the state. The stubbornly pious Saᶜīd ibn al-Musayyab (d. 712f.) is asked whether, having come upon a drunkard, one is permitted not to report him to the authorities (*sulṭān*); he tells the questioner that he should rather conceal the man (*usturhu*) under his robe, if he is able to do so.[33]

Concern not to expose a Muslim need not prevent one from forbidding wrong. Indeed Ibn al-Rabīᶜ requires admonition (*waᶜẓ*) even where the wrongdoing is something between the sinners and God.[34] But reluctance to shame a man in public does provide an excellent reason for rebuking him in private.[35] And as we saw in an earlier chapter, the scholars have a marked preference for private rebuke.[36] Thus the Ḥanafī Abū ᵓl-Layth al-Samarqandī (d. 983) says that one should perform the duty in private (*fī ᵓl-sirr*) where possible; only if this does not work should one do so in public (*fī ᵓl-ᶜalāniya*), calling upon the help of the virtuous.[37] The Shāfiᶜite Ḥalīmī points out two courses you can take to avoid the public disgrace of the offender: either you can speak about the evil in question in public without identifying the offender, or you can privately send him a message about it.[38]

3 Concluding remarks

An important feature of these Muslim ideas of privacy, if I read them right, is what might be called their procedural rather than substantive character. Wrongdoing that is confined within a home can still trigger the duty for others who live in that home: as we have seen, a wife may be obligated to rebuke her husband, and a son his parents.[39] Perhaps more significantly, someone from outside the home who for any reason happens to be there, and encounters wrongdoing, may be obligated to do something about it.[40] In other words, we do not seem to have here the notion that certain kinds of behaviour are *inherently* private, and as such immune to public scrutiny. What is protected is not 'private life' but rather 'hidden sin', behaviour

32 136 and n. 152 (and source); cf. 129 n. 111; 465.
33 81; cf. 239 no. 4.
34 380.
35 481.
36 See above, 29.
37 312; cf. 137.
38 343.
39 See above, 16, 21f., 28.
40 99f.

that happens not to be public knowledge. It is no business of ours to pry into what is unknown to us, nor to divulge what we innocently stumble upon; but once we know, we are likely to incur some kind of obligation to forbid wrong. The point is nicely made in a western Ibāḍī catechism dating from 1914 with regard to the duty of a person who has learnt of wrongdoing through spying.[41] He now has two obligations: on the one hand, he has to forbid the wrong, and on the other, he has to repent of his spying. The difference between Muslim thinking and that of the modern West is thus not simply that there is no single Muslim concept corresponding to the Western notion of privacy; it is also that the Muslim concepts seem to be of a significantly different kind.

Yet even here it is not hard to find an exception. A passage that suggests a distinction of the Western type occurs in Māwardī's discussion of the duties of the censor (*muḥtasib*).[42] Just like ordinary believers, he has no right to spy into 'forbidden things that have not become manifest'. What then if he hears the sound of music coming from a home? The answer is that he takes action outside the home, without pushing his way in, since the wrong he is addressing is a public (*ẓāhir*) one, and it is not his business to uncover a further private (*bāṭin*) wrong.

[41] 403.
[42] 482 n. 106.

CHAPTER 6

The state as an agent of forbidding wrong

From the vantage-point of the modern world, we tend to see the states of pre-modern times as shallow and flimsy constructions with little impact on the societies they purported to rule. Perhaps at some level this is an accurate picture of what the states of those times were actually like. But it is not at all how the scholars saw them. In their eyes, rulers and their associates loomed very large indeed. They wielded disproportionate power, and they used this power with some abandon for both better and worse.

In the context of forbidding wrong, this gross power of the ruler cast him in two sharply antithetical roles. On the one hand, he was better placed than anyone else to forbid wrong; but on the other, he had far more opportunity to commit it. I shall take each of these contrasting roles in turn, the first in this chapter and the second in the next.

1 The claims of the state to forbid wrong

It is no surprise that rulers liked to describe themselves, or be described, as forbidding wrong. We find examples of this here and there in the Sunnī fold. We are told that the activity was part of the daily routine of the ᶜAbbāsid caliph al-Manṣūr (r. 754–75). Likewise the caliph al-Muhtadī (r. 869–70) built a dome under which he would sit rendering justice to all; he commanded right and forbade wrong, forbidding liquor and singing-girls. In North Africa, the Almohad caliph ᶜAbd al-Muʾmin (r. 1130–63) was constantly engaged in forbidding wrong.[1] Similar language may be used of other rulers who took themselves seriously in Islamic terms, for example the Saudi Turkī ibn ᶜAbdallāh (r. 1823–34).[2] In his case the claim to forbid wrong was doubtless sincere, though in others this may be open to doubt. In 933 the ᶜAbbāsid caliph al-Qāhir (r. 932–4) forbade liquor and singing, ordering that singing-girls be sold at prices that took no account of their musical

[1] 470; cf. 300.
[2] 175; 177; cf. below, 125f.

talents. He then had them bought up for his own use at firesale prices.[3] But what concerns us here is not the sincerity or otherwise with which rulers conducted themselves, but rather their claim to the rhetoric of forbidding wrong.

This rhetoric is considerably more pronounced in sectarian contexts, where it makes frequent appearances in connection with the imamate, that is the office of imam. Among the Imāmīs, for example, there is a strain of sectarian exegesis that construes Koranic verses on forbidding wrong as referring to the imams;[4] we even find a variant reading of Q3:110 in which a small change to the consonantal text turns 'the best community' into 'the best imams'.[5] The link with the imamate is also apparent among the Ibāḍīs, both western and eastern.[6] They do not tinker with the Koranic text, but one eastern scholar achieves the same result exegetically by identifying the imams as the 'best community' when they forbid wrong.[7] Indeed among the eastern Ibāḍīs forbidding wrong was a standard part of the formula whereby allegiance to a new imam was offered and accepted.[8]

Such rhetoric is nowhere more intense than among the Zaydīs,[9] a politically activist sect with a penchant for small-scale state formation among remote mountain tribes. The initiators of these ventures were descendants of ᶜAlī who would claim the imamate in defiance of the Sunnī rulers of the lowlands. Forbidding wrong is thus a prominent theme in the life and works of al-Hādī (d. 911), the founder of the Zaydī imamate in the Yemen. In one rousing passage, he argues that commanding and forbidding are vested in the best members of the family of the Prophet, to the exclusion of Pharaohs and tyrants. His polemical target here is the anthropomorphist predestinationists (in other words, the Sunnīs) who believe that God has Himself decreed the oppression they suffer; were they to come to know God as He really is, and then to set about commanding right and forbidding wrong, their prayers would be answered and they would be delivered from their oppressors.[10] If we can judge by a biography of al-Hādī written by a contemporary, the duty coloured everything he did; it even made a simple meal of three buns and a little condiment shared by al-Hādī and one of his followers tantamount to a banquet.[11] There is little in this Zaydī tradition to suggest that forbidding wrong implied a concrete and practical programme of moral reform; rather it appears as a banner under which an ᶜAlid could rebel, establish a state and maintain his power.[12]

The rhetoric, and indeed the practice, of forbidding wrong may extend to a ruler's subordinates.[13] The ᶜAbbāsid governor of Egypt in the years 786–7 made

[3] 470 n. 3.
[4] 260–2.
[5] 261; cf. 302.
[6] 397f.; 405–7.
[7] 405f.
[8] 406.
[9] 231–7.
[10] 234.
[11] 234f.
[12] 237.
[13] Cf. also 302f.

the duty a theme of his governorship, cracking down on music and liquor (not to mention newly built churches).[14] We also hear of governors elsewhere being expected to play their part in forbidding wrong; this was so, for example, among the Zaydīs in al-Hādī's Yemen,[15] among the Ibāḍīs of seventeenth-century Oman,[16] and among the Wahhābīs of nineteenth-century Saudi Arabia.[17]

Rulers might also appoint subordinates for the specific purpose of forbidding wrong. Among the western Ibāḍīs, a ninth-century imam appointed a group to forbid wrong in the markets;[18] among their eastern brethren the 'sellers' (*shurāt*) may have had a similar role (in principle they were supposed to be religious activists who had 'sold' themselves to God in pursuit of martyrdom).[19] A nineteenth-century scholar who played a prominent role in the Saudi state speaks of the ruler's duty to send out officials in charge of religious affairs, just as he sends out tax collectors; these officials are to instruct the people, and to command and forbid them.[20] But the official we hear most of in medieval Islamic societies is of course the censor (*muḥtasib*), who was charged with the oversight of markets and morals;[21] this office was already established in the eighth century.[22]

If the state made it its business to forbid wrong in this fashion, was there not a danger that it might seek to transform its role into a monopoly? Not that a virtuous Islamic ruler would be expected to behave in this fashion. The caliph ᶜUthmān (r. 644–56) is said to have announced at the beginning of his reign: 'Whoever of you sees a wrong, let him put it right; if he lacks the strength to do so, let him refer it to me.'[23] There are nevertheless accounts which portray the Umayyad caliph ᶜAbd al-Malik (r. 685–705) and the ᶜAbbāsid caliph al-Maᵓmūn as banning the forbidding of wrong.[24] How seriously, or how literally, we should take them is another question. By way of example let us look at one of the anecdotes about al-Maᵓmūn. This is the case of the Kūfan traditionist Abū Nuᶜaym al-Faḍl ibn Dukayn (d. 834) and the lascivious soldier.[25]

The background to the story is the anarchic period prior to al-Maᵓmūn's entry into Baghdad in 819, which brought to an end a prolonged period of civil war. The elders of the city had taken it upon themselves to forbid wrong; they maintained law and order, imprisoning and punishing offenders. Now that the caliph had arrived on the scene and authority had been restored, al-Maᵓmūn proclaimed a ban on forbidding wrong. At this point Abū Nuᶜaym came to Baghdad, and happened

[14] 471f.
[15] 235 and n. 49.
[16] 407 and n. 101.
[17] 177.
[18] 397f.
[19] 412f.
[20] 177.
[21] 471 and n. 8.
[22] 471 n. 8.
[23] 472.
[24] 10; 70f.; 472f. and n. 21.
[25] 70.

to see a soldier with his hand between the thighs of a woman. He confronted the soldier; the latter then took him to the chief of police, and the matter was reported to the caliph, who had Abū Nuᶜaym brought before him. After he had been given an opportunity to display his scholarly credentials, al-Maᵓmūn told him that the ban was not directed at people like him, but only against those who turned right into wrong. Abū Nuᶜaym responded that this should have been made clear in the proclamation, and was released. Here the ban seems to be a response to a particular moment in the history of Baghdad, rather than a general assertion of caliphal authority.

Such stories are nevertheless useful in establishing the extremes of a hypothetical spectrum. At one end, we could imagine a world in which the ruler had made himself the sole forbidder of wrong; and at the other end, we could envisage one in which he had been evicted from forbidding wrong altogether. How then do the scholars see matters?

2 The scholars on the role of the state: positive views

The scholars are not blind to the claims of the state to forbid wrong. Indeed most of the material on which the preceding section is based derives from their works. What they lack, however, is a *theory* of the role of the state in forbidding wrong. All their theorising is about the role of individuals, and in the context of this concern it is only incidentally that they talk about the role of the state. And with very rare exceptions,[26] they ignore the role of the censor (*muḥtasib*).

Many scholars nevertheless speak of the role of the state in positive terms.[27] There are rare passages that, if taken literally, would indicate that forbidding wrong should be left to the ruler.[28] More commonly the scholars indicate in one way or another that the state should play a major role.[29] Thus a rather trite mirror for princes of the mid-twelfth century emphasises the duty that is incumbent on the ruler to forbid wrong because of his position of supremacy; in the case of a ruler, the scholar who wrote the book avers, forbidding wrong is more important than praying by night or fasting by day.[30] Mānkdīm distinguishes two varieties of the duty: what only rulers can carry out, and what people at large can undertake. In the first category he places such standard functions of state power as defending the frontiers and appointing governors; it is only with the second category that we enter the familiar terrain of forbidding wrong. Yet even here, he says that if there is a legitimate ruler, then it is better to have recourse to him.[31] The eastern Ibāḍī

[26] 21 and n. 36; 351 n. 91.
[27] 473–5.
[28] 43 n. 56; 342; 368; 473.
[29] 473.
[30] 470f.
[31] 215f.

scholars have similar views.[32] Thus they divide the duty into two parts: that which obligates people in general insofar as they are able to undertake it, and that which obligates the imams of justice and their officers to the exclusion of the people at large. In the context of the three-modes tradition, one eastern Ibāḍī jurist remarks that the 'hand' of the imam extends farther than that of anyone else; likewise the imams and their officers are said to be singled out to undertake the duty. The Saudi scholar ᶜAbdallāh ibn Muḥammad ibn ᶜAbd al-Wahhāb (d. 1826f.) says that the duty is incumbent on all subjects, but that the ruler has an even stronger obligation to engage in it.[33]

Ibn Taymiyya is another case in point, and a significant one.[34] He considers it to be the purpose of all state power to carry out the duty. He seems to see it as one to be performed first and foremost – though not exclusively – by what the Koran calls 'those in authority' (*ulū ᵓl-amr*). Thus in one passage he states that forbidding wrong is obligatory for 'those in authority', whom he specifies broadly as the scholars, the political and military grandees, and the elders of every community; it is their duty to forbid wrong to those of the common people who are subject to them. In another passage he also mentions kings and state functionaries. Moreover, he provides a strikingly simple justification of this association of forbidding wrong with the authorities, and in particular with the state: successful performance of the duty is obviously and critically dependent on having the power (*qudra*) to execute it, and power is something of which those in authority naturally possess the lion's share.[35]

For a good many scholars, what determines the relationship between the state and forbidding wrong is the need for recourse to violence. As we saw in an earlier chapter, they often hold that violence, or some level of it, is reserved to the state.[36] Such, of course, is the implication of the tripartite division of labour so often referred to by the Ḥanafīs.[37] Less rigid but in the same spirit is the view of some Muᶜtazilites that the imam and his deputies are better placed to undertake the duty where it involves fighting.[38] Alternatively the scholars (more especially the Imāmīs) may make recourse to violence, or some degree of it, contingent on the ruler's permission.[39] This latter idea is not restricted to narrowly scholastic contexts. A tenth-century Imāmī secretary, in a passage on situations in which the common people may need to be reined in by the state, mentions a scenario in which they set about forbidding wrong without having received the permission of their ruler, thereby neglecting their proper economic activities.[40]

[32] 412; cf. 414f.
[33] 172; cf. 179.
[34] 155.
[35] Cf. 309 n. 12.
[36] See above, 33.
[37] See above, 17.
[38] See above, 33.
[39] See above, 34.
[40] 474; 270 n. 115; cf. 329 n. 163; 356 n. 140; 459 n. 226; 472.

We also encounter a willingness among the scholars to refer cases of wrong-doing to the state, and to cooperate with the state in dealing with them.[41] Thus Mālik holds that where a neighbour openly drinks wine and the like, and ignores a rebuke, he should be reported to the imam.[42] At the same time the scholars endorse the idea that the ruler should appoint someone to see to the duty. Ḥalīmī states that since the ruler is not omnipresent, he should appoint a watchdog in each town and village; this appointee should be a learned and trustworthy man of strong and sound character.[43] One should even be prepared to accept such appointment oneself. Mālik is asked to comment on a situation in which a man who wishes to take action is unable to do so without recourse to the authorities; he approaches a ruler, who invites him to undertake the task. The man accepts on condition that he is not to sit in any appointed place, nor to have anything to do with set punishments, but is only to command and forbid. Does Mālik approve of such a man undertaking the duty at the command of the ruler? Mālik's reply is that if the man is able to perform the duty, and does it right, he should indeed undertake it.[44] Ideas of this kind are widespread enough that they cannot be dismissed as marginal.[45]

3 The scholars on the role of the state: negative views

By no means all scholars are so accommodating towards the claims of the state to a major role in forbidding wrong.[46] One unflattering account has it that the caliph ᶜAbd al-Malik was the first caliph to command wrong and forbid right – a reference to Q9:67, in which this deliberate inversion of the standard Koranic phrase is predicated of the hypocrites (*munāfiqūn*).[47] The pronouncements of the scholars are not usually so harsh or so sweeping, but in one way or another they often limit or undermine the role of the state in forbidding wrong.[48]

Much of what we need to review here is already familiar. Many scholars left individual subjects free to take up arms in forbidding wrong,[49] as in Ghazzālī's example of the man on the other side of the river who has seized a woman or is playing a flute.[50] Even Ghazzālī's notorious armed bands, about which he himself seems to have experienced some queasiness,[51] won a measure of acceptance from

[41] 136 nn. 153f.; 367; 380f.; 474f.; cf. 103; 137.
[42] 361.
[43] 342; cf. 351 n. 89; 364; 368.
[44] 361.
[45] 474f.
[46] 475f.
[47] 475 and n. 38.
[48] Cf. 349.
[49] See above, 34.
[50] See above, 30.
[51] See above, 30, 34f.

later scholars, including strong support from a western Ibāḍī.[52] Likewise the need for the ruler's permission for some level of violence may be denied;[53] such denial is found even among the Imāmī scholars.[54]

In the same vein, the familiar saying about the tripartite division of labour is occasionally subjected to closer scrutiny and found wanting.[55] Thus the Mālikī Ibn al-Ḥājj (d. 1336f.) points out that, while this distribution of roles may hold in general, there are many instances in which someone who is neither in authority nor a scholar may be obligated to take physical action.[56] Ṣāliḥī sets little store by the saying, categorising it as a weak view.[57] Birgili (d. 1573), a stern Ottoman pietist, describes it as a minority view; most scholars, he says, hold that all three modes are incumbent on everyone, and this is what one goes by in giving legal opinions.[58]

Likewise the idea of reporting wrongs to the state or cooperating with it is sometimes rejected. We have already met Saᶜīd ibn al-Musayyab's negative reaction to the idea of turning in a drunkard.[59] An eleventh-century Zaydī source says that if you come across one, you have no duty to hand him over to the authorities, but should rather keep the matter quiet and counsel him.[60] A ninth-century Spanish pietist suffered from a neighbour who would drink and sing, and considered putting the matter into the hands of the authorities; but he changed his mind on recollecting that in a similar case the great Mālikī scholar Saḥnūn (d. 854) had taken no such action.[61] All this invites comparison with the story of ᶜUqba ibn ᶜĀmir and his secretary.[62] In the same vein Sufyān al-Thawrī refuses to have anything to do with the suggestion of al-Mahdī (r. 775–85) that they join forces, sallying forth into the market to forbid wrong together,[63] and the Imāmī Muḥsin al-Fayḍ discourages a zealot in the northern Iranian province of Māzandarān who wishes to be established by the authorities as a censor.[64]

Such negative attitudes towards involving the ruler in forbidding wrong also pervade the responsa of Ibn Ḥanbal.[65] He repeatedly expresses disapproval of such action. For example, he is told by a disciple that one of his brethren is suffering greatly on account of the objectionable activities of his neighbours, who drink liquor, play lutes and commit offences that are coyly explained as having to do with women. The victim, so the disciple reports, proposes to denounce them to the

52 See above, 35.
53 See above, 34.
54 268.
55 See above, 17.
56 378.
57 163 and n. 123.
58 324; cf. 325; 326 n. 143.
59 See above, 62.
60 239 no. 4.
61 386.
62 See above, 61.
63 82.
64 287 n. 238.
65 102f.

authorities (*sulṭān*). Ibn Ḥanbal disagrees; he should admonish them and forbid them, but the authorities are to be left out of it.[66]

Cases where Ibn Ḥanbal is prepared to countenance recourse to the state are rare indeed. One such case concerns the question whether an incorrigible evildoer may be denounced to the ruler; the answer is yes – provided you know that the ruler will inflict the correct penalty. The sequel makes it clear that you are in fact unlikely to know this: Ibn Ḥanbal relates that they had had a noxious neighbour who was handed over to the authorities, received thirty lashes and died.[67] In general, it seems, the ruler is likely to go too far against an offender; and once you bring in the authorities, you are no longer in control of what happens.

Ibn Ḥanbal's reserve thus arises from the arbitrary and unpredictable character of political power. You can have no confidence that the authorities will impose the legal punishment for the offence. What they do will be too little or too much, and the chances are that they will act with lawless brutality. Such an attitude is doubtless implicit in the negative attitudes of the scholars described above. Their reservations lead naturally to our next theme: the state as an agent of wrongdoing.

[66] 90.
[67] 103.

CHAPTER 7

The state as an agent of wrongdoing

We pass now from the rhetorical claims of rulers to forbid the wrongdoing of others to their nasty but persistent habit of engaging in it themselves. We thus enter a rather different landscape. The wrongdoing of rulers, for all that it constitutes the warp and weft of the history the scholars recorded, is from our point of view of rather little conceptual interest; we will accordingly pass over it rather quickly. On the other hand, the responses of the scholars to this cornucopia of wrongdoing display a sharper focus than the discussions we looked at in the previous chapter. What they are mostly about is the bearing of doctrines of prospective harm in a context that the scholars saw as both highly significant and unusually fraught with peril. More precisely, what is involved is a special case of the question whether or not it is virtuous to forbid wrong where danger has voided the obligation.

1 The misdeeds of rulers

In his account of forbidding wrong, Ghazzālī gives a detailed and helpful survey of wrongs that are commonly met with in various contexts. He deals in turn with the mosque, the market-place, the street, the bath-house and the home (when guests are entertained there).[1] By this point, however, he has tired of enumerating wrongs, and invites his readers to continue the survey for themselves. He mentions a few places to consider, one being the offices (*dawāwīn*) of rulers,[2] but that is as far as he takes us. Fortunately other scholars writing on forbidding wrong make mention of the misdeeds of rulers from time to time, and it is on these incidental references that what follows is based.

We hear a certain amount about what might be called the personal vices of rulers and their associates, notably their liquor[3] and their music;[4] Mālik once caught

[1] 442–5.
[2] 445 no. 6.
[3] 127; 149 n. 33; 448; 461; 501; 590.
[4] 149; 383f.

a caliph in the act of playing chess,[5] and a governor of Medina ate and wore forbidden things.[6] A high-ranking Turkish military officer abducted a young woman as she left the baths.[7] Out in full public view are the ritual infractions of rulers or governors, like that in the frame-story of the three-modes tradition.[8] One ᶜAbbāsid caliph was guilty of luxurious living while on pilgrimage to Mecca,[9] another celebrated the pre-Islamic Persian festival of Nawrūz.[10] A more prosaic form of wrongdoing was fiscal extortion. Thus Saladin (r. 1169–93), like other rulers, collected illegal taxes,[11] while a governor collecting the poll-tax tortured tributary non-Muslims by forcing them to wait in the sun.[12] The greed of the authorities was also manifest in other ways. The brothels of eleventh-century Baghdad, for example, were under the protection of the Seljūq governor.[13] That a Mamlūk ruler gave the Copts power over the Muslims likewise reflects their prominence in the Egyptian fiscal bureaucracy.[14] The shrouded zealot who confronted the caliph al-Maʾmūn had other fish to fry: his grievances were the sale of wine in the army camp, the presence of slave-girls in litters with their hair uncovered and the banning of forbidding wrong.[15]

These examples may help a little to bring the misdeeds of rulers to life. But the fact is that our scholars are not generous in this respect. Often they are content to speak vaguely of oppression and injustice,[16] and sometimes they fail to supply even that. There is a striking story about a goldsmith in Marw who persistently rebuked Abū Muslim (d. 755), the architect of the ᶜAbbāsid revolution, and was eventually killed for it;[17] most accounts do not bother to mention just what it was that the goldsmith held against him.[18] Perhaps the assumption is that we all know the kinds of things that rulers do; as Ghazzālī suggests, we can be left to supply the details for ourselves. But the silence is still a little puzzling.

2 Rebuking rulers as forbidding wrong

As we will see in a later chapter,[19] our narrative sources are full of examples of pious Muslims who harshly rebuked rulers, governors and their henchmen, often

[5] 381.
[6] 63.
[7] 589.
[8] 33; cf. 62f.; 348; 501.
[9] 65.
[10] 76.
[11] 355; 501; cf. 337; 501.
[12] 60f.
[13] 121.
[14] 356.
[15] 10.
[16] 6; 464; 478; cf. 59; 336f.
[17] 3–5.
[18] Cf. 4 n. 6.
[19] See below, ch. 9, section 3.

at great risk to themselves; sometimes they got away with it, sometimes they were martyred for their pains. It is of course the scholars who tell us these stories, and they usually do so sympathetically. But how do they regard this activity when writing in a more doctrinal vein?[20]

Very occasionally we encounter statements to the effect that reproving rulers for their misdeeds is a duty.[21] But inasmuch as we find the same scholars saying things incompatible with this, it is hard to take such statements very seriously. For example, Mālik states that it is the duty of every Muslim – or scholar – to confront the wielder of political power (*dhū sulṭān*), and to forbid evil to him; it is for this purpose alone that the scholar enters into the presence of the ruler. Yet in another passage his attitude seems less resolute. When asked whether a man should command and forbid a governor (*wālī*) or the like, his answer is that he should do so if he expects that the offender will comply. To the further question whether one may omit to do so if there is no such expectation, he answers that he does not know.[22] More strikingly, a saying of Mālik's is quoted to the effect that he had met seventeen Successors – members of the generation following that of the Companions – and had not heard that they had admonished unjust rulers.[23] The effect is to undermine the idea that such admonition can be a duty in Mālik's view. Overall, as indicated above, the absence of obligation is taken for granted by the scholars. The argument is about whether or not it is *virtuous* to reprove rulers, and it is on this that the scholars disagree.

Those in favour of rebuking rulers have a much-quoted tradition on their side. In one version the Prophet says: 'The finest form of holy war is speaking out (*kalimat ḥaqq*) in the presence of an unjust ruler and getting killed for it.' The most widely attested versions lack the final reference to getting killed, but otherwise give the same support to speaking out in the presence of an unjust ruler.[24] It is thus no surprise to find a substantial body of scholarly opinion in favour of this practice. We encounter positive views among the Ḥanafīs,[25] the Shāfiᶜites, the Ḥanbalites,[26] the western and eastern Ibāḍīs,[27] and even the Imāmīs.[28]

Ghazzālī is an eloquent champion of such rebuke. To refute the view that official permission is needed to forbid wrong, he points out that we know that harsh language can be used even against the ruler; how then could it require his permission? He goes on to give examples to demonstrate the persistence of the early Muslims in rebuking their rulers.[29] Later he cites the tradition about speaking out in

[20] 476f.
[21] 135; 360.
[22] 360.
[23] 360.
[24] 6.
[25] 6f.; 309; 314; 337.
[26] 135.
[27] 402f.; 405 n. 87; 458.
[28] 259 and n. 49.
[29] 431 and n. 29.

the presence of an unjust ruler to show that it is virtuous to proceed in a case where doing so will be effective but dangerous (perhaps even when it will be ineffective and dangerous).[30] When he comes to his main discussion of the use of harsh language in rebuking rulers, he pronounces such activity forbidden if it will bring harm to others, but commendable if one fears only for oneself. Thus the early Muslims would expose themselves to such risks, knowing that to be killed in such a case was martyrdom. He then goes on to quote a series of seventeen anecdotes to illustrate their courage and plain speaking. This, he laments, is how things used to be; but today the scholars are silent, or if they do speak out, they are ineffectual, all because of their love of the things of this world.[31] At one point in all this Ghazzālī mentions the need to weigh the damage that harsh language could do to the ruler's majesty (*hayba*) against the evil of silence in the face of wrongdoing.[32] But by the time he comes to his main discussion of the issue, the ruler's majesty has long been forgotten.[33]

What of the other side of the question? One scholar who finds himself in the opposite camp is the Ḥanbalite Ibn al-Jawzī, who has to take a stand on the issue in his recension of Ghazzālī's *Revival*.[34] When he gets to the relevant passage, he admits that rebuking rulers is regarded as permissible by most scholars, but nevertheless pronounces against it. Its effect, he argues, is to provoke the ruler to an offence worse than the one the rudeness is intended to curb – rulers being constitutionally incapable of tolerating insult.[35] He then follows Ghazzālī in devoting several pages to anecdotes, but ends with a contrast that effectively voids them. In the old days, he tells us, rulers – whatever their faults – appreciated the virtues of the scholars, and accordingly put up with their rudeness. In our time, however, it is better to flee from the presence of rulers; if one cannot flee, civility is the order of the day. In short, for Ghazzālī it is the scholars who are not what they used to be; for Ibn al-Jawzī, by contrast, it is the rulers who have changed for the worse. In another of his works, he likewise recommends that in these evil days one should seek to avoid putting oneself in the position of admonishing a ruler; but he also emphasises that, if one does so, one should proceed only with the utmost tact.[36]

Ibn al-Jawzī's negative attitude to rebuking rulers had good Ḥanbalite precedent, despite the rather confusing views of Abū Yaᶜlā.[37] As Ibn Ḥanbal puts it, one should not expose oneself to the ruler since 'his sword is unsheathed'.[38] He was once consulted by a certain Aḥmad ibn Shabbawayh (d. 843), who had arrived in Baghdad

[30] 433; cf. 432 n. 40.
[31] 446.
[32] 432.
[33] 456 n. 204.
[34] 140f.
[35] Cf. 101 n. 152.
[36] 141.
[37] 135f.; cf. above, 56.
[38] 101.

with the rash intention of going in to the caliph to 'command and forbid' him; Ibn Ḥanbal discouraged him on the ground of the risk he would be running. He himself was urged by his uncle to take advantage of his involuntary presence at the court of al-Mutawakkil (r. 847–61) to go in to the caliph to command and forbid him; he refused. He likewise quotes the rhetorical question with which Sufyān al-Thawrī responded when asked why he did not go to the ruler and command him: 'When the sea overflows, who can dam it up?'[39] Long after the time of Ibn al-Jawzī, the Ḥanbalite Ibn Rajab (d. 1393) remarks that people readily entertain fantasies about confronting rulers with tough talk when they are still far away from them, but feel very differently once they get there.[40]

Another scholar who takes a stand on the issue in the manner of Ibn al-Jawzī is the Imāmī Muḥsin al-Fayḍ. In adapting the *Revival* for an Imāmī readership, he interrupts Ghazzālī to disallow rudeness to rulers, and again to discard his anecdotes about Sunnīs (he refers to them as 'people of perdition') who courted death by confronting tyrants out of a hidden aspiration to make themselves celebrities.[41] Indeed he remarks that a man who flirts with death by reproving those who wield political power is likely to go to hell for violating the Koranic prohibition of suicide (Q2:195).[42]

For this again there is good Imāmī precedent. The eighth-century imam Jaᶜfar al-Ṣādiq states that there is no reward for someone who goes up against an unjust ruler and comes to grief as a result.[43] When the tradition about speaking out in the presence of an unjust ruler is quoted to him, he explains it away: it applies only where the ruler will accept the admonition.[44] Likewise Ṭūsī in the eleventh century firmly rejects the idea that speaking out in this way and getting killed for it can be good.[45]

It is not just Ḥanbalite and Imāmī scholars who react negatively to Ghazzālī's enthusiasm. We also find a Ḥanafī and a couple of Shāfiᶜites in the same boat.[46] In a similar vein a companion of the Mālikī Saḥnūn quotes Mālik's saying about the seventeen Successors in explaining why he himself would not command and forbid a ruler who sinned.[47] The eastern Ibāḍī Ibn Baraka treats the tradition about speaking out in the presence of an unjust ruler and getting killed for it after the manner of Jaᶜfar al-Ṣādiq: it assumes a prior expectation of success in this world and the next, or that the ruler will accept the rebuke.[48]

39 53; 101f.
40 55 n. 57.
41 295; cf. 501f.
42 295 n. 286.
43 257.
44 254f.
45 281 n. 211.
46 320; 458.
47 385 and n. 219.
48 416 n. 175.

Such negative attitudes to rebuking rulers appear quite frequently among the early Muslims, for all that Ghazzālī does not acknowledge the fact. The true commander and forbidder, says ᶜAbdallāh ibn al-Mubārak (d. 797), is not someone who goes into the presence of rulers to command and forbid them, but rather someone who avoids contact with them altogether.[49] Likewise the well-known ascetic Fuḍayl ibn ᶜIyāḍ (d. 803) enjoins that you should command only someone who will accept it from you; reproving a ruler may spell disaster for yourself, your family and your neighbours.[50] Ḥasan al-Baṣrī (d. 728) is against going in to rulers to command and forbid them; he explains that it is not for a believer to humiliate himself, and that the swords of the rulers are mightier than our tongues.[51] The Companion ᶜAbdallāh ibn al-ᶜAbbās (d. 687f.) is asked by a pupil about the idea of reproving those in authority; he tells him that if he fears being killed for it, he should not upbraid the imam.[52] Asked about a man who goes in to rulers to command and forbid them, the ascetic Dāwūd ibn Nuṣayr al-Ṭāʾī (d. 781f.) replies that he fears that such a man would be whipped. But what if he can endure that? Then he fears he would be killed. And if he can endure that too? Then he fears that he would fall into the sin of self-conceit (*ᶜujb*).[53] There is also the danger, later alluded to by Ibn Rajab, that when one actually finds oneself in the presence of the ruler one will not have the nerve to go through with the intended reproof, and will instead fall into complicity with the wicked ways of the court. Maymūn ibn Mihrān al-Raqqī (d. 735f.) warns against putting oneself to the test by entering into the presence of someone in authority (*sulṭān*), even when one tells oneself that one will command him to obey God.[54]

Not all these views categorically reject the idea of rebuking rulers. It may be implied that there is no objection provided the attempt is risk-free, or is guaranteed to succeed, or at least will not bring upon one an ordeal one is unable to bear.[55] Thus the Spanish Ṣūfī Ibn al-ᶜArīf (d. 1141) circumscribes rebuking rulers with such conditions as privacy, civility and purity of intention.[56] Nevertheless the overall effect is to pour a large measure of cold water on the enthusiasm of people like Ghazzālī.

As Ibn al-Jawzī reminds us, there is also an easy way out: heroism can be celebrated, but relegated to the past. Thus the traditionist Khaṭṭābī (d. 998), in a chapter on the depravity of rulers and the need to have as little to do with them as possible, quotes the tradition on speaking out in the presence of an unjust ruler. He then laments the corruption of the age in the manner of Ghazzālī: who is there today

[49] 53.
[50] 54.
[51] 53f.
[52] 43; 54; cf. 55.
[53] 54f.; 315.
[54] 55.
[55] Cf. 54 and n. 55; 72 n. 191; 255.
[56] 465.

who goes in to rulers and does not tell them what they want to hear? Who today counsels them, and – here he begins to sound like Ibn al-Jawzī – which of them would listen? Rather, he says, the soundest course in these times, and that best calculated to preserve one's faith, is to have as little to do with rulers as possible.[57]

A rather more demanding compromise is to rebuke the powerful in private.[58] Ibn al-ᶜAbbās, after warning his pupil not to risk death, goes on to advise him that if he really must rebuke the ruler, he should do so privately.[59] Mālik upbraids a man who got himself badly beaten up as a result of his folly in rebuking a powerful figure at the gate of his own house and in the presence of his retinue.[60] An anecdote about Hishām ibn Ḥakīm ibn Ḥizām (d. 656?), an early pietist much given to forbidding wrong, is worth attention here because it brings in a Prophetic tradition in favour of such private rebuke.[61] The wrongdoer is ᶜIyāḍ ibn Ghanm (d. 640f.), the Muslim commander at the conquest of a Mesopotamian town, where he flogs a prominent non-Muslim. Hishām is very rude to ᶜIyāḍ about this, causing a break between the two men. Later Hishām goes to ᶜIyāḍ and excuses himself, but repeats his objection by quoting a Prophetic tradition according to which those who torture people in this world will be tortured by God in the next. ᶜIyāḍ then responds by quoting a Prophetic tradition of his own, to the effect that anyone rebuking a person in authority (*sulṭān*) should do so in private. He goes on to reproach Hishām for his recklessness in going up against someone established in authority by God (*sulṭān Allāh*), and thereby courting death at his hands.

This anecdote is also significant in that by the end of the story we find ourselves on the side of the commander. Something similar is true of the encounter between al-Maᵓmūn and the shrouded zealot. There the caliph concludes icily that he must have to do with a man who has deluded himself by misinterpreting the tradition according to which the finest form of holy war is to speak out in the presence of an unjust ruler.[62] Contrast the goldsmith of Marw: he too wears his shroud, but the accounts of his confrontation with unjust rule place us firmly on his side.[63]

3 Rebellion as forbidding wrong

An alternative to rebuking an unjust ruler is to rebel against him. But this, of course, is a much more drastic way to go about forbidding wrong, and as might be expected scholarly opinion is stacked heavily against it.

[57] 477; cf. above, 55.
[58] See above, 29; 170.
[59] 54.
[60] 360 n. 13.
[61] 61.
[62] 11.
[63] 3–5.

Favourable attitudes to such rebellion do exist, however.[64] They are prominent among the early Khārijites,[65] the Ibāḍīs[66] and the Zaydīs,[67] and are attested for at least one Muᶜtazilite, albeit one with strong Zaydī leanings.[68] In addition such views are, so to speak, embalmed in the heritage of the Imāmīs[69] – though the fact that for them the linkage was no longer a living one laid them open to Zaydī polemic. A couple of examples will convey a sense of this activist strain.

Let us start with al-Ḥākim al-Jishumī (d. 1101), the Muᶜtazilite with Zaydī leanings. His activism finds lively expression in a short polemical tract entitled 'The epistle of the devil to his baleful brethren'.[70] Here Jishumī has the devil explain that he has disseminated quietist notions of rendering obedience to every usurper, with the purpose of subverting the imamate, the forbidding of wrong and rebellion against unjust rule. His brethren, the devil continues, had accepted this infernal propaganda, and were busy relating traditions in support of it. (The devil's brethren are, of course, the Sunnī traditionists.) The Muᶜtazilites, by contrast, had vigorously opposed this defeatism: they stood for the imamate of the just and the forbidding of wrong, and transmitted traditions accordingly. How strongly Jishumī identifies forbidding wrong with resistance to unjust rule is apparent elsewhere from his formulation of the contrary view espoused by the Sunnī traditionists: 'Obedience is due to whoever wins, even if he is an oppressor.'[71]

The other example relates to the Zaydī polemic against the Imāmīs. In a law-book written by a follower of al-Hādī we find a refutation of the typically Imāmī view that the imam does not have to rebel, but need only be learned, pious and trustworthy. The Zaydī retort is that such a man is merely an authority on legal matters, not one to whom obedience is due, 'since he is sitting at home, neither commanding nor forbidding; for God does not enjoin obedience to one who sits, as He does to one who arises, commanding right and forbidding wrong'.[72] A later Zaydī is similarly dismissive of Imāmī quietism: if a supposed imam claims that he has not been commanded to engage in such activities as holy war, resistance to the oppressors and forbidding wrong, we ask him: 'So what *were* you commanded to do, and to what purpose?'[73]

A comparable activism is also reported from some early Muslims who did not always get as far as actual rebellion.[74] The goldsmith of Marw told Abū Muslim that he was assaulting him with his tongue only because he lacked the force to do

[64] 477f.
[65] 393f.
[66] 395f.; cf. 402f. and above, 52.
[67] 231–5.
[68] 223f.; cf. 107; 198.
[69] 260.
[70] 224.
[71] 224.
[72] 233; cf. 235 n. 46.
[73] 233 n. 39; cf. 406 n. 88.
[74] 7; 8f.; 51f.

so with his hand;[75] he had earlier tried to persuade Abū Ḥanīfa to lead a rebellion.[76] Another such figure is the well-known Kūfan Shīᶜite Ḥasan ibn Ṣāliḥ ibn Ḥayy (d. 783f.).[77] When Ṭabarī describes him as holding with action against wrong (*inkār al-munkar*) by any available means, what he has in mind is doubtless Ḥasan's notorious espousal of the sword, suggesting armed rebellion against unjust rule. 'This Ibn Ḥayy', as one of his contemporaries observed, 'has been asking to be crucified for a long time, but we can't find anyone to do it for him.' Another closet activist of this kind (though he later changed his mind) was ᶜAbdallāh ibn Farrūkh (d. 791), a Persian Ḥanafī who settled in North Africa. He considered that it would be time to rebel against unjust rulers when as many men commanding right were gathered together as had been present at the Battle of Badr – though each had to be a better man than Ibn Farrūkh himself. To do him justice, he did make one attempt to rebel, but his revolt fizzled out when only two men showed up to join him at the appointed place.[78] A later North African Ḥanafī held a similar view, but balanced it by saying that he did not hold with righting wrongs through committing worse ones.[79] As we will see in another chapter, it was quite common in the early centuries of Islam for rebels to adopt forbidding wrong as their slogan.[80]

Very occasionally such views are espoused by Sunnī scholars of later centuries. Thus Ibn Ḥazm in developing his doctrine of forbidding wrong takes the view that it is obligatory to reprove the ruler for any act of injustice, however small. If the ruler desists and submits to the appropriate penalty, well and good; if not, he must be deposed and another appointed in his place.[81] Elsewhere he maintains that, if an unjust ruler descended from the tribe of Quraysh (the tribe to which the Prophet belonged) is challenged by a rebel more just than him, it is our duty to fight for the rebel, since doing so is righting a wrong.[82] In yet another passage he endorses righteous rebellion under the banner of forbidding wrong.[83] Ibn Ḥazm, of course, was something of a law unto himself. But Juwaynī, a mainstream Shāfiᶜite, made an arresting statement in his account of forbidding wrong: if the ruler of the time acts in a manifestly unjust fashion, and does not respond to verbal admonition, then it is for 'the people of binding and loosing' to prevent him, even if this means doing battle with him.[84]

Usually, of course, such ideas are condemned in Sunnī circles.[85] Several early Muslim authorities reject rebellion as a way of forbidding wrong.[86] Thus when

[75] 3.
[76] 7.
[77] 51.
[78] 51; 315f.; 385; 477 and n. 63.
[79] 385f.
[80] See below, 108f.
[81] 390; 478.
[82] 390.
[83] 390 n. 259.
[84] 346.
[85] 311; 311f.; 478; cf. 250 and n. 163; 320.
[86] 52f.

Ḥasan al-Baṣrī is told of a Khārijite who had rebelled in Ḥīra near Kūfa, he comments that the man had seen a wrong and taken action against it (*ankarahu*), but that in seeking to right the wrong he had fallen into a worse one.[87] We have already seen how Abū Ḥanīfa, though he does not deny that the duty might in principle make rebellion mandatory, seeks to override this alarming implication by invoking the likely costs of such action.[88]

The scholars of later centuries have similar views. Abū Ḥanīfa's position is firmly endorsed by a later Ḥanafī commentator.[89] Ghazzālī excludes the use of violence by individual subjects where the wrongdoer is the ruler, since it leads to disorder and to consequences worse than the original wrong.[90] For the staunch Ḥanbalite Ibn Qayyim al-Jawziyya (d. 1350), rebellion with the aim of righting wrong (*inkār al-munkar*) is overridden by consideration of the adverse consequences it would lead to, which render it the root of all evil.[91] In saying this, he does no more than echo the view of his teacher Ibn Taymiyya.[92] Ibn Khaldūn (d. 1406) condemns the foolishness of ordinary people or scholars who mount ineffectual rebellions in the name of forbidding wrong, thus exposing themselves to mortal peril; they lack the power (*qudra*) without which there is no obligation.[93] It is worth noting that for these scholars, as for Ḥasan al-Baṣrī and Abū Ḥanīfa, rebellion is wrong because of its consequences; it is not that the intentions of the rebels are necessarily evil in themselves.

With rebellion, as with rebuke, a degree of compromise was also possible. The greatly respected Shāfiᶜite Ibn Ḥajar al-ᶜAsqalānī (d. 1449) did not find it difficult to enter a defence on behalf of Ḥasan ibn Ṣāliḥ ibn Ḥayy.[94] He observed that Ḥasan's belief in recourse to the sword was a well-known persuasion among the early Muslims, for all that it was later abandoned in the light of its results – and that in any case, Ḥasan did not actually rebel against anyone.

87 52f.
88 7f.; 308f.; 478.
89 311.
90 446.
91 394; cf. 160 n. 108.
92 153; cf. 157; see also K. Abou El Fadl, *Rebellion and violence in Islamic law*, Cambridge 2001, 273.
93 390 n. 256 (and source); 478 n. 71; cf. also 343 n. 36.
94 51.

CHAPTER 8

Is anyone against forbidding wrong?

Ghazzālī's account of forbidding wrong is marked at some points by a degree of enthusiasm. But as we saw, if we turn instead to his discussion of the advantages of the solitary life (*ᶜuzla*), we encounter a quite different tone.[1] One of its advantages, he tells us, is that the solitary is not exposed to situations in which he incurs the duty of forbidding wrong. This duty is an exigent and onerous one. You fall into sin if you ignore it and keep silent; but if you do not, you are likely to end up in the position of someone who tries to prop up a wall that is keeling over – when it falls on you, you wish you had left it alone.

Ghazzālī is not alone in pricking the bubble of enthusiasm. When the Companion ᶜAbdallāh ibn Masᶜūd (d. 652f.) is confronted with the view that one who does not command right and forbid wrong is damned (*halaka*), he replies that this is rather the fate of one who fails to approve of right and disapprove of wrong in his heart.[2] A similar mood is encapsulated in a dialogue between the ascetic Bishr al-Ḥāfī and a certain Ṣāliḥ:[3]

> Bishr: Ṣāliḥ, is your heart strong enough for you to speak out?
> Ṣāliḥ (after a silence): Bishr, do you command right and forbid wrong?
> Bishr: No.
> Ṣāliḥ: And why not?
> Bishr: If I'd known you would ask that, I wouldn't have answered you.

Sometimes the tone is more mischievous. One Ottoman scholar argues that you cannot rebuke a man simply because he has a pot of wine beside him, since after all he also has with him the means of adultery.[4] Such passages are enough to disabuse us of the notion that everyone was always zealous about forbidding wrong.

That, of course, is a conclusion that was hardly in need of documentation. Indeed, it is a natural assumption that large numbers of people in the pre-modern Islamic world simply did not care about forbidding wrong, a point we can return

[1] See above, 41.
[2] 42.
[3] 77.
[4] 319 n. 92.

to in the next chapter.[5] What concerns us here is the ideas of people – overwhelmingly scholars – who gave *reasons* for their lack of zeal. How close did their thinking ever come to overturning the duty altogether?

1 Does anyone deny the duty outright?

Straightforward denial that there is a duty to forbid wrong is very rare, and confined to the first two centuries of Islam.[6] Ḥasan al-Baṣrī is asked whether forbidding wrong is an obligation (*farīḍa*); he responds that it had indeed been so for the Israelites, but that a merciful God, taking into account the weakness of the Muslim community, had made it supererogatory (*nāfila*) for them. ᶜAbdallāh ibn Shubruma (d. 761f.) likewise states that commanding right is supererogatory (*nāfila*); he then goes on to say that those who do not perform it out of weakness have a sufficient excuse, and should not be blamed. As usual with extreme positions, there is some doubt as to how seriously to take such views.[7] Why, for example, does Ibn Shubruma find it necessary to excuse the weak? If there is no obligation, nobody needs an excuse. But taken on their own, these statements that forbidding wrong is supererogatory are unambiguous.

Though few of the scholars are on record as denying the duty themselves, they are considerably more generous in imputing such denial to others. Two groups in particular are singled out.

One is the Ḥashwiyya – a contemptuous term for anthropomorphist Sunnī traditionists such as the Ḥanbalites. They are quite often mentioned by Muᶜtazilite authors as denying the obligatoriness of forbidding wrong;[8] a comparable Ḥanafī reference to the Mujbira (predestinationists) is doubtless directed at the same target.[9] If we want to take these reports to be historically accurate, we can understand them to refer to the view we have just encountered, namely that forbidding wrong is supererogatory. But we may prefer to see them as a rhetorically inflated way of making the point that the Sunnī traditionists of the early centuries had a tendency to downplay the duty. The Ḥanafī Muᶜtazilite Jaṣṣāṣ denounces them for holding that injustice and murder may be committed by a ruler with impunity, while other offenders may be proceeded against by word or deed – but not with arms. The point is not, in his view, an academic one. It is these attitudes that have led to the present sorry state of Islam – to the domination of the reprobate, of Zoroastrians, of enemies of Islam; to the collapse of the frontiers of Islam against the infidel; to the spread of injustice, the ruin of countries and the rise of all manner of false

[5] See below, 105.
[6] 76f.; cf. 106 and n. 186.
[7] Cf. 76 n. 224; 345.
[8] 49; 201 n. 40; 206 n. 63; 224 n. 160; cf. 197; 234; 244 n. 115; 336f.; 344.
[9] 311; cf. also 390 n. 258; 396.

religions. All this, we learn, is a consequence of the abandonment of the duty to command right and forbid wrong, and of standing up to unjust rulers.[10] To an extent, there is a valid point here. For example, the classical collections of traditions, mostly dating from the ninth century, deal with forbidding wrong incidentally or not at all, leaving the impression that the subject did not bulk very large for those who compiled them;[11] and Ibn Ḥanbal, as we will see, had some curious hesitations about the duty.[12]

The other group said to deny the duty is Shīᶜite. These heretics may be referred to in a derogatory fashion as the Rāfiḍa, or more politely as a splinter-group of the Imāmīs. Again we find authors – mainly Muᶜtazilite – debiting them with denial of the obligatoriness of forbidding wrong.[13] We know of no historical Shīᶜite sect that would fit this description, so these reports are likely to be the product of exaggeration. Something more commonly said about the Imāmīs (or Rāfiḍa) in hostile sources is that they deny that forbidding wrong can be performed in the absence of their imam (who for the Imāmī mainstream has been in occlusion since 874).[14] This is not of course true,[15] but it is a recognisable distortion of the standard Imāmī doctrine that resort to violence (or some level of it) in forbidding wrong requires the imam's permission.[16] Statements that a Shīᶜite sect denied forbidding wrong to be obligatory could thus have arisen as a distortion of a distortion. Ironically, we do find among the Shaykhīs, an Imāmī subsect in nineteenth-century Iran, the doctrine that forbidding wrong is voided in most instances until the appearance of the imam.[17] Curiously enough, a similar view is mentioned as a deviant doctrine among the western Ibāḍīs.[18]

On balance we should probably not take such claims about the Ḥashwiyya and the Rāfiḍa too seriously. These categories are somewhat empty heresiographical labels. When Ṣāliḥī encountered the Ḥashwiyya in this context, he had no trouble deflecting any potential embarrassment to his fellow Ḥanbalites with a simple realignment: he identified the Ḥashwiyya as a subsect of the Rāfiḍa.[19]

Another context in which our sources speak of people who deny the duty to forbid wrong is Q5:105: 'O believers, look after your own souls. He who is astray cannot hurt you, if you are rightly guided.' This verse sounds like an invitation to forget about forbidding wrong, and the scholars devote great efforts to showing this obvious reading to be mistaken.[20] In this connection they often cite a tradition

[10] 336f.
[11] 39 n. 37; cf. 49f.
[12] See below, 88.
[13] 206 and n. 63; 345; 352 (and source).
[14] 206 n. 63; 244 n. 115; 270; 330 n. 171; 349; 430; cf. 215; 344.
[15] But cf. 260.
[16] See above, 34; cf. 206 n. 63; 215 n. 97.
[17] 301 n. 323.
[18] 399.
[19] 163 n. 122.
[20] 30; 338 n. 219; 351 n. 91.

in which Abū Bakr (r. 632–4) urges the community not to misinterpret the verse, and warns of dire consequences if they fail to right wrongs.[21] In a more scholastic vein, the exegete Ṭabarī sets out two interpretations of the verse, each of which avoids undermining the duty.[22] The first is that the verse refers to some future time when forbidding wrong will cease to be effective, so that the duty will then lapse; in other words, the verse has no application to the present. We will come back to this idea in the next section. The second interpretation does not deny the relevance of the verse to our own times, but sees a catch in the clause 'if you are rightly guided': those who fail to forbid wrong cannot be called rightly guided, and are indeed hurt by those who are astray. Ṭabarī himself opts for this second view.

Overall, the sources abound in vague references to men of straw who misconstrue the verse. For example, the Ḥanafī who speaks of the Mujbira denying the duty has them do so on the basis of Q5:105.[23] But it is rare to find an author who actually adopts such a position, or even quotes the verse to play down the duty.[24]

Altogether, credible outright denials of the obligatoriness of forbidding wrong are almost unheard of. And even the most explicit statements to such effect, those that describe it as supererogatory, imply that it is at least a virtuous thing to do.

2 Has the future already arrived?

Ṭabarī, as we saw, noted an interpretation of Q5:105 as referring to some future time. This makes sense. Everyone knows that in this world things get worse and worse;[25] the future will accordingly be bleak, and in due course the corruption of the times will be such that forbidding wrong is no longer possible. When that happens, the duty will obviously lapse, and there will be nothing further to be done about it. This idea is not part of the regular doctrine of the scholars; but many traditions link Q5:105 to the future in this way, and others convey the same message without referring to the verse.[26]

A few examples may help to convey the drift of this thinking.[27] There is a well-known tradition in which the Prophet is asked about the implications of Q5:105. In response he enjoins the believers to command right and forbid wrong until they find themselves confronted with the utter corruption of values; they should then look to themselves and forget the populace at large. In the same way the Companion Ibn Masᶜūd is present during a dispute as to whether Q5:105 overrides the duty of commanding right. He intervenes to insist that the conditions of moral disorder to

[21] 35f.
[22] 30.
[23] 311.
[24] 31 n. 85; 327 n. 158; cf. 78 n. 235.
[25] Cf. 354; 369.
[26] 39–42.
[27] 40–2; cf. 41 n. 44; 74; 228; 258 n. 40.

which the verse refers have not yet come, and instructs his hearers that until that time they should continue to perform the duty. The young Jubayr ibn Nufayr (d. 699f.) finds himself in a gathering of Companions and others in which forbidding wrong is under discussion. He foolishly quotes Q5:105, and is reproved by those present, who afterwards tell him that, since he is so young, he may in fact live into the time to which the verse refers. Kaᶜb al-Aḥbār (d. 654f.) holds that the verse will only apply when (among other things) the church of Damascus has been demolished and replaced with a mosque; a later Damascene transmitter identifies this building activity with the work carried out by the caliph Walīd (r. 705–15). Several of these traditions are Syrian, reflecting the disproportionate role of Syrian traditionists in spreading traditions that tend to play down forbidding wrong.[28] Even more striking is an Egyptian tradition in which the Prophet tells his followers to cease forbidding wrong at the beginning of the year 200 – that is, in 815.

All these traditions place the demise of forbidding wrong firmly in the future. But for those who transmitted such traditions (not to mention those who may have put them into circulation by placing them in the mouths of earlier authorities), the bad times could readily be understood to have begun already. These traditions thus lend themselves to the unusual view that the duty may have lapsed.[29] Thus the elder Ibn Rushd, after referring Q5:105 to the bleak future, observes how much his own day resembles such a time – whereas under conditions in which a helper can be found to assist in the cause of justice, no one may remain silent in the face of offences, or neglect to take action against them.[30] A few centuries later another Mālikī scholar, ᶜUqbānī (d. 1467), reproduces Ibn Rushd's discussion of Q5:105, and adds the obvious comment that if the age of Ibn Rushd was such a time, how much more so must our own be.[31] Neither of these scholars offers a firm ruling that the duty has actually lapsed, but they do not discourage the thought.

A more definite, though puzzling, position of this kind is set out by a Ḥanafī, probably of the tenth century, who is commenting on Abū Ḥanīfa's condemnation of rebellion.[32] He states that Abū Ḥanīfa's ruling against rebellion on the grounds of its adverse consequences shows forbidding wrong no longer to be in effect in our time. He explains that this activity is now directed only to bloodshed and plunder, and is not motivated by disinterested virtue. Does he really mean to say that forbidding wrong in general – and not just rebellion under its aegis – has lapsed in our time? Or is he simply using 'forbidding wrong' as a synonym for righteous rebellion? It is hard to say; but a fourteenth-century Shāfiᶜite took the passage – or rather a parallel in a related work – to refer to forbidding wrong in general.[33]

[28] 45.
[29] Cf. 464.
[30] 364.
[31] 369.
[32] 311f.
[33] 312 n. 30.

The view that worsening conditions have undermined the duty is no doubt implicit in a couple of discouraging pronouncements of Ibn Ḥanbal.[34] Asked whether forbidding wrong is obligatory, he replies that in these evil days it is too burdensome (*shadīd*) to impose, especially in the light of the easement in the Prophetic tradition – a reference to the possibility of performing the duty in the heart. On another occasion he betrays a similar sense of the corruption of the times, remarking that 'this is no time for forbidding'. Likewise Fuḍayl ibn ᶜIyāḍ, when asked about forbidding wrong, replies: 'This is not a time for speaking out, but a time for weeping, supplication, humility, and prayer.'[35]

We thus find no formal doctrine excusing Muslims of our time from forbidding wrong, though the idea is clearly in the air.

3 What do the Ṣūfīs have to say?

There are various aspects of Ṣūfism that are potentially antithetical to forbidding wrong. If Ṣūfīs are esoteric, antinomian mystics, then surely they should have no interest in the prosaic, exoteric details of enforcing the law. If they are the bearers of a relaxed tolerance unknown to the fractious Islam of the jurists, then they should be a good deal less censorious. And if they are Islam's experts in introspection, then they should be well placed to assay the motives of self-righteous pietists and find them wanting. There is something to be said for each of these expectations, and we should look at each in turn.

Did Ṣūfīs exploit the potential of their beliefs to place themselves above forbidding wrong? We do encounter occasional suggestions to this effect. ᶜAbd al-Qādir al-Jazāʾirī (d. 1883), who settled in Syria after leading the resistance to the French conquest of Algeria, argues that the mystic is not covered by the tripartite division of labour, and is thus not obligated by the duty.[36] ᶜAlī al-Qārī mentions the unusual idea that the immersion of the mystic in the depths of absolute existence might be an excuse – though an unconvincing one – for not performing the duty.[37] As we saw in an earlier chapter, the Ṣūfī Ibrāhīm al-Matbūlī puts the idea more humbly: performance with the heart is for gnostics whose contempt for themselves precludes their forbidding anyone.[38] A thirteenth-century North African typology of saints moves in three stages from the most sociable to the least so. The first group comprises those who live in the world, making a living as other people do, but leading scrupulously virtuous and observant lives; one aspect of this is their cultivation of forbidding wrong. By contrast, there is no mention of it in the accounts of the other two – manifestly superior – types of saint.[39]

[34] 106.
[35] 76f.
[36] 467 n. 288.
[37] 318.
[38] See above, 37.
[39] 466f.

An interesting if somewhat obscure passage in a letter of Ibn ᶜAbbād al-Rundī (d. 1390), a Ṣūfī from Spain, takes us a little deeper.[40] He is responding to people who have been troubled by a saying of a deceased Ṣūfī; he endorses the saying, but unfortunately does not quote it. He then goes on to explain that there is in fact no contradiction between, on the one hand, excusing people's misdeeds by looking upon them with the eye of the mystic (*ᶜayn al-tawḥīd*), and on the other, commanding right and forbidding wrong to them. One reason he gives for this is that the mystic is considering things from the viewpoint of esoteric truth (*ḥaqīqa*), whereas forbidding wrong is a matter of exoteric law (*sharīᶜa*), and between the two there is no contradiction. Ibn ᶜAbbād ends by expressing his surprise that his addressees should have failed to see something so obvious. It is a pity that we know no more about the crack that he is papering over here.

Turning to Ṣūfī toleration, there is an intriguing polemic against certain heretics (*malāḥida*) in the treatise on forbidding wrong written by the Indian Ḥanafī ᶜIṣmat Allāh of Sahāranpūr.[41] These heretics, he tells us, take as their doctrine the principle of leaving people in peace (*tark taᶜarruḍ al-khalq wa-īdhāʾihim*) and having pacific relations with everyone (*ṣulḥ al-kull*). Worse yet, they claim this to be the doctrine of the Ṣūfīs, and hold to the literal meaning of a saying widely current among the common people: 'Do not bother anyone, and do whatever you wish; for in our law there is no sin other than this.' (In fact this is a verse from a poem by the Persian poet Ḥāfiẓ (d. 1389), though our author does not say so.) These heretics ingratiate themselves, he continues, with every errant sect of infidels – Jews, Brahmins, Zindīqs and others – and hate the Muḥammadan community.

This is as much as ᶜIṣmat Allāh tells us about the heretics and their views. They were clearly Muslims, in their own view if not in his; they claim that their doctrine is Ṣūfī, and as we will see they are refuted by appealing to Muslim authority. They were presumably a feature of the Indian environment. The principle of having pacific relations with everyone (*ṣulḥ-i kull*) was well known in Moghul India, where it justified friendly interaction with the followers of native Indian religions.

ᶜIṣmat Allāh begins his refutation by impaling the heretics on the horns of a dilemma. Either they accept what the authoritative texts say about forbidding wrong, or they do not. If they do not accept it, they have abandoned Islam, and there is no possibility of dialogue with them; if they do accept it, their doctrine collapses. For were it pleasing to God to leave people alone, He would not have sent the prophets, nor established their laws, nor called to Islam, nor voided other religions, but would rather have left people to their own devices, untroubled by divine visitations; nor would He have imposed on them the duty of holy war, which involves suffering and death for both Muslims and infidels. He further emphasises that Ṣūfīs – pantheists included – have made it abundantly clear that they neither practise nor preach an indiscriminate toleration. What is more, distinguished Ṣūfīs

[40] 466.
[41] 467f.

have written on forbidding wrong. Even apart from all this, the fact that the prophets were sent to command right and forbid wrong is enough to establish that it is both good and obligatory. In short, if leaving people alone were praiseworthy, then forbidding wrong would not be a religious duty. This is a rousing polemic, but it is hard to tell from it whether the heretics had mounted an explicit attack on the doctrine of forbidding wrong.

What then of introspection?[42] The key point here is one of ascetic psychology. Forbidding wrong can be an act of great altruism, but it can also become an ego trip. It will be remembered that Dāwūd al-Ṭāʾī, an early precursor of Ṣūfism, feared that a man capable of rebuking a ruler at the cost of his own life would fall into the sin of self-conceit.[43] But the classic formulation of the idea is that of Ghazzālī.[44]

Speaking of exhortation, Ghazzālī observes that there is a mortal peril to be avoided, namely that the scholar becomes puffed up with his sense of his own superior knowledge, and of the inferiority of the person he is instructing – an attitude that is a greater wrong than the one he is seeking to right. Only someone who knows his own faults is safe from this, for there is a tremendous egotistical pleasure to be had from knowing better and assuming authority over others. As he points out, one can detect this vice in oneself by a simple introspective test. Ask yourself what would please you more: for the offender to be corrected by your intervention, or for the agent of correction to be someone else, perhaps the offender himself. Anyone who finds the duty unwelcome and wishes someone else would do it for him should in fact go ahead, because his motives are genuinely religious. But if it is the other way round, then he is simply looking for an ego trip, and should start by reforming himself.

The insight that concerns us is not, of course, one attainable only by Ṣūfīs. It was also vouchsafed to Abū ʾl-Layth al-Samarqandī, who illustrated it with a story about a zealot who set out to cut down a sacred tree, but was waylaid by the devil, who cleverly corrupted his motivation.[45] Yet sensitivity to the lure of egotism has at least an elective affinity with Ṣūfism. Sunāmī in the early fourteenth century clearly regarded it as a Ṣūfī idea, since he remarks that the Ṣūfīs add to the conditions for forbidding wrong that one's ego should not be involved – if it is, one should not proceed.[46]

Two anecdotes related by Ghazzālī and others may serve to illustrate the sensibility behind this thinking.[47] One concerns Abū Sulaymān al-Dārānī (d. 820f.), an ascetic of Dārayyā near Damascus. This saintly man tells us that he once heard a caliph say something objectionable, and wanted to take a stand against it. But he knew that he would lose his life if he did so, and decided not to. What stopped him,

42 Cf. 450.
43 See above, 78.
44 439.
45 313 and n. 38 (and source); cf. 325.
46 461f.
47 462.

he explained, was not the prospect of being killed; rather it was that there were many people present, and he feared that he might be motivated by vanity. The second anecdote is about the Ṣūfī Abū ʾl-Ḥusayn al-Nūrī (d. 907f.). It starts with the observation that he was a man given to minding his own business, but would right a wrong if he saw one. One day at the riverside he noticed a boat with a suspicious cargo of thirty amphorae. He pressed the boatman to tell him what was in them, and learnt that the cargo was wine belonging to the caliph al-Muʿtaḍid (r. 892–902). Nūrī thereupon broke all of the amphorae but one. For this he was taken before the caliph, who, among other things, was curious to know why he had left that single amphora intact. Our Ṣūfī explained that in the course of his rampage his inner state had changed: at first he had acted because God was demanding that he do so; but when he came to the last amphora, he became aware of self-conceit, and desisted.

In short, there is no lack of ideas linked to Ṣūfism that downplay forbidding wrong in one way or another. But there is no mainstream Ṣūfī doctrine rejecting the duty as such, and Ṣūfīs can readily be found discussing or practising the duty; one Moroccan Ṣūfī who journeyed to the east around 1500 would forbid wrong wherever he was, so that if he failed in one place, he would move on and try somewhere else.[48] In the end, the fact of the matter is that Ṣūfīs were Muslims like anyone else – and many or most Muslims were Ṣūfīs.

4 ʿAbd al-Ghanī al-Nābulusī

ʿAbd al-Ghanī al-Nābulusī (d. 1731) was a Damascene Ḥanafī and Ṣūfī. He was also, among many other things, the author of a commentary on a work of the sixteenth-century Ottoman pietist Birgili (whom we met in an earlier chapter).[49] The tone of Birgili's discussion of forbidding wrong in that work had been distinctly enthusiastic. He had endorsed martyrdom, arguing that the duty is even more binding than holy war.[50] In response to this enthusiasm, ʿAbd al-Ghanī set out a new and chastening doctrine of the duty. It rested on two pillars.[51]

The first is a firm distinction between forbidding wrong and censorship (*ḥisba*) – two terms that the influence of Ghazzālī had tended to render synonymous among Ḥanafīs and others alike. So on the one hand, we have forbidding wrong. This is a quite general duty to command right and forbid wrong – that and no more. It is purely a matter of the tongue, and carries with it no power or duty of enforcement. Either people listen or they don't: 'No compulsion is there in religion' (Q2:256).

[48] 460f.; 465f.; 468 and n. 296; M. Winter, 'Sheikh ʿAlī ibn Maymūn and Syrian Sufism in the sixteenth century', *Israel Oriental Studies*, 7 (1977), 284; and see above, 38f.
[49] See above, 71.
[50] 324f.
[51] 326–8.

And on the other hand, we have censorship (*ḥisba*), the duty to enforce right conduct (*ḥaml al-nās ʿalā ʾl-ṭāʿa*). This activity is reserved to the authorities (*ḥukkām*), though with one qualification: when an offence is actually being committed (but not after the event), the ordinary believer may intervene (but has no duty to do so). Failure to make this distinction between forbidding wrong and censorship is common among supposed scholars in our time, and leads to disastrous results. ʿAbd al-Ghanī's tone in this part of his argument is discouraging, but his substantive doctrine would not in itself preclude much of the activity that is usually seen as part of forbidding wrong.

This is not the case with the second pillar of ʿAbd al-Ghanī's doctrine. In a familiar Ṣūfī vein, he lays great stress on having the right motives, and laments the prevalence of the wrong ones in his time: people set out to command and forbid because they crave an ego trip, or see it as a way to establish a role of power and dominance in society, or to gain the attention of important people, or to win fame, or to attain proximity to the portals of rulers. What is significant here, apart from the unusual elaboration of the theme, is the doctrinal conclusion he draws from this moralising: those whose motives are corrupt are obligated not to undertake the activity at all. (He contrives to derive this conclusion from the classical danger condition.)[52] And who in this age of ours could even think, let alone be sure, that his motives were pure? Certainly not those whose obsession with prying into the faults of others makes them blind to their own; so the chances of any scholar in this day and age attaining the martyrdom of which Birgili spoke are negligible. What we need, in short, is less self-righteousness and more self-knowledge.[53] This is something that can only be attained through a deep knowledge of Ṣūfism, which alone confers knowledge, not just of the holy law, but also of how to practise it. The combination of the redrawn distinction between forbidding wrong and censorship, on the one hand, and of the Ṣūfī critique of egotistical and self-righteous pietism, on the other, effectively closes the door to the activity Birgili had considered so binding. What is all this about?

We have here one of those rare but rewarding moments when a tradition of academic commentary suddenly gets real.[54] Birgili had been more than an author of much-copied books. He was the inspiration of the Qāḍīzādeli movement, a puritanical reformism that gripped seventeenth-century Istanbul. Its leaders held official positions as preachers in the major mosques of the city, combining popular followings with support from within the Ottoman state apparatus. Their prime target was none other than Ṣūfī innovation – in other words, a religious tradition to which ʿAbd al-Ghanī was strongly committed.

Yet at the time no clear doctrinal issue regarding the duty seems to have emerged between the Qāḍīzādelis and their opponents.[55] Forbidding wrong was indeed a

[52] Cf. 327 n. 155.
[53] Cf. 327 n. 158.
[54] 328.
[55] 329f.

bone of contention between the two parties, since it was what the Qāḍīzādelis took themselves to be doing. Hence Kātib Chelebi (d. 1657), in a little work which he contributed to the controversy, devoted a section to forbidding wrong, and in the course of it set out a rather rambling account of the conditions of obligation borrowed from Ashᶜarite sources. His purpose in piling up caveats was to cool the ardour of latter-day 'pretenders', in other words the Qāḍīzādelis. But while he stated that the common people were ignorant of the restrictions he dwelt on, he gave no indication that the Qāḍīzādelis themselves subscribed to a doctrine that formally sanctioned their more reckless activities. The clash articulated in Kātib Chelebi's tract was not between rival doctrines of forbidding wrong, but rather between the zeal of the Qāḍīzādelis and his own realism and common sense. As he remarks elsewhere in the work, once an innovation has become firmly rooted it is fatuous to try to eradicate it in the name of forbidding wrong; the plain fact is that, for better or worse, people will not give up what they are accustomed to. It is only with ᶜAbd al-Ghanī al-Nābulusī that the friction over the practice of forbidding wrong is elevated to the level of a doctrinal dispute.

ᶜAbd al-Ghanī's new doctrine thus comes close to closing the gate to forbidding wrong. But it was not taken up by posterity.

5 Minding one's own business

The scholars never tired of pointing out that forbidding wrong was an activity likely to provoke negative responses. By far the most insistent of these can be rendered as: 'Mind your own business! This has nothing to do with you!'

The scholars did not, of course, approve of this response, and did not portray it sympathetically.[56] Ibn Masᶜūd says that it is one of the worst of sins when someone is told to fear God, and responds: 'Look to yourself!' The devil asks the zealot who sets out with his axe to cut down the sacred tree: 'What's it got to do with you?' Abū ᵓl-Ḥusayn al-Nūrī, pressing his inquiries regarding the thirty amphorae containing the caliph's wine, is described by the boatman in charge of them as a 'meddlesome Ṣūfī' (*ṣūfī fuḍūlī*).[57] Ibn Ḥanbal predicts that a time will come when the believer who sees occasion to forbid wrong will be declared a busybody. In this day and age, laments the Egyptian Shāfiᶜite Ibn al-Naḥḥās (d. 1411), one who performs the duty is reviled for his meddlesomeness, while one who fawns on people is praised for his ability to get along with them.

We also hear about this reaction in a less rhetorical and more juristic vein when the Ḥanafī scholars list irreligious statements (quoted in the Persian vernacular) the utterance of which may constitute unbelief.[58] One man says to another: 'Go to the

[56] 498f.
[57] Cf. 461.
[58] 499.

home of so-and-so and command him right!'; the other replies: 'What wrong has he done to me that I should command him right?' Or he may reply 'What has he done to me?', or 'How has he bothered me?', or 'What have I to do with such meddlesomeness?' Or he may say to someone who is commanding right: 'What a commotion we have here!'

Nor are we exclusively dependent on the scholars to articulate this widespread counter-cultural value for us. The poets express it directly.[59] Ḥāfiẓ says that it is nothing to do with you whether he is good or bad; in the end each of us will reap what he himself has sown. He tells the ascetic not to find fault with the profligate; the sins of others will not be debited to his account. He asks the preacher what all the fuss is about, and tells him to go about his own business. Such poetry had wide resonance in the traditional culture of Iran.

In itself, however, minding one's own business is perfectly Islamic.[60] As the Prophet says, one of the things that makes a good Muslim is that he stays clear of what does not concern him (*tarkuhu mā lā yaᶜnīhi*). Nūrī, it will be remembered, was a man given to minding his own business, for all that the boatman regarded him as a meddlesome Ṣūfī (as events were to prove, with some reason). Does not God Himself tell the believers to 'look after your own souls', since those who are astray cannot harm them – provided, of course, they are 'rightly guided' (Q5:105)? The issue, in other words, is not whether one should mind one's own business, but rather just what the limits of one's business should be. Clearly those who invoked this value against unwanted commanding and forbidding had their own ideas as to these limits. But our sources scarcely tell us what these ideas were.

There is one vivid exception.[61] During his westward journey through North Africa on his way to establish the Almohad state, Ibn Tūmart (d. 1130), found the people of Dashr Qallāl near Fez engaged in making music in mixed company. He sent two of his followers to forbid this wrong, but the response they met with was: 'This is how we do things.' When the disciples insisted to the offenders that Ibn Tūmart was commanding them right (*maᶜrūf*), they received the retort: 'We go by our kind of right, and you go by yours; go away!' The replies are laconic, but they clearly assert the moral sovereignty of the local community and the wider moral relativism this implies.

We thus find no doctrinal rejection of forbidding wrong based on the principle of minding one's own business. But we do at least come face to face with an attitude that must have been widespread – though it was by no means universal among ordinary people. When in 1357 the authorities in Damascus paraded a group of pietists in chains, proclaiming 'This is how people are punished who interfere in what is none of their business,' the punishment met with strong popular disapproval.[62]

59 499.
60 499f.
61 591f.; cf. 458f.
62 500 n. 247; cf. 472.

6 Concluding remarks

Two points are worth noting by way of conclusion. One is that despite the variety of negative responses to forbidding wrong, no consolidated doctrine directed against it ever emerges bar that of ᶜAbd al-Ghanī, which achieved no wider success. The other is that none of the basic ideas found in these responses come from outside the standard repertoire of Islamic values.[63] Consider the encounter between the caliph al-Maʾmūn and the shrouded zealot. This story is unusual in inviting us to identify squarely with the caliph; in that sense we can see it as a fine articulation of the 'thèse caliphale'. The story can also be relied on to warm the heart of any secularist. The caliph is clear-headed, sober and responsible; the zealot is fanatical, pretentious and stupid. But the caliph's position is in no way that of a secularist. It is not just that he derives considerable moral advantage from the placement of the story in the context of holy war against the infidel. More than that, he mounts no argument that has its point of departure outside the religious tradition of Islam, and concludes that the man must have misinterpreted a Prophetic tradition. Likewise ᶜAbd al-Ghanī bases his most innovative and devastating argument on the danger condition. Perhaps non-Islamic values played their part in the popular dismissal of pietists as busybodies; but the only context in which we glimpse them is Ibn Tūmart's visit to Dashr Qallāl.

[63] 497f.

CHAPTER 9

What was forbidding wrong like in practice?

At the end of all this analysis of the doctrines of the scholars, it is natural to ask what forbidding wrong was really like in the pre-modern Islamic world. But in attempting to answer this question, we are almost entirely at the mercy of the same scholars. They are not just the guardians of doctrine; they are also the authors of the biographical works that give us most of our material for the study of the practice of the duty. We have no journalists, anthropologists, novelists or secularists to give us different perspectives. We thus have almost no way to emancipate ourselves from the world-view of the scholars, short of not believing a word they say. With rare exceptions, the best we can do is to use common sense to discount some of what they tell us, and occasional cunning to go behind it. This chapter will accordingly describe the practice of forbidding wrong pretty much as the scholars saw it.

As already indicated, one of the best sources for this enterprise is biographical literature. The Muslim scholars devoted biographical works to such groups as poets, grammarians, Koran reciters, and even women – but above all to their fellow scholars. Before modern times the idea does not seem to have occurred to anyone to collect into a single work biographical material on those who forbade wrong. But the broad range of biographical literature contains much scattered evidence of the practice of forbidding wrong by individual Muslims. The material is uneven and can be threadbare; a writer may tell us no more than that the subject of a biography was assiduous in forbidding wrong. But sometimes the anecdotal detail is rich and colourful. Particularly in the early centuries, biographers were in the business of holding the attention of their audiences.

It is to our advantage here that forbidding wrong can provide a biographer with good stories. Typically the activity is an individual performance, and as such fits well into a biography. It is easy for the reader to take sides: there is a bad guy who is busy doing wrong, and a good guy who fearlessly forbids him. Moreover the enterprise on which the hero embarks is quite unlike prayer or fasting, duties any normal person can adequately fulfil just by keeping at them. It also differs from them in that the conditions under which it is undertaken, and the eventual outcome, can be very varied indeed. To succeed in forbidding wrong takes courage, skill, nerve and judgement – not to mention having God on your side. A superior performance is likely to be dramatic, distinctive and highly eligible material for a biographer. But of course there is another side to this coin. It is doubtless the good stories that we come to hear, not the far more common bad or indifferent ones; and the good stories are likely to have been improved in the telling.

But for the moment let us leave aside the heroes and villains, and concentrate on the wrongs themselves.

1 What wrongs do people commit?

As we have seen, Ghazzālī provides a survey of wrongs that are commonly met with.[1] He stresses that his survey is selective, and at a certain point he hands over the task of continuing it to the reader. It nevertheless provides a convenient introduction to the subject; we can use it as a basis with which to compare what we find in biographical and related sources. Ghazzālī presents his wrongs under five contextual headings: the mosque, the market, the street, the bath-house and hospitality.[2]

His wrongs of the mosque include sloppy prayer, faulty recitation of the Koran, a practice whereby pairs of muezzins make a duet of the call to prayer, needless repetitions of the call to prayer after daybreak and preachers who mix heresy into what they say. Preachers are a particular problem: Ghazzālī warns against the young, elegantly dressed preacher whose delivery is full of poetry and gesture and whose circle is frequented by women. He also denounces the sale of medicines in the mosque, not to mention the presence of madmen, boys and drunks.

Ghazzālī's wrongs of the market fall into three categories. The first is commercial dishonesty, such as concealing defects in goods, or passing off reconditioned second-hand clothes as new. The second is engaging in transactions that violate the law – usurious ones, for example. The third is the sale of forbidden goods: musical instruments, toy animals (which would count as images) sold for small boys during festivals, gold and silver vessels, silk clothes such as can only be worn by men, or are locally known to be worn only by them. These, we might comment, are matters that would naturally fall within the province of the officially appointed censor (*muḥtasib*). But Ghazzālī is concerned only with the duty of the individual Muslim. Thus if a man says, 'I bought these goods for – say – ten and I'm taking a profit of such-and-such,' and he is lying, then anyone who is aware of this has a duty to inform the prospective buyer of the deceit.

Ghazzālī's wrongs of the street are violations of the principle that streets are for public use. They include unnecessarily transporting loads of thorns in narrow alleys, slaughtering animals on the street, scattering watermelon rind, discharging

[1] See above, 73.
[2] 443–5.

water from spouts into narrow lanes, leaving puddles, mud and snow on the streets and keeping dogs that bother passers-by.

Ghazzālī's wrongs of the bath-house begin with the image found either at the entrance to the bath-house or inside it (though images of trees and such are not a problem). Then follow the issues of nudity, touching and impurity that inevitably arise in such places. In addition, there is the matter of slippery surfaces and the liabilities to which they give rise.

Ghazzālī ends the systematic part of his survey with wrongs of hospitality. These include laying out silk coverings for men, using censers made of silver or gold, hanging curtains with images on them and listening to musical instruments or singing-girls. Then there is the scandal of women gathering on roofs to watch men when there are youths among them who could give rise to temptation. Or forbidden food may be served, or the house may be one occupied illegally, or someone present may be drinking wine or wearing silk or a golden signet ring, or a heretic may be holding forth about his heresy, or some joker may be regaling the party with ribald and untruthful humour. (Humour that is neither untruthful nor indecorous is acceptable in moderation, provided it does not become a habit.) On top of all this there may be extravagance and wastefulness.

If we look at Ghazzālī's wrongs through our eyes rather than his, we can sort them in a rough-and-ready fashion into three piles. First, there are those that violate narrowly religious norms, such as praying faultily or holding forth about one's heresy. Second, there are wrongs that offend against puritanical norms, such as liquor, music and improper relations between the sexes. Finally, there are wrongs we could term secular, those that straightforwardly violate the rights of other humans in this world; examples are blocking the streets they need to use or exposing them to the risk of slipping and falling in the bath-house. We do not need to decide in each and every case to which category we would assign Ghazzālī's wrongs. What is clear is that those he surveys are a good mix: all three categories are well represented – though it is worth noting that there is no sign within the secular category of a concern for what we might call social justice.

What happens if we go looking for Ghazzālī's wrongs in the sources that concern us in this chapter? Most of them simply do not appear. Some make occasional appearances. This is the case with sloppy prayer[3] and impropriety in the bath-house;[4] if we leave aside the specific context in which Ghazzālī mentions them, the same is true of heresy[5] and images.[6] But the fact is that the narrowly religious wrongs are not a prominent concern of our sources,[7] and still less the secular ones. Thus Ghazzālī's concerns about the street find no echo in these sources, and I have

[3] 76 n. 222; 92; 149.
[4] 115 n. 3, no. (5); cf. 69.
[5] 355 n. 134; 387; 403.
[6] 93; 115 n. 3, no. (10); 329.
[7] Cf. 355 nn. 128, 138.

encountered few references to cheating customers[8] – though one of them is unusually colourful. According to a thirteenth-century geographer, a custom was observed each year in Gīlān in the north of Iran that amounted to a sort of scholars' carnival.[9] The scholars would seek permission from the ruler to command right. Once they had it, they would round up everyone and flog them. If a man swore that he had neither drunk nor fornicated, the scholar would ask him his trade; if he said he was a grocer, the scholar would infer that he cheated his customers, and flog him anyway. This is a nice story, but it does not encourage us to think that what I have called the secular component of forbidding wrong enjoyed much salience in practice.

It is thus the puritanical norms that dominate the recorded practice of the duty. What our sources tell us is that the overwhelming concern of those who forbade wrong was with wine, women and song. In fact liquor and music are by far the most widespread wrongs in our sources. Women come in a poor third – a fact that may surprise anyone familiar with the salience of prostitutes in the public life of as ancient an Islamic city as Damascus in the eighteenth century.[10]

We have already met liquor in connection with the private misdeeds of rulers,[11] but it appears in many other settings.[12] Ibn Taymiyya, for example, once toured the taverns of Damascus with a group of disciples, smashing bottles and splitting skins.[13] Ibn Karrām (d. 869), the founder of a pietistic Sunnī sect known after him as the Karrāmiyya, was less abrasive.[14] Walking with a group of his disciples, he encountered some young men drinking wine. The indignant disciples wanted to right this wrong and put a stop to the drinking, but Ibn Karrām told them to hold off so that he could show them how to command right. He then went up to the tipplers and greeted them. One of them stood up and handed Ibn Karrām a cup; Ibn Karrām took the cup, and addressed them. He referred to their custom of talking about those they loved as they drank, and suggested that instead they contemplate their own mortality. On this theme he waxed so eloquent that the young men arose, broke the instruments of their depravity, and repented. The anecdote implicitly acknowledges the sheer normality of drinking as a social practice in the medieval Muslim world. The eastern Ibāḍī sources even complain about women who gather to drink.[15]

Music is as common in our sources as liquor, perhaps even more so.[16] This time the eastern Ibāḍī sources add variety by complaining about African and Indian

[8] See also 400 n. 43; 421.
[9] 474.
[10] A.-K. Rafeq, 'Public morality in 18th century Ottoman Damascus', *Revue du Monde Musulman et de la Méditerranée*, 55–56 (1990), 183f., 189f.
[11] See above, 73f.
[12] 67f.; 91f.; 118f.; 121; 149; 383 n. 195; 386; 409; 463; cf. 241; 474.
[13] 150 n. 42.
[14] 489.
[15] 409.
[16] 68; 90f.; 118f.; 148f.; 149; 382f.; 386; 409f.; 591f.; cf. 241.

music.[17] One example among many of a bold confrontation with the evil of music is an incident that took place in 1072.[18] A Ḥanbalite scholar came upon a singing-girl who had just been performing for a Turk. Undeterred by the military connection, he grabbed her lute and cut its strings; she went back and complained to the Turk, who retaliated by raiding the scholar's home.

Improper relations between the sexes are less often mentioned, but still prominent.[19] Men engage women in conversation,[20] soldiers wax lascivious,[21] women have the coquettish habit of wearing squeaky sandals[22] and so forth. But nothing reported from the heartlands of the Islamic world quite matches the customs of the town of Jenne as brought to the notice of the North African jurist Maghīlī (d. 1503f.) by the ruler of Songhay: 'All the most beautiful girls walk naked among people with no covering at all.'[23]

Before concluding this survey, it is worth returning briefly to the matter of social justice. Here perhaps we are scraping the barrel, but we do not come out entirely empty-handed. For one thing, we may suspect that puritanism directed at the luxurious living of the elite may on occasion take on a populist colouring,[24] as when pietists rebuke the privileged for their arrogant gait.[25] Sometimes the wrong-doers we hear of maltreat those less powerful than themselves: a master beats his slave,[26] a brother may deprive his sisters of their rights of inheritance,[27] henchmen of the governor rob a woodcutter of his wood.[28] Sometimes the forbidder of wrong clearly represents a larger constituency: one scholar protests to the ruler about illegal taxes, another about the overweening power of the Copts.[29] But it would be a mistake to see forbidders of wrong in general in such a light. The Shāfiᶜite Abū ᵓl-ᶜAbbās al-Sarrāj (d. 925) of Nīshāpūr used to command right and forbid wrong riding on his donkey, telling his teaching assistant ᶜAbbās to do away with this and break that; but when he was brought in to remonstrate with the ruler, he disappointed everybody by bringing up a point about the ritual of prayer in the mosque, instead of furthering the material interests of the city.[30]

The main conclusion of this survey concerns neither the ritual of prayer nor the interests of cities, but rather the recurrent puritanical agenda of forbidding wrong. An eighth-century Tunisian pietist upbraided a colleague for failing to rebuke his

[17] 409f.
[18] 119.
[19] 68; 92; 121; 383; 384 n. 208; 459; 591f.; cf. 463; 474; 589.
[20] 68.
[21] 70; 250f.
[22] 368.
[23] 386f.
[24] 501.
[25] 69.
[26] 72.
[27] 93.
[28] 383; 384.
[29] 355; 356; 501.
[30] 348; 501.

brother, who had just come in from the countryside and was talking endlessly in a religious circle about matters of rain and grain.[31] The Ḥanbalite vizier Ibn Hubayra (d. 1165) once considered it his duty to leave a distinguished scholarly gathering at his home to administer a reproof for a cry that had gone up in the private quarters on the death of his infant son.[32] If we trust our sources, puritanism was what forbidding wrong was mostly about; and I see no reason to set their testimony aside.

2 Who actually forbids wrong?

As we saw in an earlier chapter, the scholars did not usually lay claim to a monopoly of forbidding wrong.[33] But in the literature that concerns us here, it seems clear that those who engage in the activity are overwhelmingly scholars.[34] This centrality of the role of the scholars is confirmed unthinkingly by Ghazzālī in his lament about the decay of the art of rebuking rulers. This is an activity in which in principle any man of sincere piety could participate effectively; but what Ghazzālī laments is that today the *scholars* are silent or ineffectual.[35]

A corollary of this is that the forbidding wrong we hear about is predominantly urban, like the scholars themselves.[36] Again, Ghazzālī unreflectingly assumes this when he says that it is the duty of every scholar who can do so to go out from his town to the rural population around it.[37] Conversely, we learn that when the people of Toledo could no longer endure the zeal of a scholar who forbade wrong among them in the early tenth century, he retired to a village.[38] But there were exceptional regions where scholars lived in the countryside, as in the Ḥanbalite villages of northern Palestine.[39] The rural Ṣūfīs of Morocco in later centuries offer a parallel.[40]

The scholars who forbade wrong – perhaps in contrast to many of their colleagues – are unlikely to have been quiet scholars. Two of them, one in the eighth century and the other in the twelfth, are described as liable to experience acute psychosomatic symptoms if unable to right a wrong.[41] Likewise our sources present those who forbid wrong as courting danger. The Damascene Ḥanbalite ᶜAbd al-Ghanī al-Maqdisī (d. 1203) was possessed of an electrifying presence and a remarkable self-confidence, and had a way of getting into trouble wherever he

[31] 383.
[32] 129; cf. 93; 410; 414.
[33] See above,17f.
[34] 114f. n. 3; 127f.; 148f. and nn. 33, 37; 163 and n. 124; 250f.; 316; 348 and n. 71; 354–6; 381–6; 387; 403; 458f.; 474; 489; cf. 385 and n. 218; 487.
[35] 446; 488; cf. 140f.
[36] 487.
[37] 445; 487; cf. 487 n. 149.
[38] 382; 487; 500.
[39] 163 n. 125; 487.
[40] 387.
[41] 65; 355 n. 129; 492 n. 192.

went; once when he was pouring away wine the irate owner drew his sword, and ᶜAbd al-Ghanī simply grabbed it.[42] His brother got himself beaten up,[43] and another contemporary lost a tooth.[44] The Ḥanbalite Maḥmūd al-Naᶜᶜāl (d. 1212), who once confronted a gathering of grandees and destroyed their supply of liquor, was several times beaten up in the course of such incidents.[45] One tenth-century Mālikī got himself killed,[46] a slightly later one was expelled from his city.[47] It is thus a surprise to find a pietist who forbade wrong in fourteenth-century Fez described as shy, solitary and painfully modest.[48] Nevertheless the authority invoked in forbidding wrong is a narrowly moral one; the righteous scholar is a very different figure from the perfect gentle knight of medieval European chivalry.[49]

At the same time, we encounter cases from time to time where it is clear that a scholar who forbids wrong has a constituency. We saw a couple of examples of this in the previous section, and there are others to hand. The shy pietist is said to have had wide support for his activity.[50] A Ḥanbalite in twelfth-century Ḥarrān escaped a flogging after pouring out the ruler's wine thanks to his standing with the common people of the city.[51]

Sometimes it is clear that the support such figures received from their constituencies amounted to more than just approval. In early tenth-century Baghdad, the Ḥanbalite Barbahārī was manifestly a demagogue.[52] The traveller Ibn Baṭṭūṭa (d. 1368f.) describes an ascetic preacher in Herat with whom the townspeople had entered into agreement to right wrongs; they would put right any wrong, even if it took place at the court of the ruler.[53] He adds a story in which 6,000 of them saw to it that the prescribed punishment for drinking was inflicted on the ruler in his palace. Moreover it is not uncommon for our sources to speak of people forbidding wrong as part of a group.[54] Thus Hishām ibn Ḥakīm ibn Ḥizām used to forbid wrong with a group of Syrians; no one had authority over them, and they would wander around selflessly putting things to rights and giving counsel.[55] Maḥmūd al-Naᶜᶜāl is described in 1176f. as the leader of a group that took horrendous risks in the cause of forbidding wrong.[56] These were clearly groups with a long-term existence, but others might be formed for the purpose in hand. The practice of the

42 148f.; 492; 493.
43 149; cf. 69f.; 72.
44 149.
45 127.
46 384; cf. 114 n. 3, no. (1); 316.
47 387; cf. 316.
48 492 n. 193.
49 489f.; 492f.
50 387; 500; cf. 472.
51 149 n. 33; 500.
52 116–18; 500.
53 500f.
54 73f.; 91 n. 21; 97f.; 119f.; 128; 150 n. 42; 384; 403; 493f.; 589; cf. 394; see above, 34.
55 60.
56 127.

ascetic Muḥammad ibn Muṣᶜab (d. 843) is a case in point.[57] On hearing the sound of music coming from a house, he would knock at the door and demand the offending instrument in order to break it. If the inmates failed to cooperate, he would sit at the door and recite the Koran till a noisy crowd gathered round, and the inmates had second thoughts.

The reader may have noted that in the last few paragraphs we have had occasion to mention some figures who do not look quite like scholars: the shy pietist of Fez, the ascetic preacher of Herat and the ascetic Koran reciter are cases in point. Are these a marginal phenomenon, or are they the tip of an iceberg?

Some of these figures are recognisable as members of the religious elite in a broad sense. The ascetics just mentioned may belong in this category, as do other preachers,[58] not to mention the Ṣūfīs we encounter forbidding wrong.[59] One Damascene scholar who died in 1517 apparently practised forbidding wrong in a phase of his life when he had dropped out of academia and taken up asceticism.[60]

Others do not sound like scholars at all.[61] Perhaps the shy pietist belongs here. One eleventh-century figure who would right wrongs with a group of pietists is unidentifiable as a scholar, and probably was not one.[62] A tailor of Baghdad to whom we will come in a later chapter is another such case.[63] An eleventh-century Baghdādī Ḥanbalite was a decorator in his youth, and would forbid his fellow craftsmen to make images; he gave up the trade after an episode in which he smashed images in the home of a grandee.[64] Likewise the followers of the Qāḍīzādeli preachers can hardly qualify as scholars. One of them got into trouble in eastern Anatolia when he felt it his duty to mutilate the illustrations in a fine copy of the *Shāhnāma*, the Persian national epic. He regarded this as forbidding wrong; the local authorities considered it vandalism, and had him flogged for it, telling him he had no commission to forbid wrong.[65]

I have encountered no cut-and-dried case of a woman forbidding wrong as an individual Muslim.[66] But an unusual case of a non-scholar forbidding wrong is an eighth-century dog.[67] Its owner was Sulaymān ibn Mihrān al-Aᶜmash (d. 765), a noted Kūfan traditionist with a reputation for being boorish and disagreeable. It was characteristic of his meanness towards students in search of traditions that when they visited him they would be harassed by this vicious animal. One day, however, they found that the dog had died, and eagerly rushed in. On seeing them,

[57] 98.
[58] 328f.; cf. 387f.
[59] 388; 463f.
[60] 355 n. 138.
[61] See also 472 n. 13.
[62] 493f.
[63] 589; see below, 166.
[64] 115 n. 3, no. (10).
[65] 329 and n. 163.
[66] 82f.; 95; 153 n. 68; 402; 485f.
[67] 83.

Aᶜmash wept and remarked of the dog: 'He who used to command right and forbid wrong has perished!'

Aᶜmash's dog apart, our basic problem concerns the relationship between our sources and the wider society. Our sources, as we have seen, give us the impression that with few exceptions it was only the religious elite of the society that forbade wrong. The question is whether they give us this impression because that is how it was, or because the religious elite had a marked proclivity for talking about itself. We have no satisfactory way to answer this question. But one point suggests that we should accept the broad outline of the picture given us by our sources. There was a good deal of ethical writing in the Islamic world that was not specifically Islamic in character, deriving rather from the pre-Islamic Greek and Persian traditions. Some of this writing is highbrow, some inclines to the popular. But to my knowledge, it is almost untouched by the idea of forbidding wrong;[68] a marginal exception is an account of the duty given by Avicenna (d. 1037) in the course of developing a kind of philosophical Ṣūfism.[69] This would support the idea that forbidding wrong was largely a preserve of the religious elite.

Sometimes, of course, nobody forbade wrong. Visiting the city of Laodicea (the modern Denizli) in western Anatolia, the traveller Ibn Baṭṭūṭa was moved to comment: 'The people of this city do not right wrongs, nor do the people of this entire region.' He went on to give a vivid picture of the prostitution of Greek slave-girls. He was told that their owners included the judge of the town, and that these prostitutes freely entered the bath-houses in the company of their clients.[70]

3 Forbidding the wrongs of rulers

So far in this chapter we have seen that in practice forbidding wrong was mainly a matter of members of the religious elite pursuing a puritanical agenda. The annals of confrontation with the wrongdoing of rulers fit quite well with this pattern.

As we have seen, the personal vices of rulers and their associates are largely a matter of liquor and music.[71] Moreover, where the wrongdoing of ruling circles is spelled out in the sources that concern us in this chapter, it quite often falls in this category.[72] Thus ᶜAbd al-Ghanī al-Maqdisī breaks mandolins being transported to a drinking-party given by members of the family of Saladin.[73] Even clearer is the tendency for those who rebuke rulers to be scholars, or failing that members of the broader religious elite,[74] just as Ghazzālī took for granted. For example, we are

[68] 494–7.
[69] 495f.
[70] 316.
[71] See above, 73f.
[72] 119; 384f.; 462.
[73] 149.
[74] 3; 55 n. 60; 56; 58f.; 59; 62f.; 64; 65; 66; 127f.; 163 n. 124, no. (3); 316; 355 n. 135; 356; 381f.; 384f.; 387; 388; 464; cf. 348; 385 and n. 218.

told that the Ayyūbid al-Malik al-ᶜĀdil (r. 1196–1218) confessed to being terrified of ᶜAbd al-Ghanī; when ᶜAbd al-Ghanī came into his presence, he said, he felt as though a wild beast had come to devour him.[75] Another such case is the Shāfiᶜite scholar Khubūshānī (d. 1191), who when confronting Saladin about illegal taxes went so far as to poke him with a stick, knocking off his headgear.[76]

We may, of course, suspect that the accounts our sources give us of run-ins with rulers are particularly likely to have been enriched by those who recounted them. Did Sufyān al-Thawrī really compare the caliph's viziers unfavourably to those of Pharaoh?[77] Did a traditionist brought before al-Maʾmūn for violating his ban on commanding right really tell the caliph that he did not command right, but did forbid wrong?[78] (The caliph had him flogged anyway, but subsequently released him.) Did a pietist who began his rebuke of Hārūn al-Rashīd (r. 786–809) by calling out 'Hey Hārūn!' really deflect the charge that he had had the temerity to address the caliph by name with the inspired riposte that he did the same to God?[79] (He was released without further ado.) When Nūrī, the Ṣūfī who broke all but one of the caliph's amphorae,[80] was asked by the irate ruler to explain who had appointed him to the censorship (*ḥisba*), did he really respond 'He who appointed you to the imamate'?[81] It seems reasonable to suspect a measure of embellishment in such cases, though we should not forget that people do at times succeed in saying apt things on the spur of the moment.

But there is a more serious distortion that needs to be taken into account. By and large, stories about confrontations with rulers and their henchmen are better value than those in which the wrongdoers are ordinary people. Consequently their salience in our sources is unlikely to reflect their relative frequency in real life.[82] Consider the case of Muḥammad ibn al-Munkadir (d. 747f.) and the baths of Medina.[83] Ibn al-Munkadir and a companion went into the baths and while there they reproved a man – we are not told what his offence was. This man then went to the governor and complained that there were Khārijites in the baths; the governor accordingly had them whipped, without bothering to inquire more closely into the matter. When Ibn al-Munkadir was humiliated in this fashion, the people of Medina reacted by gathering around him; he seems to have calmed them by telling them that anyone worth his salt must expect to incur such suffering when forbidding wrong. It is clear that in this story the narrator has no interest in what happened between Ibn al-Munkadir and the man in the baths; we hear of the scene only

[75] 148.
[76] 355.
[77] 65.
[78] 71.
[79] 59.
[80] See above, 91.
[81] 448; cf. 459 n. 226; 583 n. 139.
[82] Cf. 384.
[83] 69f.; 72.

because it provides the background to the clash with the governor. The same is true of the story of Abū Nuᶜaym, the lascivious soldier and al-Maʾmūn: we hear of the confrontation with the soldier only because it brought Abū Nuᶜaym face to face with the caliph.[84] An incident that makes the same point in a different way took place in Oman around the beginning of the sixteenth century.[85] One Muḥammad ibn Ismāᶜīl saw a man chasing a naked woman whom he had come upon while she was washing; our hero grappled with the pursuer and brought him down, while the woman escaped. The story is preserved only because it made political history: people were sufficiently impressed with Muḥammad ibn Ismāᶜīl's strength in forbidding wrong that he was chosen to be imam, and ruled for over thirty years.

Something else that invites suspicion is an occasional mismatch between words and deeds. We usually expect people to talk more bravely than they act. Yet in a couple of instances we find it to be the other way round.[86] When Sufyān al-Thawrī is asked why he does not go in to rebuke those in power, he responds with a graphic metaphor about the futility of trying to dam up the sea. Yet he himself goes in to the caliph and as good as tells him that he is Pharaoh. Shuᶜayb ibn Ḥarb (d. 811f.) is the pietist who courted death by calling out 'Hey Hārūn!' Yet the same Shuᶜayb responds with these words to a questioner who asks him about forbidding wrong: 'But for the sword, the whip, and things of that ilk, we would command and forbid. If you are up to it, go ahead.' In cases like this, stirring deeds are perhaps more likely to be fictitious than prudent words. To a biographer, the temptation to have Sufyān al-Thawrī confront the caliph face to face and treat him like Pharaoh may well have been irresistible; but the doctrinal discussion of this dangerous activity tended to be more measured.[87]

There is also a curious dissonance regarding the performance of Mālik in rebuking rulers. Within the school, we hear only good news,[88] which contrasts with the rather half-hearted tone of the relevant sayings of Mālik.[89] Yet even here, there is an undertone of embarrassment, as if the impression had to be avoided that Mālik mixed too often and too easily with those in power. There is a concern to show that Mālik made no concessions to the corrupting and intimidating ambience of the caliphal presence, and that in any case his visits were justified by the results. Thus Mālik protests that if he did not visit the authorities, not a single normative custom (*sunna*) of the Prophet would be put into practice in Medina. And not to worry: he swore that whenever he went in to see someone in authority, it was God's habit to remove from his heart the awe that such figures inspire, and to enable him to come out with the truth. Thus far the Mālikī version. Outside the

[84] See above, 67f.
[85] 425.
[86] 66f.
[87] See above, ch. 7, section 2; cf. also 300f.
[88] 381f.
[89] See above, 75.

school, we encounter a quite different image.[90] It takes the form of an unfavourable comparison between Mālik and the Medinese traditionist Ibn Abī Dhiʾb (d. 775f.). In the presence of the authorities, we are told, Ibn Abī Dhiʾb would speak out, commanding and forbidding; meanwhile Mālik would remain silent.

We may in any case discern an element of play-acting underlying many of these encounters between piety and power. This game had its rules, as we can see from a case in which one party accused the other of breaking them. Members of the Aghlabid family, which in the ninth century ruled what is now Tunisia, used to visit a blind saint to derive blessing from him.[91] But on one occasion the saint refused to admit the ruler and his retinue. The enraged ruler responded: 'Listen you, we've come to you so you can command us right, and we then hasten to do it, and forbid us wrong, and we then restrain ourselves from it. But you've humiliated me and kept me out here, me, your ruler!' His protest was of course in vain, and after further slights he departed, full of appreciation for the saint.

4 Forbidding wrong and rebellion

A hostile anecdote about the Moroccan rebel Abū Maḥallī (d. 1613) relates that in his youth he and his coeval Maḥammad ibn Abī Bakr al-Dilāʾī (d. 1636) once spent the day in contrasting pursuits: Abū Maḥallī in fractious and fruitless attempts to forbid wrong, and Ibn Abī Bakr in washing his clothes, saying his prayers and the like. It was, of course, Abū Maḥallī who developed the pretensions to temporal power that led to his early death, whereas Ibn Abī Bakr lived to a ripe old age as the head of a major centre of religious culture in Dilāʾ.[92]

As we move from rebuke to rebellion, we leave behind the normal range of scholarly puritanism. We have, of course, already attended to the doctrinal aspect of the link between forbidding wrong and rebellion in an earlier chapter;[93] our concern at this point is with historical events. Here the main thing we learn from the sources is that 'commanding right and forbidding wrong' was a slogan readily adopted by rebels. Examples are to be found among the Khārijites, including the Ibāḍīs,[94] among the Shīʿites, including the Zaydīs,[95] and among the Sunnīs, especially the Mālikīs.[96] Some instances of such rebels in the early centuries of Islam are Jahm ibn Ṣafwān (d. 746) in late Umayyad Transoxania, Yūsuf al-Barm in Khurāsān in 776f., Mubarqaʿ in Palestine in 841f., Ibn al-Qiṭṭ in Spain in 901 and

90 382.
91 385.
92 389.
93 See above, ch. 7, section 3.
94 393f.; 396; 397; 406.
95 231–5.
96 388–90.

an ᶜAbbāsid who rebelled in Armenia in 960.[97] In a more recent example, from nineteenth-century Oman, forty men, against the wishes of their relatives, resolved on 'selling' themselves to God, donned shrouds, and went forth to command right and forbid wrong. However, the group went to pieces after they agreed to accept presents sent by the sultan, and they all went home.[98]

The slogan also played its part in political ventures that cannot be categorised as rebellion for lack of a functioning state to rebel against.[99] The years 816–17 were fertile in this respect. In Alexandria in 816, under conditions of political chaos, we are told that there appeared in the city 'a group called the Ṣūfīs' who commanded right, or so they claimed, and challenged the local governor; they had a leader who was one of their number.[100] How we should understand their activity is not clear: were they seeking to enforce moral puritanism on the population, to restore public order or to seize power? The situation in Baghdad in the following year is clearer. Here popular movements emerged aiming to restore public order in the absence of effective authority.[101] At least three leaders were active: Khālid al-Daryūsh, Sahl ibn Salāma and the young Aḥmad ibn Naṣr (who was to perish in an abortive rebellion in 846). All three acted under the banner of forbidding wrong. Two of them, Khālid and Sahl, are said to have begun with appeals to their neighbours, and then to the people of their quarters. They were separated by a significant doctrinal difference regarding the duty. Khālid (who was clearly the less successful leader) categorically opposed performing it against a ruler. Sahl, by contrast, proposed to fight anyone who opposed the Koran and the normative practice (*sunna*), irrespective of whether he was a ruler or not – a view that may well reflect a Muᶜtazilite affiliation. We are told that Ibn Ḥanbal disapproved of Sahl's enterprise, and reproved one of his followers;[102] and as we have seen, al-Maʾmūn is said to have been moved by these events to declare a ban on forbidding wrong.

This leads to a curious paradox. While forbidding wrong can express the claims of rebels to political authority, it can also provide an alibi for those who do not wish to challenge an incumbent state too openly or directly. One instance of this is found in a letter of imam Yaḥyā Ḥamīd al-Dīn of the Yemen (r. 1904–48) written in 1909, during a period in which the Ottoman governor had adopted a conciliatory policy, and Yaḥyā's rebellion was more or less in abeyance.[103] Here imam Yaḥyā speaks of the grant of autonomy he is seeking from the Ottomans as 'the transfer into our hands of the execution of the important duty of commanding right and forbidding wrong in the region of Yemen'. Likewise in a letter written to the Ottoman governor in 1906, he had sworn that he was not seeking power, and had no ambition

[97] 388f.; 477.
[98] 406.
[99] See also 390 n. 256.
[100] 461.
[101] 107 and n. 190.
[102] 104 and n. 173.
[103] 478.

beyond forbidding wrong.[104] Another such case is Muḥammad ibn ᶜAlī al-Idrīsī (r. 1908f.–1923), who in the last years of Ottoman rule established a state in ᶜAsīr that was later annexed by the Saudis.[105] In the early years of his venture, he liked to portray himself as a local religious reformer who was loyal to the Ottoman state. In this connection he described himself, both in correspondence with the Ottoman authorities and in propaganda directed to the local population, as forbidding wrong. Others spoke of him in the same vein.

5 Concluding remarks

In this chapter we have considered what the reality of forbidding wrong may have been like in pre-modern Islamic societies. The broad conclusions that emerge are fairly clear. In terms of its targets, our sources present the activity as driven largely by puritanical attitudes. In terms of the identity of those who participated, our sources point to the members of the religious elite, and above all the scholars. On neither point is there good reason to doubt the testimony of the sources. Where we can fairly suspect them of embellishment and of giving us an unbalanced picture is in their accounts of verbal confrontations with rulers. But the link between forbidding wrong and rebellion is unproblematically historical.

[104] 660.
[105] 478f.

CHAPTER 10

What has changed for the Sunnīs in modern times?

The doctrines of forbidding wrong that we examined in previous chapters form part of a medieval scholastic heritage. Such heritages excite the fascination, and sometimes the wonder, of historians, but as living traditions they are no longer really at home in the modern world. What actually becomes of them depends on a range of factors that have little to do with their intrinsic intellectual merits. They may, for example, be dismissed as irrelevant and forgotten, or relegated to iconic status, or perpetuated through institutional inertia.

In the case of the medieval Islamic scholastic heritage, the key factor is the resurgence of Islam in the second half of the twentieth century. Islamic fundamentalism, to use a convenient term, is committed to believing in the relevance of the Islamic tradition – or at least of select parts of it – to the conditions under which Muslims live in the modern world. This faith has guaranteed continuing attention to the substance of medieval doctrines of forbidding wrong. But it has not, of course, given them any immunity to the tidal forces of modernity. The effects of these forces begin to be visible in the last decades of the nineteenth century,[1] and it is with the outcome of this process that this and the following chapter are mostly concerned.

Before we begin, we need to revisit one of the themes of the introduction of this book: religious allegiances.[2] The road-map supplied there is no longer very helpful in the modern period.

1 Religious allegiances in the modern Islamic world

One of the ways in which the Western impact has profoundly changed the Islamic world is that many of the old divisions no longer matter much. The significant cleavages in Islamic thought today are not those between Ḥanafīs and Shāfiʿites, or Ashʿarites and traditionalists. Even the sectarian divisions between Sunnīs,

[1] Cf. 506f.
[2] See above, ch. 1, section 2.

Zaydīs and Ibāḍīs no longer support much in the way of intellectual superstructure, whatever role they may play in the communal politics of the relevant parts of the Islamic world. Of the main sects and schools whose views we have referred to in previous chapters, only the Imāmī Shīᶜites are still strongly differentiated from the broad spectrum of modern Islam.

This remaining division, however, is very real. It is not simply that the heritages of the Sunnīs and Imāmīs are in some ways very different in content and character, and that the two traditions have yet to set aside their long history of mutual hostility. One contrast that will occupy us in the next chapter relates rather to the dissimilar fates of the two scholastic traditions.[3] That of the Sunnīs has become precisely a heritage (*turāth*): rather like a revered monument, it is cherished by people who no longer truly inhabit it. The Imāmī scholastic tradition, by contrast, can still be described as a living one, owing its continuity and adaptation to scholars who operate within it. It may be that the difference is in some ways more apparent than real, and that in the long run it will disappear. But to date it remains a striking one. It is for this and other reasons that I treat the modern development of Imāmī thinking in a separate chapter.

Alongside the ancient division between Sunnīs and Imāmīs, a new one has appeared within the Sunnī fold. It is generally agreed among the more educated and committed Sunnī believers that Islam as practised in recent centuries has been in serious need of reform. The question, of course, is what kind of reform, and in essence there are two rival products on the market. Both, of course, seek to restore Islam to its original purity as understood by the reformers in question. One, which appeared in the first half of the twentieth century, is Islamic modernism. It could be summed up as the conviction that Islam should be restored in such a way as to enable its adherents to live comfortably in the modern world. It would be cynical, but perhaps not unduly so, to see this as a somewhat disguised project for Westernising Islam – which is in fact how the fundamentalists see it. The other reform project, which took shape in the second half of the twentieth century, is fundamentalism: a hardline restoration of Islam that seeks to move it away from, not towards, the Western culture that dominates the modern world.

The first of these projects was very predictable, and it arose in relatively complex urban societies that experienced Western dominance early in their modern histories. Egypt provides the leading example. The second project had a more curious genealogy, and in the event took the world by surprise. Reform movements seeking to restore a pristine Islam were, of course, nothing new in the history of the religion. One such movement happened to be born in eighteenth-century Najd, in the desolate interior of Arabia; it is known as Wahhābism from the name of its Ḥanbalite founder, Muḥammad ibn ᶜAbd al-Wahhāb (d. 1792). It was this movement that gave rise to the Saudi state in its three successive incarnations – roughly,

[3] See below, ch. 11, section 6.

those of the eighteenth, nineteenth and twentieth centuries. This reformism had arisen in a purely indigenous and pre-modern context; but by an accident of history, it was there to provide inspiration for fundamentalists across the Islamic world in the face of the inroads of the modern West.

2 The interaction with the West: attraction and repulsion

Wrestling with an alien but dominant culture is bound to produce mixed feelings, and it is not hard to detect both attraction and repulsion in Muslim reactions to Western culture in modern times. This is as true in the context of discussions of forbidding wrong as it is in general. Let us begin with attraction.

One of the clearest indices of the attractive power of Western culture in the modern Islamic world has been the energy put into the enterprise of proving that all good things found in the West are Islamic. Here forbidding wrong has been called in to smooth the appropriation of a whole set of Western political values, ranging from constitutionalism to revolution.

Some examples will help to show what is involved.[4] A prime instance of the invocation of the duty in order to sanction constitutionalism is provided by Rashīd Riḍā (d. 1935), one of the key figures of Islamic modernism. Building on a hint provided by his teacher Muḥammad ᶜAbduh (d. 1905), he discovers in Q3:104 a foundation for government by a representative assembly such as is found in republics and limited monarchies. Likewise the Tunisian Khayr al-Dīn Pāshā (d. 1890) sets up an analogy between, on the one hand, representative assemblies and freedom of the press in Europe, and, on the other, the duty of the scholars and notables of the Islamic world to engage in righting wrongs; in both cases the point is to check the arbitrary behaviour of rulers.[5] The Young Ottoman reformist ᶜAlī Suᶜāvī (d. 1878), in a constitutionalist article he published in 1868, set out a syncretic myth of an ancient Islamic and Ottoman constitution.[6] He described Islamic government as originally limited: if anyone sought to transgress the limits of the holy law, the scholars would come to its defence – an action termed forbidding wrong. In the same way the Ottoman sultan Suleymān (r. 1520–66) bestowed on the scholars and viziers the privilege of forbidding wrong in relation to generals and sultans, the object being to secure the preservation of the law-code he had established with the help of the scholars and statesmen of the day. Writers linking forbidding wrong to revolution have rather more to appeal to in their heritage. In a careful discussion of the question, the Indian Jalāl al-Dīn ᶜAmrī calls to witness such scholars as Ibn Ḥazm and Juwaynī; his conclusion tends to support their radical views. Likewise the Egyptian Muḥammad ᶜUmāra finds in forbidding

[4] 511f.
[5] 511 n. 37.
[6] [ᶜAlī Suᶜāvī], 'Uṣūl-i meshveret', *Mukhbir* (London), 14 March 1868.

wrong a duty of political participation; if non-violent participation is ineffective, then revolution becomes a duty. ᶜUmāra does not reveal his source of inspiration here, but to the extent that it is not simply modern, it is likely to be Zaydī and Muᶜtazilite: he has a liking for these sectarians unusual in someone of Sunnī background. In the recent efflorescence of literature on Islam and human rights, forbidding wrong occasionally appears in yet another role: as a fundamental guarantee of human rights in Islam. Thus Shaukat Hussain considers that 'the greatest sanction for the practical implementation of Human Rights' is the duty of forbidding wrong.

Alongside these rather broad invocations of the duty, we also find it linked with particular political rights from the Western liberal tradition.[7] Occasionally it is used as a foundation for freedom of association. Thus the deputy postmaster-general of Peshawar quotes Q3:104 as his proof-text for this right, commenting that God has thereby 'given the right to form association for pursuit of righteousness'. But the standard equation, and it is an old one, is with freedom of speech (or expression, or opinion). Muwayliḥī (d. 1930) adumbrates this in a jocular passage in which he identifies journalists as playing the part of 'those who command right and forbid wrong to whom Islamic law refers'.[8] A typical example of the linkage is found in a work of Saᶜīd Muḥammad Aḥmad Bā Nāja. He cites Article 19 of the Universal Declaration of Human Rights regarding freedom of opinion and expression, emphasising at the same time that governments – both Eastern and Western – have imposed serious restrictions on it. He then turns to Islam, and to the high status it confers on freedom of opinion as an individual right. Forbidding wrong, he points out, is among the most important duties of Islam, and its realisation necessarily requires freedom of opinion, as is apparent from many Koranic verses. He goes on to explain that this is not, of course, a right to propagate views contrary to Islamic beliefs or morals. (As we have already seen, political rights in their Islamic versions tend to be rights to do or say good Islamic things, not bad un-Islamic things.) Numerous authors associate forbidding wrong with freedom of speech in these or similar terms. Some make separate reference to a right of protest or the like against rulers, and they too have no problem grounding it in forbidding wrong.

The results of this syncretic activity are uneven. Sometimes they are quite plausible, as when forbidding wrong is linked to protest and revolution. But where the match is with liberal values, the effect can be jarring. The reason is not far to seek. Islam, within certain limits, tells people what to believe and how to live; liberalism, within certain limits, is about leaving them to work this out for themselves. It is this incompatibility that lies behind the unhappy notion of a right to freedom of opinion that protects only good opinions. What makes the disparity so salient in the discussions that concern us is the fact that forbidding wrong is

[7] 512f.
[8] Cf. 509.

precisely a practice for telling people what to believe and how to live – for imposing family values, not for enabling people to choose their lifestyles. This incompatibility has not been lost on modern Muslim writers, who have long been critical of excessive freedom in the West.

Here, then, the forces of repulsion are at work, and again some examples will help. We should perhaps give pride of place to Sayyid Quṭb (d. 1966), the founding father of Islamic fundamentalism.[9] He remarks that in the pagan (*jāhilī*) societies of the world today, debauchery and sin are considered to be 'personal matters' in which no one else has a right to interfere. You tell people: 'This is wrong!' But they respond: 'On the contrary, it's not wrong; it used to be wrong in the past, but the world "evolves", society "progresses", and attitudes vary.' Likewise the Syrian fundamentalist Saᶜīd Ḥawwā (d. 1989) lists among the insults that do not dispense one from performing the duty accusations of reactionariness and backwardness.[10]

A more earthy writer contemporary with Quṭb opens his discussion of forbidding wrong with a characterisation of the modern, as opposed to the Islamic, fashion (*mōḍa*).[11] The modern fashion has it that people are free, nobody having any authority over anyone else, or any right to interfere in his affairs; if you see someone naked in a tram, or bad-mouthing religion, or drinking wine, or gambling, or kissing girls in the middle of the street, so what? The characterisation he then offers of the Islamic fashion stresses that the community is a single body; a public wrongdoer does harm not just to himself, but to you as well. He invokes a well-known Prophetic tradition about a group of people in a boat who will perish or survive together: it depends on how they react to some of their number who set about making a hole in the hull – a clear indication that the modern enemy is not just libertinism but also individualism.

The Algerian preacher ᶜAlī ibn Ḥājj (Ali Belhadj) also deserves a place here.[12] In an article in an Algerian fundamentalist journal, he attacks those who seek to emasculate the duty on the pretext that we live in a time of democracy and liberty, and that every individual is a free agent – as if democracy could abrogate this duty, which many today denigrate as interference in the lives of others. He invites the believers to sympathise with some upstanding young men who had gone to break up a dancing-party, and were received by the police with a hail of tear-gas bombs. In the same journal, anonymous participants in a bottle-smashing incident which took place in B'rrāqī near Algiers in 1989 give a vivid account of the affair. They highlight the outrageous response of the vintner: 'Boumedienne permits taverns for wine and mosques for prayer; it's up to you to choose!' It was with some foresight that Louis Gardet once wrote that forbidding wrong as moral reform ('réforme des moeurs'), though currently held in check by the modern state, was

[9] 514.
[10] 510.
[11] 514f.
[12] 515.

alive in the sentiments of the Muslim people, and could well re-emerge in favourable circumstances.[13]

In all this there is a strong sense of cultural pollution at work.[14] For example, we are told that at a time of military misfortune the Egyptian khedive Ismāᶜīl (r. 1863–79) was reproved by an unnamed scholar at the Azhar, the reproof consisting of a well-known Prophetic tradition on forbidding wrong. Later, in private, the scholar elaborated: how could the khedive expect succour from heaven when the Mixed Courts operated under a law that allowed usury, when fornication was permitted, and the drinking of wine was legal? The khedive's response was: 'What can we do now that foreigners live side by side with us, and this is their civilisation?' As the Lebanese Shaykh Fayṣal Mawlawī put it in 1984 to an audience of Muslims living in France, 'European countries are nothing but wrongs'; to the traditional repertoire he adds the cinema. Bayānūnī, a Syrian who published a book on the duty in 1973, is worried about a whole slew of wrongs: the sale of photographs of women, physical contact between males and females in crowded buses, posters advertising dirty films, cafés, playing-cards, and music on the radio and television. But his most insistent concern is with the un-Islamic practice of shaving beards.[15]

A context in which the forces of both attraction and repulsion are in play is the role of women in forbidding wrong. As we saw in an earlier chapter, this group had traditionally received rather little attention.[16] It now gets significantly more.[17] While no author actually denies that women are eligible to perform the duty, ᶜAmrī comes close to it: although he is clearly composing his account with Ghazzālī's in front of him, he chooses to open his analysis of the conditions of obligation by stating that 'a man' must be legally competent. By contrast, an Egyptian academic writing on Zaydī thought reacts to the exclusion of women by Yaḥyā ibn Ḥamza with the remark that he sees no ground for stipulating that the performer be male. The Palestinian exegete Muḥammad ᶜIzzat Darwaza (d. 1984) understands Q9:71 to establish the equality of women with men, in particular with regard to forbidding wrong. The fact that he is alone in raising the question among the seventeen modern Sunnī exegetes whose commentaries I checked may suggest some reluctance to broach a sensitive issue. Outside Koranic exegesis, however, the verse is quite often invoked to include women. Ibn Ḥājj takes it to say that the duty is incumbent on women as well as men – though he adds that women are a special case. Muhammad Sharif Chaudhry interprets the verse to mean that Muslim men and women 'are severally and jointly responsible for enjoining the right and forbidding the wrong'; appropriately, his book has an introduction penned by his wife, Dr Nasreen Sharif of the Fatimah Jinnah Medical College. Fatḥī ᶜUthmān cites the verse to show that

[13] 515.
[14] 509f.
[15] Cf. 301 n. 322; 379 n. 168.
[16] See above, 14–16.
[17] 519–21; cf. 332.

in Islam women are not stripped of rights and duties, nor denied legal personality and social responsibility.

A particularly strong proponent of female participation is ᶜAbd al-Ḥalīm Muḥammad Abū Shuqqa, a pupil of the well-known scholar Nāṣir al-Dīn al-Albānī.[18] He adduces Q9:71 as a proof-text, and finds examples in tradition of women performing the duty against men. One of these is a story set among an Arab tribal group that converted to Islam after the conquest of Mecca in 630. The best they could do for a prayer-leader was a boy of six or seven who happened to have learnt some of the Koran from travellers. Unfortunately his garment was so short that his bottom was exposed each time he prostrated himself. In response to this spectacle, a tribeswoman called out: 'Aren't you going to cover up your Koran-reciter's bottom from us?' The tribesmen thereupon made the boy's day by providing him with a shirt. This is an original use of a tradition that plays no part in pre-modern discussions of forbidding wrong, whether by women or anyone else.

What is less common is for these writers to face squarely the tensions between such views and the traditional subordination and seclusion of women. A generation ago ᶜAbd al-Karīm Zaydān published a work in which he held that women should be involved in Muslim public affairs (though not in elections); he spoke of them as forbidding wrong to members of the family, neighbours and other women – but not, by implication, to men at large. In a massive work on the legal status of women in Islam published a quarter of a century later, he is emphatic that women are obligated to perform the duty just as men are; but again, he does not seem to think that they should do it to men, at least not outside the immediate family. Instead, his earlier mention of women doing it to other women now reappears as a programme for endowing women with a parallel public space of their own. Thus where the state organises the duty officially, it may open a college to train female officers to perform it (*muḥtasibāt*). Likewise Muslim women at the present day should undertake the duty as organised groups, forming female associations for the purpose. These associations should operate among women, whether seeking them out in their homes or inviting them to their centres; they should publish weekly or monthly magazines, and arrange classes, lectures and discussions.[19]

This, of course, is a more progressive position than many would care to adopt.[20] A conservative attitude is represented by the Saudi Khālid al-Sabt. Following Ghazzālī, he has no hesitation in taking the position that to be male is not a condition of obligation. However, he goes on to make it very clear that we are talking about a woman in her own home; this is no licence for women to go outside their homes to practise the duty, involving themselves in religious and other affairs, as unfortunately happens so much these days. Another conservative Saudi author, ᶜAbd al-ᶜAzīz al-Masᶜūd, states that for women the normal mode of performance

18 520.
19 520f.
20 521.

of the duty with respect to men is in the heart. He does, however, take the view that they should do it to other women, and verbally to those males who are related to them. This includes their husbands, and, of course, their children; as he points out, they are well placed to perform the duty with regard to their children since, unlike men, they spend all their time at home.

3 Living with the modern state: activism and quietism

What of the role of the state in forbidding wrong? This has always been a focus of tension, and it has become even more so with the rise of the modern state – under whatever ideological aegis – in the Islamic world. Thus Ḥawwā aptly remarks that the state in our epoch has come to hold sway over everything: education, instruction, the economy, the army, society, politics, intellectual life, culture.[21] In some Sunnī countries this has issued in forbidding wrong becoming a function of the state apparatus; we will come to this later. Elsewhere there are broadly speaking two very different ways to react to the new salience of the state. One is to give ground and limit the performance of the duty to what modern conditions permit; the other is to confront the state in the name of Islam.

An early example of limitation is found in a series of articles on forbidding wrong published in 1918 by the Ottoman Shaykh al-Islām Ḥaydarīzāde Ibrāhīm Efendi (d. 1931).[22] Though he omitted to mention the fact, what he did was mostly to summarise and occasionally modify Ghazzālī's account. One point of divergence for which he had precedent among his fellow Ḥanafīs was his negative attitude towards the use of violence by ordinary believers in forbidding wrong. He therefore insists that the permission of the authorities is indispensable for the use of violence against the person of the offender. Moreover, he later returns to this issue in a paragraph that is clearly his own. Here he states that, given the requirements of our time and the present organisation of the state, even harsh language and attacks on offending objects would run foul of the criminal law. Accordingly, the view of those scholars who hold the permission of the authorities to be a condition for the performance of the duty is to this extent to be accepted. This shift away from Ghazzālī's position is likely to reflect two things: one is the traditional Ḥanafī inclination not to rock the boat, but the other is the pressure of modern conditions to which Ḥaydarīzāde explicitly refers.

Similar reservations are in evidence in other modern confrontations with the views of Ghazzālī.[23] Several authors are clearly embarrassed. Thus Jamāl al-Dīn al-Qāsimī (d. 1914), in his epitome of Ghazzālī's *Revival*, omits all of Ghazzālī's levels involving violence to the person, and limits the destruction of offending

[21] 522.
[22] 331–3.
[23] 526f.

objects to officialdom. Another epitomiser discreetly omits to mention armed conflict, not to speak of armed bands. Khālid al-Sabt lists Ghazzālī's levels, and gives a few pages each to the first two; but thereafter he tacitly forgets them, turning instead to the three modes. The many examples of performance 'with the hand' that he proceeds to give convey the message that it consists of violence directed against things (breaking and pouring) rather than people. He has thus spared himself the awkwardness of confronting Ghazzālī's more aggressive levels of performance; and with regard to recourse to arms, he offers only the passing remark that more than one scholar has made this conditional on the ruler's permission. A similar strategy is adopted by his fellow Saudi ᶜAbd al-ᶜAzīz al-Masᶜūd. His account of the levels simply drops those involving violence to the person, and restricts performance 'with the hand' to objects. He too requires the permission of the ruler for recourse to arms.

The most characteristic expression of such tendencies in the Arab world is the view that carrying out the duty 'with the hand' is reserved for those in authority.[24] This idea is not new; but whereas it was rare outside Ḥanafī circles in traditional Islam, it is significantly more common in modern writings. Perhaps surprisingly, it seems to owe its prominence to the leading Islamic activist of the first half of the twentieth century, Ḥasan al-Bannā (d. 1949). In the years immediately preceding the Second World War, the Muslim Brothers were divided by a dispute over the proper means of moral reform in Egypt. A group which in due course seceded from the movement believed in proceeding 'with the hand' in accordance with the three-modes tradition; Bannā himself, by contrast, inclined rather to the 'good admonition' (*al-mawᶜiẓa al-ḥasana*) of Q16:125. This association with the founder of the Muslim Brotherhood has probably bestowed a certain prestige on an idea that might otherwise have seemed merely time-serving.

As could be expected, this notion is current in Egypt in quarters friendly to the state.[25] Thus it is the main theme of an interview given by the Muftī of the Republic, Muḥammad Sayyid Ṭanṭāwī, in an Egyptian magazine in 1988. He argues, among other things, that if everyone could right wrongs 'with the hand', the result would be anarchy. (He is, of course, against anarchy: he brings up the awful example of Lebanon.) It is not that he limits the requisite authority to the state. He himself, for example, has such authority over his children – but not over the children or wives of others. Confronted with the view that Ibn Taymiyya had approved of performing the duty 'with the hand', the Muftī avers that great scholar to have been innocent of any such thing. This interview should not be seen in isolation; it belongs to a period marked by vigorous polemical exchanges on the issue. Some of these are described by the Azhar scholar ᶜAbd al-ᶜAẓīm Ibrāhīm al-Maṭᶜanī, himself a careful critic of the position represented by the Muftī – he regards the view restricting performance 'with the hand' to the authorities as a recent Egyptian heresy.

[24] 523.
[25] 523f.

The views held by the Muftī have also had less exalted adherents.[26] One Aḥmad Ḥusayn tells a story about his youthful involvement in some activity 'with the hand' against liquor stores, and his subsequent change of heart in prison; the setting is the same schism among the Muslim Brothers. Another author joins the chorus making the point that for individuals to take to executing the duty 'with the hand' would lead to anarchy. Outside Egypt the same thinking can be found in Saudi Arabia, as also in a European setting in the preaching of Mawlawī. Action against wrong 'with the hand', he says, is only for someone in authority within his proper sphere (*ṣāḥib al-sulṭān fī sulṭānihi*); and you are not such a person. Darwaza is clearly thinking along the same lines: he ties the role of individuals to ethical and personal matters in which their activity will not lead to anarchy or the like.

This view of performance 'with the hand' is both a flagrant divergence from the mainstream of traditional Islamic doctrine and an unmistakable assertion of political quietism. The combination guaranteed that it would not prove generally acceptable in a period of highly politicised Islamic resurgence.[27] Writers with more respect for the heritage, or less respect for existing states, were naturally disinclined to go against the plain sense of the three-modes tradition. Thus the Egyptian ᶜAbd al-Qādir ᶜAwda (d. 1954), repeating the standard rejection of the view that the permission of the ruler is required, makes it clear that he believes individuals to have the right to perform the duty 'with their hands'; and ᶜAmrī takes the position that ordinary people – or at least ordinary men – are entitled to perform the duty by force.

But those who reject the view that only the authorities may proceed 'with the hand' are not necessarily in favour of violence.[28] Maṭᶜanī, who considers the view to be without foundation and has no difficulty in proving his point, deplores the waves of terrorism and violence sweeping over Egypt. He eventually makes it clear that, in his view, violence has no part in the performance 'with the hand' that is the province of individual subjects. His key argument, or rather assumption, is that the use of violence constitutes punishment, and as such is reserved to the ruler and his subordinates.

Others, within limits, are more comfortable with some degree of violence. Again, this can be seen from some interactions with Ghazzālī's account.[29] Thus ᶜAmrī approves the use of force, but dislikes the idea of armed bands. ᶜAwda in his discussion of the use of violence follows Ghazzālī without flinching, even espousing his views of armed conflict and armed bands, though he does adopt Ghazzālī's position that the subject may not use violence against the ruler. Some recent figures lack even these inhibitions. Thus Ḥawwā strongly endorses Ghazzālī's views on violence, and Ibn Ḥājj quotes Ghazzālī's passage on armed bands with obvious relish.

[26] 524f.
[27] 525; also ᶜAbd al-Munᶜim Muṣṭafā Ḥalīma, *Ṣifat al-ṭāʾifa al-manṣūra*, Amman 1994, 42–6.
[28] 525f.
[29] 527f.

Against this background, it seems at first sight paradoxical that it is precisely one of the most radical of fundamentalist visions that has gone farthest in modern times towards voiding the duty of the individual to forbid wrong.[30] When Quṭb comments on Q3:104, he seems almost to deny the existence of this duty: 'commanding' and 'forbidding' are things that only someone in authority (*dhū sulṭān*) can do, and accordingly we need an authority (*sulṭa*) to perform the duty. This authority would seem to be the Muslim community; there is no mention of the Muslims as individuals.

It is not until he comments on Q5:79 that we learn what has become of the duty of the individual. Here Quṭb remarks, promisingly, that the Muslim community is one in which no one who sees another person act wrongly can say 'What's that to me?' But there is a catch. A Muslim society is indeed one that enables a Muslim to devote himself to forbidding wrong, without his attempts being reduced to pointless gestures or made impossible altogether, as is the case in the pagan societies that exist today. The real task is thus to establish the good society as such, and this comes before the righting of small-scale, personal and individual wrongs; such efforts are vain when the whole society is corrupt. All the sacred texts bearing on forbidding wrong, Quṭb argues, concern themselves with the duty of the Muslim in a Muslim society. Thus in commenting on Q9:112, he invokes the early history of the Muslim community in support of his view: the followers of the Prophet first devoted their efforts to establishing the Muslim state and society, and only then turned to forbidding wrong in secondary matters. It is noteworthy that this rationale for voiding forbidding wrong in the present is very much Quṭb's own. Thus he does not invoke the authority of the eschatological traditions which foretell such a time. He does at one point make use of the notion of performance in the heart, but it plays no central role in his argument.

Although known to have remained current among his followers, Quṭb's renunciation of forbidding wrong in the pagan present has not become standard fundamentalist doctrine.[31] Thus Muḥammad Aḥmad al-Rāshid, after quoting Quṭb's commentary to Q9:112, feels compelled to add that this does not mean that missionaries (*duʿāt*) should not instruct themselves and their followers in their Islamic duties, or that they should abstain from forbidding the kind of secondary wrongs that can in fact be stopped. Mawlawī takes the view that in a non-Islamic society – particularly in Europe – it is utterly inappropriate for us to cut off relations with (Muslim) offenders, since all it does is to isolate us; instead we should persist, warning them once, twice, thrice, even ten times. Likewise Khālid al-Sabt points out that lots of wrongs can be dealt with perfectly well even in the absence of an Islamic state. Still less would we expect a radical such as Ibn Ḥājj to share the quietist doctrine of Quṭb. Though Ibn Ḥājj does not mention Quṭb, he makes a

[30] 528f.
[31] 529f.

point of identifying many of the Koranic verses he discusses as revealed in Mecca; he asks rhetorically if the Prophet told his followers to be silent and abstain from performing the duty till they were established in Medina. He too rejects the idea that one can do away with forbidding wrong on the pretext that we do not live in an Islamic state. The activist tinge of this passage is likely to reflect his role as a populist leader in a revolutionary situation. Thus he strongly endorses heroism, and directs himself to a youth that is zealous in performing the duty and needs only to be instructed in its principles.

Of course the Islamic revolution has not taken place in Algeria. But what if it had? What becomes of forbidding wrong in an Islamic state?

4 Towards forbidding wrong in an Islamic state

The core of the traditional conception of forbidding wrong was a personal duty to right wrongs committed by fellow believers as and when one encountered them. It is this conception that Ghazzālī set out with such force and clarity in his *Revival*.

But under modern conditions this medieval doctrine may begin to look irrelevant. This is evident from a separate printing of Ghazzālī's account that appeared in Beirut in 1983.[32] It was accompanied by a short introduction by a scholar well known in the West, Riḍwān al-Sayyid. Sayyid's main concern in these pages is clearly to forestall the likely disappointment of the Muslim reader. You might expect, he tells him, that Ghazzālī would take the opportunity of a discussion of forbidding wrong to set out the social and political problems confronting the Muslim world of his day, and propound solutions to them. And yet for whatever reason, Ghazzālī elected not to do this. Sayyid's sense of what the contemporary reader might be looking for in a tract on forbidding wrong is doubtless accurate. There are, of course, passages here and there in Ghazzālī's discussion that such a reader will find intensely rewarding, but all in all they are few and far between. The core of Ghazzālī's message, however well articulated, is not one that speaks to the concerns of political Islam today. In the face of the problems facing the Muslim world, the individual activity he prescribes seems doomed to be ineffective. Quṭb, as we saw, argued that such activity is pointless when the whole society is corrupt.

Instead, the core of the modern conception of forbidding wrong has become the organised propagation of Islamic values. This insistent concern with organisation is very much a sign of the times; it is the result of living in a world in which the competition tends to be far more organised than ever before.

ᶜAbduh's commentary on Q3:104 as developed by Riḍā is an early example of such concern.[33] On the assumption that the 'community' who are to perform the

[32] 554.
[33] 516.

duty are a subgroup of the community at large, they proceed to discuss the nature of this subgroup. Sometimes, as we have seen, they appear to be talking about constitutional government. But in one extended passage, they seem rather to be thinking of missionaries, whether their efforts be directed towards Muslims or non-Muslims. This enterprise, they explain, needs organisation: it should be in the hands of what these days is called an association (*jamᶜiyya*), and it must have a leadership to direct it.

Since then, this emphasis on organisation has become widespread.[34] Thus Zaydān stresses the need for the duty to be performed by organised groups, and he is far from alone in this. Likewise Ḥawwā explains that Muslims living in a corrupt Islamic state (*dawla Islāmiyya munḥarifa*) should organise performance of the duty 'with the hand'; this operation should avoid collision with the state, and should take as its target wrongs perpetrated by individuals (he mentions musical instruments, pictures of nudes, liquor and the flaunting of female sexuality). Sometimes, however, it is hard to tell whether it is the society or the state that is to create the desired organisation; but the former is clearly envisaged in the Islamic human right of free association for the purposes of forbidding wrong. Such societies for forbidding wrong have indeed been established from time to time; one was set up in Palestine under the Mandate, another is mentioned in Egypt.

A sense of what has changed with this espousal of organisation can be obtained from Rāshid's work.[35] His concern is to show that the great authorities of the past proclaimed the legality of collective action in forbidding wrong, and thus to refute the claim that such action is an innovation alien to Islamic norms. To this end, he collects from medieval sources examples of traditional figures who are said to have performed the duty together with a group of associates. Texts such as these, he remarks, are valuable discoveries that should take their place in the law of Islamic activism (*al-fiqh al-ḥarakī*). He then quotes Ghazzālī's view that the permission of the ruler is not needed for the performance of forbidding wrong by armed bands. This text, he adds, is one that should be written in letters of gold, and memorised by missionaries (*duᶜāt*); it shows that the literature of the heritage (*kutub al-turāth*) abounds in sources for the law of activism. Two things are noteworthy here. One is the gap between the precedents Rāshid invokes and the current practice he seeks to legitimise: the occasional examples of group action in the literature of the heritage never involve the kind of formal associations that have sprung up in the Islamic world under Western influence. The other is the sense of surprise that he displays. He takes it for granted, not that his concerns and those of the heritage are identical, but that they come from different worlds; the relevance of the views of the medieval scholars to his own world is not an axiom but a discovery. Not surprisingly, Ibn Ḥājj is also very partial to Ghazzālī's statement about armed bands.[36]

[34] 516f.
[35] 517f.
[36] 518 n. 86.

Who is to engage in all this organised activity? The religious scholars, the group that had traditionally been at the centre of forbidding wrong, get remarkably little attention. Two authors who still take them seriously are Fārūq al-Sāmarrāʾī and Muḥammad ʿAlī Masʿūd.[37] Much of what Sāmarrāʾī says about the scholars is negative; but his high-flown rhetoric regarding the horrendous consequences of their silence in the face of wrongdoing does at least pay them the compliment of supposing that they matter. And in one of his rare expressions of personal opinion, he tells us that he feels it to be better for the duty to be undertaken by the scholars. Of course it may happen that wrongdoing will become so rampant that they alone cannot handle it; in that case the individual members of the community will be obligated to act – but under the leadership of their scholars. The other author, Masʿūd, seems to have in mind the old saying about the tripartite division of labour, though he does not quote it. The duty, he says, is to be performed in three modes. First, there is the mode of the rulers, who alone can use force. Second, there is that of the scholars, who are to perform the duty with their pens, tongues and ideas – but not with violence. Finally, there are the common people, for whom he reserves a fairly energetic version of performance 'with the heart' – again without violence. This certainly ascribes a major role to the scholars, though Masʿūd's concept of them is a broad and somewhat modernised one: it includes authors and school-teachers alongside preachers and spiritual guides.

If individuals are more or less irrelevant and the scholars are tacitly shunted aside (as they usually are), then we are left to consider the rulers. Inasmuch as most Muslim countries cannot count as Islamic states by fundamentalist standards, this is a largely futuristic concern. Thus for Quṭb, as we saw, forbidding wrong will begin only when we have an Islamic state; as he says, we need an authority to perform the duty. But whatever the future may hold, there are a couple of countries where this manner of forbidding wrong already has a track record.

One is Afghanistan, where between 1996 and 2001 the Ṭālibān held sway and established a department – later a ministry – for forbidding wrong.[38] One example among many of the activities of this organisation is shown in a photograph that appeared in a Madrid newspaper in 1997: a member of the religious police armed with a scissors is good-humouredly cutting the fringe of a malefactor with curly hair at a crossroads in Kabul (he was apparently the fifty-seventh offender to get an involuntary haircut that day).[39] This initiative is the more striking in that the Ṭālibān seem otherwise to have invested remarkably little effort in the normal business of government; thus they left caring for the everyday needs of the population in the hands of international agencies, for all that in other countries Islamic

[37] 518f.

[38] 522; Ahmed Rashid, *Taliban: militant Islam, oil and fundamentalism in Central Asia*, New Haven and London 2001, 105–7, 217–19; Amy Waldman, 'No TV, no chess, no kites: Taliban's code, from A to Z', *The New York Times*, 22 November 2001, A1 and B5.

[39] 522 n. 121.

fundamentalists have shown a talent for social work. The other country with an apparatus for religious policing is Saudi Arabia. Though the system is not widely discussed by fundamentalists outside the country,[40] it has much greater historical depth than the ill-fated attempt of the Ṭālibān. It may therefore be worthwhile to sketch the history of the Saudi system.

5 Religious policing in Saudi Arabia

In the first Saudi state (1745f.–1818) we hear of religious policing only in one context: Saudi rule in the Ḥijāz in the years following the conquest of 1803. What we see there may be typical of the workings of the first Saudi state, or it may be a response to the distinctive context of the Ḥijāz; we do not really know.

A Meccan chronicler describing the conquest tells us that the Saudi ruler had a bonfire made of tobacco-pipes and stringed instruments, after recording the names of their owners. He also reports that in 1806 the Sharīf of Mecca, now a Saudi protégé, issued orders to the people of Mecca and Jedda banning tobacco, requiring attendance at mosques, and imposing on the scholars readings of epistles of Muḥammad ibn ᶜAbd al-Wahhāb. A European observer confirms that as a result of the conquest the Meccans were 'obliged to pray more punctually than usual', and to desist from smoking in public; he too mentions a bonfire of 'Persian pipes', which took place in front of the Saudi ruler's headquarters. In addition, he attests roll-calls at prayers in Medina during the Saudi occupation.[41] There is also evidence from the Saudi side. ᶜAbdallāh ibn Muḥammad ibn ᶜAbd al-Wahhāb quotes a speech of the Saudi ruler to the Meccans in which he affirms that one of the points at issue between the two sides is forbidding wrong, of which only the name is to be found among the Meccans. But when ᶜAbdallāh comes to the practicalities of the duty, his tone is conciliatory. We forbid, he tells them, only innovations tending to polytheism; those apart, we tolerate such things as coffee, love poems, eulogies of kings, the war-drum, and the tambourine at weddings – but not, of course, musical instruments at large.[42] The main Saudi chronicler for the period tells us that during the pilgrimages to Mecca led by the Saudi ruler in 1809–12, men were appointed to patrol the markets at the times of prayer and to order people to pray; smoking vanished from the markets, or at least was no longer to be seen in public.[43]

Turning to the second Saudi state (1823–87), we find pointers to the official, not to say officious, character of the duty.[44] Those charged with it engage in

40 522 and n. 122.
41 168 n. 18.
42 172.
43 168.
44 177f.

investigation (*tafaqqud*). Thus one ruler orders his emirs to seek out people who gather together to smoke tobacco. A scholar of the period says that the scholars and emirs should keep a check on the people of their towns with regard to prayer and religious instruction. Performance of the pilgrimage is likewise to be monitored. Holding religious meetings (*majālis*) is another aspect of the system; those known for their failure to attend are to be reported to the authorities. The same ruler stipulates that people who obstruct the forbidding of wrong are to be punished with exile. We also encounter the inevitable accompaniments of this official meddlesomeness: corrupt motives on the part of those performing the duty, and sniggering on the part of those exposed to it. And we have a most vivid description of the system from the pen of the notoriously unreliable traveller W. G. Palgrave, who claims to have visited Riyāḍ in 1862.[45] He describes the appointment of twenty-two 'Zelators', the vices they sought to stamp out (such as absence from prayer, smoking tobacco, making music), their dress and their mode of operation. This included 'unexpectedly entering the houses to see if there is anything incorrect going on there' and roll-calls of names in the mosques; he gives an account of an 'indignant Zelator' who collects 'a pious band armed with sticks and staves' to investigate absences from prayer. It is hard to know what to make of all this, but some of it fits. We also hear of religious policing in the eastern province of al-Aḥsāʾ while it was under Saudi rule.[46]

The picture is clearer for the third Saudi state (established in 1902); or at least, it becomes so from the time of the conquest of the Ḥijāz in 1924–5. Before that date our evidence is fragmentary. But a foreigner who visited Riyāḍ in 1922–3 recounts that floggings were commonly inflicted in the city for smoking, non-attendance at prayer and other such offences. He was told of regular roll-calls to check attendance at prayer in every mosque in the city. Offenders were visited by some kind of group, and were flogged if they did not mend their ways.[47]

The Saudi conquest of the Ḥijāz, with its juxtaposition of Wahhābī puritanism and the laxer attitudes of the wider Muslim world, was a prescription for trouble. It was here, it seems, that the current Saudi system of religious policing took shape, in an effort to give Wahhābism its due without gross disruption of the valuable pilgrim traffic.[48] The key step was the establishment of a new institution in Mecca in 1926. This was the 'Committee for Commanding Right and Forbidding Wrong'. Contemporary sources show that its job was to impose prayer-discipline, curb foul language and the like. By the late 1920s the committee was well established. From that period we have a document that sets out the scope of its activity in twenty articles; they cover such matters as prayer-discipline, liquor, smoking and the segregation of women.[49] The final article declares the headmen of quarters

[45] 178 n. 90.
[46] 179 n. 95.
[47] 181.
[48] 182–5.
[49] 185f.

in the town to be responsible for offences committed in their quarters; they were to be deemed accomplices if they attempted to conceal them. At this point the committee was made up of scholars and notables, both Ḥijāzī and Najdī. By now similar institutions were also to be found in Jedda and Medina.[50]

Further information on the early history of the institution is provided by some British reports from Jedda dating from a slightly later period.[51] These reports describe a swing from a soft line to a hard one and back that took place in early 1930, and a similar shift in the summer of 1931. During the first of these cycles, one dispatch describes the confiscation of mouth organs from small boys in Jedda; the street-urchins subsequently took their revenge by waylaying the president of the local committee and pelting him with melon rind – the only instance of open resistance to the activities of the committees that I have encountered. In the second period, Ibn Saᶜūd (r. 1902–52) had been trying to move away from Wahhābī puritanism, and to cultivate the image of a monarch 'who not only likes to see his people have a bit of fun, but is democratic enough to join in it' (the reference is to his participation in a Najdī war-dance). In this relaxed atmosphere the committees had apparently disappeared. Then, within a few months, the line shifted: the committees were reconstituted, and the war on vice took on a new lease of life. In addition to the traditional targets of the duty, we now encounter an instrument of music-making unknown to the Ḥanbalite law-books: the gramophone. Stocks of needles were seized, and it was said that as a result they could only be purchased from the police.

It was shortly after this that a plaintive report was penned by the Indian vice-consul Munshi Ihsanullah after his return from a visit to Mecca. He was greatly disturbed by the shift of power from local to Najdī hands. Previously, he suggests, the committee had been something of a body of notables, where local figures would exercise a moderating influence, and in particular ensure that the well-to-do were properly treated. Now, he reports, the committee had been given summary powers, and it was backed by groups of Najdī soldiers – twenty to a quarter, 260 in all – whose savage approach to prayer-discipline he found particularly appalling.

It seems that after its establishment in the Ḥijāz, the system was rapidly extended to the rest of the Saudi kingdom.[52] There has also been a move towards greater centralisation. Until 1976, there were two mutually independent directorates, one in the Ḥijāz and the other in Najd; in that year they were amalgamated into a unitary structure under a general director with the rank of cabinet minister. Nor does the institution seem to have remained confined to urban settings: we hear of the existence of a committee in a village in the southern Ḥijāz with a population of 1,600 souls.

[50] 187 n. 135.
[51] 186f.
[52] 187f.

Some further light is shed on the activities of the committees in the responsa of a distinguished Saudi scholar, Muḥammad ibn Ibrāhīm Āl al-Shaykh (d. 1969).[53] The most striking theme in these responsa, though hardly a surprising one, is the vein of hostility to which the activities of the committees give rise. Thus a Meccan judge had allowed a man accused of drunkenness to attack the credibility of the testimony of the committee members; Ibn Ibrāhīm roundly condemns the judge. Where members of committees have been over-zealous in the performance of their duties, he enjoins leniency; they have enemies among the reprobate who would be unduly encouraged if such lapses were dealt with severely. Where members of committees go astray, they should be discharged only if they can be replaced with others known to be of better character. In a case from Jedda involving serious sexual misconduct, the main informant had disappeared, leaving three witnesses among the committee members liable to the penalty for defamation; Ibn Ibrāhīm rescues them by finding a loophole in the law, urging that to impose the prescribed penalty would diminish their authority in carrying out the duty. We also learn of a novel offence: the committee in Zilfī was concerning itself with young men who made it a practice to ride out into the countryside at night on their motorcycles.

A more recent work that provides concrete detail on the activities of the committees is a voluminous treatise on the institution of the censorship (*ḥisba*) in Islam by ʿAlī ibn Ḥasan al-Quranī (the book was published in Riyāḍ in 1994).[54] He includes a sympathetic study of the committee system, in the course of which he devotes some pages to its present functioning. In particular, he gives an account of some of the offences encountered by the committee in Riyāḍ in 1984. One was sodomy; the offenders were Filipino in one case, Sri Lankan and British in another, but not, it seems, Saudi. Two Saudis were, however, furtively engaged in pushing eau de Cologne among young people. Another was peddling liquor together with two Yemenis; they were also found to have 2,555 forbidden pills in their possession. Four Yemenis had 3,773 Seconal pills. A young Saudi picked up in an unusual state had been sipping paint. A mixed group of Saudis and Yemenis had been producing liquor; the plant was raided and destroyed. The pattern of wrongdoing in Riyāḍ in 1984 was obviously not lacking in either variety or ethnic diversity.

More recently, in March 2002, the religious police received unwelcome publicity in the Saudi and international press in connection with a fire at a Meccan school in which fifteen schoolgirls died.[55] It was alleged, and subsequently denied, that members of the religious police impeded attempts to rescue the girls; they were said to have barred male rescue workers from the school on the ground that the girls were not wearing the Islamic dress required in public.

53 189f.
54 190f.
55 *The New York Times*, 16 March 2002, A7; 19 March 2002, A6. For attitudes of young Saudis to the religious police, see Mai Yamani, *Changed identities: the challenge of the new generation in Saudi Arabia*, London 2000, 123–5.

As might be expected, there is little direct evidence of the practice of forbidding wrong in Saudi Arabia outside this official framework. The striking exception is ᶜAbdallāh al-Qarᶜāwī (d. 1969) of ᶜUnayza, a pupil of Ibn Ibrāhīm.[56] One of his biographers, who owed his elementary education to Qarᶜāwī, describes his teacher's activities in the town. In the course of forbidding wrong, he would roam the streets and markets, belabouring with his tongue and stick any man who held back from communal prayer, and any woman whose dress flaunted her sexuality; there is no indication that he did this in an official capacity. Another biographer describes how, in the years after 1940, Qarᶜāwī mounted a large-scale (and officially approved) campaign to spread education in the extreme south-west of the country; on Thursday evenings he would take his senior students out to visit the tribes to preach, instruct and forbid wrong, supervising his students' efforts and showing them how to perform the duty nicely. But Qarᶜāwī seems to have been an unusual figure.

6 Forbidding wrong and privacy

The strength and reach of modern states does not bode well for the privacy of those they rule, and this is particularly so for states of a strongly ideological complexion. Here the legacy of the privacy concerns of the medieval scholars is in some tension with the collective and political orientation of the Islamic revival. It is no surprise that in the event privacy gets relatively little attention from the fundamentalists.

It is not that the topic is ignored altogether.[57] But while the old material may be repeated, it does not generate much excitement. Thus ᶜAwda stipulates that a wrong must be manifest without spying or prying, among other things because God has said so (Q49:12), and because of the inviolability of homes and persons until such time as sin is apparent. To emphasise the point he relates the story of the three sins of the caliph ᶜUmar. But when there is reliable evidence or good reason to believe that someone is engaging in covert wrongdoing in his home, ᶜAwda tells us that these restrictions no longer apply. The presentation is clear and balanced, but there is nothing electric about it. Likewise Khālid al-Sabt has some short discussions of aspects of privacy, in one of which he sets out the conditions under which it may or may not be permissible to refrain from exposing sins. But he says nothing of conditions under which one has an actual duty to refrain, or of any rights of sinners to privacy. Nobody suggests writing anything Ghazzālī had said about privacy in letters of gold.

56 191.
57 556.

CHAPTER 11

What has changed for the Imāmīs in modern times?

The Imāmīs differ from the Sunnīs in some obvious ways. They are very much in a minority within the Islamic world as a whole; their geographical distribution is more concentrated; the role of the clergy in their religious life was traditionally more salient, and in the last century has become even more so. By way of introduction to modern Imāmī thought about forbidding wrong, it may be helpful to start with some implications of these contrasts.

1 Comparing Imāmīs and Sunnīs

One significant effect of the minority status of the Imāmīs is that it makes for asymmetrical literary relations between the two communities.[1] It is rare indeed for Sunnī authors to show awareness of Imāmī views, let alone a willingness to learn from them. A few Egyptian writers sympathetic to the Muᶜtazilites make occasional reference to the Imāmīs in accordance with their catholic approach to the resources of the wider Islamic tradition. But for all their openness, they know little about traditional Imāmī thought, and nothing about modern developments. Imāmī scholars, by contrast, are often prepared to make some use of the resources of Sunnī Islam. They like to draw on the first modern commentary on the Koran, that of ᶜAbduh and Riḍā; it even finds its way into the newspapers of the Islamic Republic. Imāmī authors also go back to older Sunnī sources. On occasion they quote Ghazzālī, the favourite author of modern Sunnī writers on forbidding wrong;[2] and they develop a liking for some Sunnī Prophetic traditions, such as the one about the people in the boat. They also show a marked interest in the classical institution of the censorship (*ḥisba*) and the Sunnī literature that it generated; this seems to have been a discovery of Murtaḍā Muṭahharī (d. 1979).

At the same time the relative geographical concentration of the Imāmīs has helped to make their modern political experience very different from that of the

[1] 549–51.
[2] Cf. 507–9.

Sunnīs.[3] The Sunnī world is enormously diverse and confusing. There is no one country whose politics set the pace, no single defining event in the community's recent past, and considerable variety in the relationships between fundamentalists and regimes. Small wonder that the history of Sunnī political values as seen in modern Sunnī doctrines of forbidding wrong should show no clear and unequivocal evolution. On the Imāmī side, by contrast, the picture is much more clear-cut. The fact that Iran is a major Islamic country, and also the only major Imāmī one, has given it an indisputable predominance in the Imāmī community. This is fully reflected in the intellectual role of Iran: most of the Imāmī authors we shall be concerned with in this chapter are Iranian, and it is the Iranian political scene to which their thinking is primarily related. The defining event is thus the Islamic revolution of 1979 that toppled the Shah (r. 1941–79) and brought Khumaynī to power for the next ten years. Before the revolution, the choice was between putting up with the secular state and confronting it. Since the revolution, the state has been Islamic by definition; the choice is between identifying fully with the regime and pursuing a mildly dissident course within the limits of the system.

That leaves the role of the clergy.[4] Among the Imāmīs, as among the Sunnīs, the resurgence of Islam as a political doctrine in a modern setting has been a development of the last two generations. But whereas in the Sunnī community the revival has mostly been the work of laymen, this is not so in the Imāmī case. There have certainly been Imāmī laymen who have concerned themselves with religious matters: ᶜAlī Sharīᶜatī (d. 1977) is an obvious example. At least one layman, Mahdī Bāzargān (d. 1995), was involved in the rethinking of the doctrine of forbidding wrong at an early stage. But the evidence indicates that it was the clerics who got there first.[5] In any case the events of the Islamic revolution, and the subsequent consolidation of the clerical regime, have tended to eclipse lay thinkers. It is the role of the clerics, and the continuing vitality of their literary tradition, that distinguishes and dominates the Imāmī experience.

Against this background, we can now turn to the development of the Imāmī doctrine of forbidding wrong over the last half century. I shall organise what follows in terms of the same major categories as in the Sunnī case, and some notable parallels will emerge; but there will also be some striking differences.

2 The interaction with the West: attraction and repulsion

From the early decades of the Western impact on Iran, we encounter the same lax syncretism that we saw on the Sunnī side.[6] Initially this is the work of laymen.

[3] 551f.
[4] 532f.
[5] 532f. n. 199.
[6] 531f.

A fine early example is a brief account of freedom of expression given by Mīrzā Yūsuf Khān Mustashār al-Dawla (d. 1895f.). He states that resistance to oppression is a law (*qānūn*) in Europe, which explains European prosperity; this value is also enjoined in several passages of the Koran, of which the first he quotes is Q3:104. One of the benefits of this law, he continues, is that freedom of expression has become prevalent. This too, he says, is in accordance with the law of Islam, and he proves his point by quoting an account of forbidding wrong from a work of Ṭūsī's. He then goes on to freedom of the press, and remarks that some aspects of this fall within the scope of forbidding wrong. He adds that in Paris there are 100 presses and 600 bookshops. The same idea appears in a discussion of 'freedom of speech and pen' by Mīrzā Malkum Khān (d. 1908). This freedom, he says, which all civilised nations recognise as fundamental, is one that Muslims have established for the whole world in the two phrases 'commanding right' and 'forbidding wrong'. What positive law has proclaimed this freedom more explicitly? The Constitutional Revolution of 1906 was likewise defended in terms of forbidding wrong. Indeed such thinking still continues. In 1997 the dissident cleric Ḥusayn-ᶜAlī Muntaẓirī is reported to have issued a responsum calling for the formation of political parties in Iran as a modern way to apply the principle of forbidding wrong. In all these cases the motivation of the syncretism is to render a Western idea acceptable in a Muslim context; but as on the Sunnī side of the fence, we also find the same device used to defend Islam against the charge of deficiency. Thus when the Iraqi clergyman Muḥammad Bāqir al-Ḥakīm wishes to argue the superiority of Islam in providing guarantees of human rights, he too quotes Koranic verses on forbidding wrong.

The force of repulsion is also in evidence, just as among the Sunnīs. Imāmī authors attack Western individualism in the same way that Sunnīs do, and they frequently report and rebut the invocations of freedom and charges of meddlesomeness made by those subjected to forbidding wrong.[7] An Iranian cleric complains that attempts to forbid wrong now meet with the riposte: 'What's it to you? I'm free, it's a free country, it's a democracy, everybody does whatever he wants!' The opening question is traditional, but the continuation most certainly is not.[8] One work on forbidding wrong gives a list of the objections wrongdoers come out with, and provides apt replies to assist the pious forbidder of wrong. Alongside the traditional 'This has nothing to do with you!', or 'Don't interfere!', we again find 'I'm free!' The author of a very popular little book on the duty says that of course forbidding wrong means interfering in other people's affairs, and naturally people with their heads stuffed full of Western ideas don't like it. Another complains that as a result of Western influence, contemporary society regards forbidding wrong as meddlesomeness; yet another describes freedom as a holy word in the shadow of which thousands of unholy deeds are done.

[7] 556 and n. 361.
[8] 595.

As among the Sunnīs, the forces of attraction and repulsion no doubt combine to tug at the question of the role of women in forbidding wrong; but in the Imāmī case the repulsion is less in evidence.[9] The issue is one that the Imāmī scholars of the past had not thought to raise. Those modern scholars who discuss the question – and many do not – usually quote Q9:71 and infer that women too are obligated. Imāmī exegetes are significantly more likely than their Sunnī counterparts to highlight this aspect of the verse: of the fifteen modern Imāmī Koran commentaries I consulted, five did so. But there is little discussion of how other aspects of the legal position of women might affect their performance of the duty. Aḥmad Ṭayyibī Shabistarī (d. 1971) says that Muslim women must participate in the duty 'shoulder to shoulder' with Muslim men, which certainly suggests that segregation should not be much of a barrier; and although his youthful enthusiasm is unlikely to represent settled clerical opinion, his phrase is echoed by two recent clerical writers of a more or less liberal bent. Khumaynī himself was once consulted by a nurse who was concerned about her duty with regard to war-wounded patients who failed to pray because of the inadequacy of their faith; he replied that it was her duty to forbid wrong.

3 Living with the modern state: from quietism to activism

In contrast to what we saw among the Sunnīs, the modern development of the Imāmī doctrine of forbidding wrong moves sharply in a single direction: from quietism to activism. The traditional Imāmī teachings had displayed a marked political quietism on two points. One was the danger condition, which in its Imāmī version voided not only the duty to proceed but also the virtue of doing so – as we saw, the old Imāmī scholars had no use for heroism. The other point was the requirement that the imam give permission for any serious recourse to violence. Recasting the Imāmī heritage as an ideology of political revolution was likely to put some strain on both these traditional tenets.

As might be expected, one response to the problem was to unearth elements in the Imāmī tradition that went against the grain of the settled doctrine of the sect. Thus politically engaged Imāmīs were fortunate to find in a work of the tenth-century author Ibn Shuʿba a speech of the martyr Ḥusayn (d. 680) in which forbidding wrong is the central term of a cascade of revolutionary rhetoric.[10] They also made great play of the long activist tradition in which the imam Muḥammad al-Bāqir speaks contemptuously of those who consider forbidding wrong to be a duty only when they are safe from harm.[11] But the Imāmī clerics of modern times did more than this. They set about formally reshaping their inherited doctrine.

9 548.
10 552.
11 538 and n. 227; 540 n. 241; cf. above, 54.

The best starting-point with regard to the danger condition is an account of forbidding wrong written by Khumaynī himself.[12] The framework of this account is provided by a set of brief and unremarkable general statements of doctrine; each such passage is followed by a string of specific points, most of them of no particular political significance. The presentation of the danger condition initially conforms to this pattern, and much of what is said is fully compatible with the traditional doctrine. Thus one of the points Khumaynī makes is that the prospect of any significant harm to the performer or those associated with him voids the obligation, while another is that if he fears for his life or honour, or those of other Muslims, it is forbidden for him to proceed.

But in the middle of this generally familiar scholastic material, we come upon a jarring block of fourteen points that transparently relate to a contemporary political context, the confrontation between Khumaynī and the Shah. Many of these points do not in fact relate to forbidding wrong in any obvious way, but rather prescribe the boycotting of religious institutions controlled by the regime. The first six points are the ones that concern us. Taken together, they enunciate the doctrine that there is a category of wrongs of such relative weight (*ahammiyya*) that the obligation to right them overrides the danger condition, particularly for the clergy; typically such wrongs involve some threat to the very basis of Islam. This new doctrine is inserted without any attempt to integrate it with the old.

Khumaynī was not alone among the major scholars of his generation in qualifying the danger condition.[13] Kāẓim Sharīᶜatmadārī (d. 1986) holds that what the condition excludes is suffering harm over and above the intrinsic inconveniences of performing the duty, and on a scale that outweighs the utility of the initiative; it is not every kind of harm that voids the duty. Abū ᵓl-Qāsim al-Khūᵓī (d. 1992), after stating the danger condition in the usual way, makes a rather clumsy addition to it in which he says that – provided the efficacy condition is satisfied – what has to be considered is the relative weight of the two considerations; forbidding wrong could thus be obligatory even with actual knowledge of consequent harm. Khwānsārī (d. 1985) argues that some wrongs are to be forbidden even if this results in bearable harm; he draws an analogy with the duty of pilgrimage, which in the past was not voided by virtue of the protection money that used to be levied on the pilgrims. Muḥammad Ḥusaynī Shīrāzī in a short treatment of the duty states that the condition is overridden when Islam is in danger. Even Muḥammad Amīn Zayn al-Dīn (d. 1998), who as the head of the schismatic Akhbārī community in Baḥrayn might have been expected to stand apart from developments among the Imāmī mainstream, adopts the principle of relative weight with regard to the danger condition.

12 533f.
13 535f.

It is no surprise to find more recent scholars following Khumaynī.[14] Thus his pupil Muṭahharī, in a talk given in 1970, expresses his regret that some Imāmī scholars of the past, from whom one would have expected better, had maintained the danger condition without qualification. He accepts that the duty may be overridden when the result would be greater harm to Islam; but, appealing to the example of Ḥusayn, he does not accept that mere personal harm dispenses one from performing the duty. It may be, he says, that what is at stake is something on which Islam sets a higher value than it does on life, property or dignity – as when the Koran is in danger. ᶜAlī Tihrānī, a cleric who was active in Mashhad, composed before the revolution a work on forbidding wrong in which he quietly adopts much material from Khumaynī; in his treatment of the danger condition, he integrates Khumaynī's new thinking more closely with the rest of this material. Pupils of Khumaynī who have published legal handbooks for their followers tend to follow him closely, though again they may make changes to smooth over the intrusiveness of Khumaynī's innovation. In a work free of the constrictions of this genre, Muntaẓirī – at one time Khumaynī's designated successor – takes the position that since the duty is one intended for the reform of society and the eradication of evil and corruption, one must weigh the prospective harm against the targeted wrong, and give precedence to the weightier. He goes on to speak of the kinds of evil where a modicum of harm could hardly be held to override the duty; these include contagious social ills and threats to the foundations of Islam. Ḥusayn al-Nūrī al-Hamadānī in a rather noisy monograph on forbidding wrong gives a lengthy discussion of the danger condition, mounting a sustained attack on the traditional Imāmī view. Like others he argues that, just as there can be no holy war without cost, so also there can be no forbidding wrong without cost. He greatly widens Khumaynī's view of the circumstances in which the condition is overridden: stopping a single act of fornication is worth a bloody nose. And he strongly rejects any suggestion that martyrdom is tantamount to suicide – indeed he suspects that the hidden hand of colonialism might have played a part in creating and spreading this misconception. (His problem here is that he finds the misconception already present in a twelfth-century Koran commentary.) A more recent monograph on the duty is that of Muḥsin al-Kharrāzī. His approach is dry and scholastic, and he avoids Nūrī's flights of rhetoric. But he accepts the principle of relative weight where omission to perform the duty would have major untoward consequences.

An interesting figure who does not fit the analysis given above is Ṭayyibī Shabistarī, who nevertheless provides the prototype for much of Nūrī's work.[15] A cleric who had not passed the age of forty when he died in 1971, he wrote a rather hot-headed work on forbidding wrong that was published soon after his death. What is remarkable about it in the present connection is that Ṭayyibī, in his

[14] 536–9.
[15] 539f.

revolutionary enthusiasm, was not content to qualify the danger condition more or less heavily; instead he rejected it outright, as he also rejected the knowledge and efficacy conditions. As we have seen, not even Nūrī follows him so far.

The other quietist feature of the traditional doctrine was the requirement of the imam's permission.[16] Here one possibility would have been to reject the requirement altogether, a position that had distinguished representatives among the classical Imāmī jurists. However, recent Imāmī scholars have shown no interest in reviving so drastic a manoeuvre. Instead they have opted to render the necessary permission more accessible. This has been done most explicitly through the modification of a minority view that had appeared in the sixteenth century: that such action could be undertaken by a suitably qualified jurist.[17]

Again, we can best begin with Khumaynī.[18] He starts by telling us that, according to the stronger view, wounding and killing require the permission of the imam; he then goes on to say that in our time the jurist who satisfies the relevant conditions takes his place – the reference being clearly to any suitably qualified jurist. Some, though not all, of Khumaynī's contemporaries say similar things. Among more recent writers, Nūrī echoes Khumaynī. Kharrāzī, however, adapts the doctrine to the conditions of the Islamic Republic: such action is reserved to the Supreme Guide to the exclusion of other jurists. Thus where Khumaynī had originally allowed righteous violence to be unleashed by individual members of the clergy, for Kharrāzī it has become a monopoly of the state. Unsurprisingly, this latter view has the endorsement of the current Supreme Guide: Khāminaʾī declared in a speech of 1992 that in an Islamic society the duty of ordinary people is to forbid wrong with the tongue; if the matter would lead to violence, it is for the authorities to step in.

4 Towards forbidding wrong in an Islamic state

The other major innovation in modern Imāmī thought on forbidding wrong parallels a development we have already sketched on the Sunnī side: an increasing sense of the importance of getting organised.

Again, there is no lack of examples.[19] In a talk of 1960, Muṭahharī observes that individual action is not very effective, particularly in the world as it is today; what is needed is cooperation. Ten years later he simply equates forbidding wrong with fellow feeling, solidarity, cooperation and other such qualities. Ṭayyibī speaks of the need for institutions and for an Islamic state. Shīrāzī remarks that in this age commanding and forbidding require something like industrial planning. Nūrī argues that in our time the forces of evil are well equipped, and we have to respond in

[16] 540.
[17] 286; 299.
[18] 540f.
[19] 542.

kind. What is called for today is accordingly something much more concerted and systematic than the view of the duty enshrined in the old juristic tradition. It is not the business of the writers who concern us to tell us exactly what this revamping should consist of; but one cleric infers from Q3:104 a duty to form a group of guardians of Islam, and requires the Islamic state to establish a ministry of forbidding wrong (which it has not in fact done).

In the same vein we find a tendency to downplay the humble traditional core of forbidding wrong.[20] Sharīᶜatī denounces the reduction of the duty to a merely personal one, and the restriction of its scope to such trivialities as beards, hair and dress – this at a time when the wrongs that really matter are such things as international imperialism, world Zionism and colonialism old and new, not to mention cultural infatuation with the West. Ṭayyibī describes forbidding wrong as 'the most social of social questions'; he laments the fact that in recent centuries its 'social, progressive, and revolutionary content' has been distorted, reducing the duty for the most part to a personal affair of little or no significance. Muntaẓirī speaks a trifle dismissively of the performance of the duty by 'ordinary people in minor contexts'; in this petty form it is clearly not much of a contribution to the grand objective of 'reforming society and extirpating corruption and wrong' – the purpose for which, he avers, the duty was created. Nūrī formalises this attitude by distinguishing two circles. In the first, our agenda is the total reform of society – moral, credal, economic and social – through the preparation and organisation of the means appropriate for the realisation of right in its broadest sense. In the second, we are simply concerned with specific rights and wrongs that are actually happening or likely to do so. God, as might be expected, is much more concerned with the first circle. Other Imāmī scholars express similar attitudes.

In this new emphasis on organisation, the Imāmīs sound very like the Sunnīs. Where they differ from them is that the Imāmīs have moved to provide a conceptual foundation for this emphasis through a development within their scholastic tradition. Specifically, what is involved is a new twist in the handling of three conditions of the classical four: the knowledge, efficacy and danger conditions.

It will be simplest to begin with Nūrī's account, since this presents the ideas in a fully developed form, and then to go back to sketch their evolution.[21] What Nūrī argues is more or less as follows. In a situation in which performance of the duty has been aborted because one of these three conditions was not satisfied, we might be tempted to assume that we are thereby morally in the clear: we had no duty, and accordingly did nothing. But what such an outcome in fact suggests is that we were negligent in a prior duty to prepare ourselves for such eventualities. If the problem was that we did not know right from wrong, we should have been at pains to educate ourselves in advance. If the problem was that we lacked the means to

20 553f.
21 543.

perform the duty effectively, we should have expended effort to prepare those means beforehand. And if the problem was that we were in danger, that points to a weakness which we should have had the foresight to remedy.

This style of thought does have a root in the older Imāmī doctrine of forbidding wrong.[22] In discussing the knowledge condition, scholars of the sixteenth century had suggested circumstances in which one might have a duty to get to know. It is a condition for valid prayer that one be in a state of ritual purity; but failure to put oneself into such a state does not mean that one is entitled to forget about prayer. In the same way, might it not be argued that in certain circumstances one has an obligation to inform oneself about right and wrong?[23] These jurists were not engaged in confronting a burning contemporary issue; rather, in a style that was very typical of them, they were simply being clever. But the idea they put forward was one that could be applied to all three of the relevant conditions, and used to quite different effect.

The first scholar to move significantly in this direction seems to have been Sharīᶜatmadārī.[24] After raising the question with regard to the conditions in general, he discusses the knowledge condition, and concludes that it is of the kind that one must take action to fulfil. With regard to the efficacy condition, his position is more complicated. He has already introduced a typically modern distinction between a social and a personal form of the duty; the former, unlike the latter, is performed by an organised group of suitably trained and qualified people. He now says that in the case of the social and collective form of the duty – as opposed to the personal form – there is an obligation to satisfy the efficacy condition; we must lay the foundations for the social duty so that its performance will be effective. He does not discuss the question when he comes to the danger condition, though he remarks in his account of it that students of the Islamic sciences in particular need to be prepared to carry out the social duty.

This style of thought does not seem to have been widespread in Sharīᶜatmadārī's generation.[25] Shīrāzī shared it, but only with respect to the knowledge condition; Khumaynī was untouched by it, which helps to explain its rather unsteady progress. Two younger authors who took it up were Muṭahharī and Ṭayyibī. Muṭahharī showed no familiarity with it in his talk of 1960, though his plea for logic – by which he meant something like creativeness and ingenuity in social engineering – could be construed as a concern to secure the means of efficacy. (For example, if we want to put a stop to vicious gossip among our traditional Iranian women, pious exhortations will get us nowhere; we have to think of some other way for them to relax in their spare time.)[26] In his talk of 1970 he continued to speak of logic. But

22 543.
23 See above, 47f.
24 544.
25 544f.
26 544 n. 274.

he also insisted on the duty to secure the power needed for efficacy. The response of Islam to the man who says he doesn't have the power to perform the duty is: 'Fine, but go and acquire the power!' The other author who adopted the doctrine of prior duty, and with regard to all three conditions, was Ṭayyibī. His position is essentially Sharīᶜatmadārī's, but extended to cover the danger condition, and expressed in a language suffused with political activism. Views of the kind we have been considering are by now widely known, but they have not achieved the same recognition as the revision of the danger condition. The intellectually conservative Kharrāzī, in his recent monograph on forbidding wrong, does not pay much attention to them; nevertheless, an equally recent commentator on one of Khumaynī's accounts adopts them.

The kind of religious policing to which such thinking leads has been a prominent feature of life in the Islamic Republic.[27] According to the constitution, the duty is one that must be fulfilled 'by the people with respect to one another, by the government with respect to the people, and by the people with respect to the government'. In practice, the first and third have been relatively muted by the din of the second. Iran, like Saudi Arabia, has become a society in which forbidding wrong is predominantly a function of the state apparatus, in this case involving a plurality of organs that do not always act in concert. A case in point is an incident in which the ᶜAlī ibn Abī Ṭālib Foundation organised a competition to test the general public's knowledge of forbidding wrong. The foundation ran into a storm of criticism because it had announced that one of the prizes would be a video – this at a time when traffic in videos had been declared illegal, and there were daily reports of clashes between the forces of order and the owners and distributors of these pernicious devices.[28]

Because Iranian society is culturally richer than that of Saudi Arabia, and Iranian politics more open, there is a no doubt a better story to be told here, and more material with which to tell it.[29] 'It has been bad all morning', a pious Iranian confided to an American journalist regarding his task of forbidding wrongdoing by couples hiking in the mountains behind Tehran in the high summer. 'When we see couples go up the peaks, we must follow to make sure they are brothers and sisters or are married,' the poor man explained.[30] 'But all this climbing, all this walking, is hard. By the end of the day I collapse.' That morning it had been one thing after another. 'Girls in baseball caps, covered with makeup, coming up here without proper headscarves. And the boys use words I can't repeat and strip off their shirts. It is a dirty, lonely job. But we must be ready to die for God.' I regret not having attempted a fuller study of religious policing in the Islamic Republic.

27 545f.
28 546 n. 286.
29 546.
30 546 n. 288.

At this point we should perhaps turn back to the performance of the duty 'by the people with respect to one another'.[31] To judge by the section on forbidding wrong in a collection of responsa of Khumaynī dating mostly from the early years of the revolution, this individual form of the duty retained a place alongside the activities of the state. One question put to Khumaynī is about our obligation with regard to strangers 'under today's conditions'; but with few exceptions, the common thread of the questions is a concern about our duty towards people with whom we have regular social relations. Can one, for example, be friends with an observant Muslim who lacks faith in the authority of the Supreme Guide (*wilāyat-i faqīh*) and has an eclectic style of thought? Many of these problems concern family ties. Every Iranian family, it seems, is unhappy in the same way: one member or another remains mired in the immorality, irreligion or political allegiances of the fallen 'Ṭāghūtī' regime. One questioner has four nephews and a niece who are not in the least religiously observant, make their living mostly from gambling and drug-peddling, and even now live in hope of a Ṭāghūtī restoration – may they never see it even in their dreams! A woman laments that her father does not believe in God, the Prophet or the world to come, never prays, and is strongly opposed to the revolution – whereas her mother, sister and brothers are all believers. Talking to him nicely doesn't work, and things are getting worse by the day. At this point she mentions that she is married, and explains that matters have now reached a point at which her husband refuses to visit her parents' house. What is she to do? One husband of an impious wife complains that she never performs the dawn prayer. Another has a wife who prays only once in a while, and then after much aggravation; he suffers mental anguish, and is worried as to whether he will be held responsible at the Resurrection. Where ties of kinship are at issue, Khumaynī tends to warn against severing such bonds, and to enjoin counselling or reproving the offender.[32]

It remains that the organised forbidding of wrong is what has excited Imāmīs and Sunnīs alike in recent decades – rather than the duty of the individual to right wrongs as and when he comes across them, and to the best of his knowledge and abilities. The driving concerns of both communities are at once more ambitious and characteristically modern, even when authentic features of the tradition can be adduced in support.

5 Forbidding wrong and privacy

We saw in the previous chapter that modern Sunnī writers on forbidding wrong do not have very much to say about privacy.[33] Among the Imāmīs, where it was never

[31] 546f.
[32] 547 n. 296.
[33] See above, ch. 10, section 6.

a standard topic in the traditional discussion of the duty, we tend to hear even less of it.[34] Themes connected with privacy appear here and there in the modern Imāmī literature, but there is no move to consolidate them into a bulwark against abuse, whether perpetrated by the state apparatus or by individual pietists.

To this there is one significant exception,[35] though it is not entirely isolated inasmuch as the author in question owes some of his inspiration to Muṭahharī. One of many recent books on forbidding wrong published in Iran by junior clerics is by Sayyid Ḥasan Islāmī Ardakānī. This one, published in Qumm in 1996, is nicely produced and skilfully written. It opens with a graphic scene of a city asleep – we are not told when or where – and a man patrolling the streets. He comes to a house, sniffs wrongdoing, finds the door closed, and enters by climbing over the wall and descending through the roof. He catches a man and a woman in their cups, and denounces the man as an enemy of God for his sin. The malefactor immediately responds by accusing the intruder of not one but three contraventions of divine law: spying on him, entering his home other than by the door, and doing so without asking his leave or greeting him. Thus someone who sought to expose the sin of another found that he himself had fallen into no less than three mortal sins. It is only now that the lay reader, who might at first have been under the disturbing misapprehension that the scene was set in our own dear Islamic Republic, gets to learn that the triple sinner was the caliph ᶜUmar.[36] Not being an old-fashioned Imāmī bigot, Islāmī does not curse this traditional enemy of the Shīᶜites; but neither does he find it necessary to bless him. All told, this is not a story calculated to raise ᶜUmar in the esteem of the Imāmī reader;[37] by the same token, and more to the point, it is well calculated to give intrusiveness a bad name among good Imāmīs today.

Later in the book, Islāmī uses another strategy to the same effect. In line with Muṭahharī and those who followed him, he gives considerable attention to the Sunnī institution of the censorship (*ḥisba*) as a mechanism for forbidding wrong. By the time Islāmī was writing, of course, the novelty of Muṭahharī's discovery had long worn off. What excites Islāmī is not so much the institution itself as the reasons for its decay over the centuries. Of these reasons, there is one that he presents with particular eloquence: the abusive behaviour of those purportedly engaged in forbidding wrong. In this way the very institution that was supposed to be the solution itself became part of the problem. Islāmī returns to the theme of abuse in the context of the question why the duty is in such a bad way in our own age, for all that we live at a time when Islam is being revived and an Islamic republic has been established. He reviews a number of factors, but one stands out: abuses that have given the duty a bad name. There is, he says, no need to call witnesses; we have all encountered shamefully abusive conduct on the part of people

[34] 556f.
[35] 557–60.
[36] See above, 58.
[37] Cf. 454 n. 185.

supposedly engaged in forbidding wrong – people whose actions lead in fact to the ruin of the duty, and indeed of religion itself.

He then enlists in this protest an almost incontrovertible authority: the martyred Muṭahharī, a man who devoted his life to reviving the duty and died for the cause of establishing an Islamic government. In his talk of 1960, Muṭahharī had indeed shown strong antipathy to thuggery and intrusion. Referring to some recent activities carried out in the name of forbidding wrong, he commented that, if this was indeed what forbidding wrong amounted to, it was better that it should remain in oblivion. We only have the right to intervene, he insisted, where wrongs are out in the public domain; we have no right to engage in spying and interference in matters relating to people's private lives. He had then told a searing story of over-zealous religious students who raided a wedding by scrambling across the rooftops, smashing musical instruments and boxing the ears of the bride; later they were roundly rebuked by a senior cleric for their multiple sins. Islāmī, of course, makes excellent use of this material.

All this is exciting, but also perhaps a trifle alarming: is the virtuous reader not in danger of being drawn into a profoundly subversive attack on the entire apparatus of religious enforcement in the Islamic Republic? Islāmī has thought of this, and slips in a timely reassurance. Fortunately, he tells us, the horrible activities to which Muṭahharī was alluding are quite unknown today, and it is devoutly to be hoped that such things will never again sully the purity of Islam. The reader relaxes, albeit still slightly puzzled by the information that we have *all* witnessed abuses of this kind. Many of us can scarcely remember the bad old days before the revolution; and even if we do, over-zealous religious policing is not conventionally included among the crimes of the fallen regime.

When it comes to legal prescription, Islāmī again has a strategy. He proceeds by enlarging and enriching a category that had originally been developed by Ghazzālī: the 'norms' (*ādāb*) of the duty. Happily, Islāmī is able to find an Imāmī precedent for the category; in any case, as he goes on to indicate, bringing a number of points together under this heading is to an extent just a matter of convenience. Having justified his use of the category, he goes on to present his set of ten norms. The first is that there must be no spying. Indeed the most important point there is to be made about forbidding wrong, he tells us, is that the forbidder should abstain from interference in the private lives of others and from prying into their worldly affairs. What Islam requires is the elimination of manifest sin; secret sin is reserved for the jurisdiction of God. The second, closely linked norm is that there should be no 'curtain-ripping', in other words no exposure of hidden sins. In all this, Islāmī's leading quoted sources are Ghazzālī and another Sunnī, the Persian littérateur Sa^{c}dī (d. 1292); Imāmī authorities tend to take a back seat. Looming behind these Sunnīs, it does not take a very sharp eye to discern the ghostly presence of Western conceptions of rights. Sinners, Islāmī remarks, are human like us; they too have rights, and these are not to be trampled underfoot.

Islāmī's ideas are not representative of the prevailing religious culture in Iran. But they are likely to have considerable resonance for a significant part of the educated population.

6 Concluding remarks

By way of conclusion, it is worth coming back to a comparison introduced at the beginning of the previous chapter:[38] the relationship of modern to medieval thought as it appears among the Sunnīs, on the one hand, and the Imāmīs, on the other.

In the Sunnī world, the austerely traditionalist intellectual heritage of the scholars has combined with their marginalisation by social and political change to make it hard for their scholasticism to provide convincing Islamic solutions to modern problems.[39] Maṭᶜanī's literary polemics on righting wrongs 'with the hand' provide a good example of their predicament.[40] It is not just that neither the state nor 'religious youth', the two forces that define the political context of his thinking, are likely to pay much attention to him. What he says is in itself problematic. When he attacks the view that action 'with the hand' is reserved to the authorities, the traditional Sunnī horror of doctrinal innovation is on his side. Like many a medieval scholar, he wins by rightly insisting that his position is not some innovation he thought up for himself. In the same vein, he describes the view he is rejecting as an unknown and innovatory interpretation, and as a recent opinion that not one of the scholars of the community had held in the past. Having said all this in the manner of a medieval traditionalist, it is superfluous for him to argue that the position he is attacking is a bad idea. But when he puts forward his own idea – severely limiting the type of action 'with the hand' permitted to individuals – he is hoist with his own petard. We wait in vain for the roll-call of authoritative opinions from the past that alone could make his view respectable. Among the Sunnīs, therefore, new thinking – and in a new world there has to be some – cannot easily take place within the framework of the scholastic heritage; instead the locus of intellectual creativity of necessity shifts outside it.

Among the Imāmīs, with their markedly more rationalist heritage, this does not have to be so.[41] In their discussions of forbidding wrong, the modern Imāmī scholars have attacked and gone behind the traditional view of the conditions of obligation in a way that Maṭᶜanī could never have done. Ṭayyibī, for example, invents a novel conception of a 'collective obligation'. He then considers the possibility that someone might object that it is new, and responds 'So be it!' Other Imāmī scholars are not so brazen, but they are significantly less constricted than

[38] See above, 112.
[39] 555.
[40] See above, 119, 120.
[41] 555f.

their Sunnī colleagues; witness the elaboration of the essentially novel doctrine of the prior duty to secure the prerequisites for forbidding wrong. There is also a strain of purely academic scepticism in the treatment of inherited doctrines that does not feature in the more practically oriented discussions considered in this chapter;[42] this too is without parallel among the Sunnī scholars.

42 285; 295f.; 299; 535 n. 210; cf. 298.

CHAPTER 12

Do non-Islamic cultures have similar values?

As we have seen, forbidding wrong is a prominent Islamic value. But is it peculiarly Islamic? Or are values that resemble it to be found in other cultures? If so, how close do they come to the Islamic value, and in what ways are they different? Such parallels, if they exist, could validly give rise to two projects that are in principle distinct. One is genetic: here the questions are whether the Islamic conception of forbidding wrong has identifiable pre-Islamic origins, and how far it has influenced non-Islamic cultures. The other is comparative: it is often illuminating to compare and contrast analogous, perhaps genetically unrelated, phenomena in different settings. In what follows, however, I have not formally separated the two projects. What begins as an inquiry into the origins of the Islamic value will end up as an attempt to identify and explain what is distinctive about it. But before embarking on this quest, it may be prudent to narrow the field somewhat.

1 What are we looking for?

It is not hard to find non-Islamic parallels to the expression 'command right and forbid wrong'.[1] Thus a German legal document of 1616 offers the phrase 'recht gebieten und unrecht verbieten' with regard to the conduct incumbent on the judge of a certain court. In the next century William Blackstone (d. 1780), in his celebrated treatise on the laws of England, defines municipal law as 'a rule of civil conduct prescribed by the supreme power in a state, commanding what is right and prohibiting what is wrong'. His definition echoes one already adopted in antiquity by the Stoics. Thus Chrysippus (d. 207 BC) opened his book on law with the statement that the law must, among other things, command what should be done and forbid what should not be done. This in turn echoes Aristotle (d. 322 BC). Perhaps, then, this ancient wording, like the owl on Athenian coins, found its way to pre-Islamic Arabia.

[1] 561.

Yet it would be hard to argue that all attestations of such a phrase must go back to a single origin. In a text preserved in the Pāli canon, the Buddha (*c.* fifth century BC) includes among the virtues of the good friend who tells one what one needs to do that 'he restrains [one] from wrong; he establishes [one] in right'.[2] In a second passage in the same text it is the parents who do this to their child, and in a third it is the leaders in religious life who do it to the young layman of good family. In China in the T^{c}ang period (618–907) it was reckoned one of the duties of the historian 'to encourage good and to reprove evil'.[3] Again the phrase is old: it goes back to a work composed between the fifth and first centuries BC. It would doubtless be possible to find further parallels lurking elsewhere in the world's literatures.

If the phrase has such echoes in other cultures, should we think of the duty itself as a universal human value?[4] The basic principle involved is that if one encounters someone engaged in wrongdoing, one should do something to stop them. My guess is that this principle, or something like it, is to be found embedded (though not necessarily articulated) in just about all human cultures. That is to say, I would think that in almost any culture there will be occasions – not tied to specific social relationships or material calculations – when it makes sense to say something like: 'You can't just stand there and let him do that.' I have no idea how one might amass the empirical evidence that would put such a guess on a firmer foundation. The principle does not have a name either in common English or in the technical language of anthropologists; consequently ethnographers are not looking for the value, and if they happen to describe it, they are unlikely to signal this in a way that makes the information easy to locate in their ethnographies. In what follows, I shall simply assume that the value is more or less universal.

The existence of this hypothetical uniformity would still leave room for a great deal of variation between cultures, not to mention the individuals who belong to them. Most obviously, there are extensive differences between cultures regarding what is considered right or wrong: witness the collision between West African and Islamic attitudes to female nudity. But while such differences are clearly crucial for the practice of the value, they are not intrinsic to the way in which it is conceived.

More interestingly for our purposes, there are likely to be considerable variations regarding the extent to which our value is identified or emphasised in the moral vocabularies of different cultures. The same is true of the relative weight attached to it in relation to such antithetical principles as minding one's own business and keeping out of trouble. It would be a plausible guess that the vernacular subcultures of the Islamic world have tended to assign more weight to such antithetical principles than the mainstream religious tradition has done; and it would not be surprising to find comparable differences obtaining between cultures at large. This would

[2] 579.
[3] 580 and n. 121.
[4] 562f.

surely apply even within the set of the world's historic literary cultures. Here again, I do not know how one would go about making comparisons on a serious scale – neither the tables of contents nor the indexes of ethnographies being of much assistance in this regard. I have accordingly made no serious attempt in this direction, except in one case of obvious historical significance: pre-Islamic Arabia.

There is, however, a relevant difference between the literary heritages of high cultures that is relatively accessible to comparative exploration. This is the extent to which they subject our value to formal, systematic elaboration. I have consequently made it my business to ascertain which cultures distil their local versions of our value into scholastic doctrines. It is, for example, a striking and perhaps historically relevant fact that in the world of late antiquity, monks would rebuke the powerful with the same abrasiveness as ascetics in the Islamic world.[5] There was, moreover, an old Greek term for such outspokenness (*parrhēsia*). But for all that the phenomenon was there, and possessed of a name, it does not seem to have given rise to any body of systematic thought in the Christian literature of the time. Other cultures may have more to offer. If we can collect some scholastic doctrines from different cultures, we can attempt to compare them with what we have found in Islam. But first, let us attend to pre-Islamic Arabia.

2 Pre-Islamic Arabia

There are two separate (though related) questions to ask about the role of pre-Islamic Arabia in the origins of the Islamic conception of forbidding wrong.[6] The first concerns the terminology of the duty. Is the language used to describe it in Islam inherited – in whole or in part – from the Jāhiliyya? Or is it new to Arabic, perhaps derived from some extra-Arabian source? The second question is about the idea of the duty. Did Arabian society give prominence to the notion that it is a man's business to right wrongs and seek to prevent their occurrence? Or was such activity highly valued only when it took place within the limits of specific social relationships that required it? In an attempt to answer these questions, let us first examine two traditions relating to Mecca in the late pre-Islamic period, and then consider the evidence of Jāhilī poetry.

The first tradition concerns Ḥakīm ibn Umayya, a member of a family that belonged to the tribe of Sulaym but was well established in Mecca.[7] He was a confederate of the Umayyad clan, and later converted to Islam. It is reported that in pre-Islamic Mecca he exercised the role of restraining and disciplining the hot-blooded young men of Quraysh, with the general consent of the tribe. In this connection he is referred to in some sources as a censor (*muḥtasib*); these sources then

[5] 563.
[6] 563–9.
[7] 564.

go on to describe him as '(commanding right and) forbidding wrong'. Altogether their wording is so similar that their testimony must be treated as reflecting a single source. With regard to their terminology, are these authors then reporting actual Jāhilī usage, or are they merely retrojecting Islamic usage onto a Jāhilī phenomenon that happens to remind them of an Islamic one? Since they do not make any explicit claim to be reporting Jāhilī usage, the safest assumption is that they are retrojecting. With regard to the activity itself, what we have here is – as these authors indicate – a precedent for the official censorship (*ḥisba*), rather than for the duty of the individual believer.

The case is somewhat different with a much more widely attested institution of pre-Islamic Mecca, an alliance (known as the *ḥilf al-fuḍūl*) that was created for the purpose of righting wrongs.[8] A typical account of the formation of this alliance is the following. A member of the Yemeni tribe of the Banū Zubayd came to Mecca with commercial goods which he sold to a member of the Banū Sahm, a clan of Quraysh. The purchaser, however, failed to pay for them. The public protest of the wronged merchant (in verse, of course) gave rise to such concern among Quraysh that several clans gathered and made a pact in the following terms: 'If anyone is wronged in Mecca, we will all take his part against the wrongdoer until we recover what is due to him from the one who has wronged him, whether he is noble or humble, one of us or not.' As a result the Sahmī wrongdoer was prevailed upon to pay the Zubaydī merchant his due. Thereafter, if anyone wronged anyone in Mecca, the members of the alliance were there to put matters right. Again, we are in the generation before the rise of Islam; the Prophet himself is reported to have been present at the formation of the alliance. To my knowledge, there are no other reports of such institutions in pre-Islamic Arabia, except that it is said by some that the alliance owed its name to a similar alliance that had been formed in the tribe of Jurhum, the somewhat shadowy possessors of the Meccan sanctuary in an earlier period. The story tends to suggest – though not very strongly – that righting wrongs in general was not the business of the individual; rather, it would seem to have required a formal agreement to establish a group pledged to do this in a single locality.

Here again there is a question of terminology.[9] A thirteenth-century author remarks that forbidding wrong was known to the pre-Islamic Arabs, and he establishes his point by adducing our alliance. He does not actually attribute the phrase to the pre-Islamic Arabs, but a report transmitted by a ninth-century scholar does just that: it explicitly includes 'commanding right and forbidding wrong' in the terms of the agreement. Here, then, we have a clear ascription of the phrase to the Jāhiliyya. But the report is an isolated one among our many accounts of the agreement, and this suggests that we would be well advised to regard it as anachronistic.

[8] 565f.
[9] 566.

In a similar way our sources are happy to impute statements about forbidding wrong to the Byzantines.

The other source that calls for our attention is Jāhilī poetry. There are, of course, considerable problems regarding the authenticity of poetry ascribed to the pre-Islamic period; but as will be seen, these problems are not of overriding significance in the present context. The main points are as follows.

First, the words I regularly translate as 'right' (*ma^{c}rūf*) and 'wrong' (*munkar*) are widely attested in pre-Islamic poetry.[10] Moreover, they are not infrequently used as antithetical terms. In their etymological senses of 'known' and 'unknown', they are already paired in a much-repeated hemistich of Muraqqish al-Akbar, who is perhaps our oldest Arab poet: speaking of dusty deserts, he tells of crossing the unknown wilderness to reach the known (*qaṭa^{c}tu ilā ma^{c}rūfihā munkarātihā*). In more evaluative senses, we find the words similarly paired by several Jāhilī poets. There is even a precedent for one of our Islamic phrases for taking action against a wrong (*ankara ʾl-munkar*). This latter might be dismissed as retrojection, since it is not widely attested. But it would require a categorical rejection of the corpus of pre-Islamic poetry to dispose of the attestations of 'right' and 'wrong', and a high degree of scepticism to disallow the evidence for their pairing.

Second, the locutions 'commanding right' and 'forbidding wrong' are unknown to pre-Islamic poetry.[11] They only begin to appear – and then sporadically – in poetry of the early Islamic period. The most that can be said is that one of these early Islamic attestations purports to be describing a scene set in the pre-Islamic period. In other words, it would require a high degree of credulity to find in poetry evidence that these phrases were used before the appearance of Islam.

The situation is thus fairly clear-cut.[12] Pre-Islamic Arabia knew well the terms 'right' and 'wrong', and seems to have paired them. But if we can judge by its poetry, it did not possess the notions of 'commanding' or 'forbidding' them. Nor, to my knowledge, is there evidence in poetry of such a value expressed in other terms. Protecting those who have been wronged is a familiar theme in pre-Islamic Arabia; but it is a protection extended to those who seek it, not to the wronged as such.

From what has been said in this section, we can conclude that the Koran owes its terms for 'right' (*ma^{c}rūf*) and 'wrong' (*munkar*) to pre-Islamic Arabia. But what of 'commanding' and 'forbidding' them? We have no serious precedent for such a usage from within Arabia; nor, to my knowledge, do we have any from outside it that is likely to be historically relevant, unless perchance we invoke the Stoics and their heirs. It is accordingly an obvious hypothesis that the usage from which the Islamic duty takes its name was a Koranic innovation.

[10] 567f.
[11] 568.
[12] 568f.

The religious recognition of the duty is another matter. As we saw, it is by no means clear whether the Koranic verses that speak of 'commanding right and forbidding wrong' are in fact talking about the duty we know from later Islamic thought, an opacity reflected in early exegesis.[13] We also saw that an early usage that clearly does refer to our duty speaks not of 'forbidding' wrong but rather of 'righting' it.[14] We thus have some reason to put the Koranic terminology to one side, and to look elsewhere for the antecedents of the duty itself. In any case we need some parallels, whether or not they are genetically related.

3 Rabbinic Judaism

Ignaz Goldziher, in an extended discussion of the duty published in 1903, adduced two parallels from outside Islam.[15] One was the institution of the censorship in Confucian China; to this he might have added the more familiar censorship of republican Rome. Both were institutions maintained by the state, and as such might bear comparison with the Islamic censorship (*ḥisba*) – itself a special case of forbidding wrong. But they are quite unlike the general Islamic conception of an executive power of individual believers existing outside any institutional framework. The other parallel adduced by Goldziher is from Rabbinic Judaism, and this is considerably more to the point.

In the first place, a comparable duty is already prescribed in the Bible: 'you shall reprove your neighbour (*hokheaḥ tokhiaḥ et-ᶜamitekha*), or you will incur guilt yourself' (Lev. 19:17).[16] This is adduced by the rabbis, appropriately enough, to show that if a man sees something unseemly in his neighbour, it is his duty to rebuke him. (Here and below, all the Jewish sources I draw on are pre-Islamic, unless otherwise indicated.) He also has the duty of repeating his rebuke if the offender does not take the point (*lo qibbel*). How much come-back does he have to put up with in the performance of the duty? Here there is disagreement: till he is beaten? till he is cursed? till the offender becomes angry? There is also dispute as to where one's duty lies if one's initiative will be of no avail. One rabbi declined to rebuke the members of the household of the Jewish exilarch in Babylonia on the grounds that they would not accept it from him; another held that he should rebuke them notwithstanding. There should be no respect of persons: a disciple has the duty of rebuking a teacher. Failure to perform the duty can lead to collective divine punishment: Jerusalem was destroyed because 'they did not rebuke one another'. On the other hand, there is a preference for private rebuke: Jeroboam merited the kingship because he reproved Solomon, but was punished for reproving him in

[13] See above, 3.
[14] See above, 4.
[15] 569f.
[16] 570f.

public. Reproving people is not a way of making friends: if a young scholar is popular with his fellow townsmen, it is because he does not rebuke them in religious matters. As might be expected, the duty does not flourish in the present: no one in this generation is able to reprove, or able to accept reproof, or even knows how to reprove.

In the second place, there is a duty (perhaps to be equated with the preceding) to protest (*le-maḥot*) at the misdeeds of others.[17] This duty is aired in connection with the scandal of Rabbi Elᶜazar ben ᶜAzariah's cow. This cow would go out on the Sabbath with a strap between its horns, a practice on which the sages looked askance, though Rabbi Elᶜazar himself deemed it permissible. So far, these commotions hardly concern us. In the Babylonian Talmud, however, a discussion takes place that puts a quite different complexion on the matter. Here it is suggested that the cow was not in fact Rabbi Elᶜazar's at all, but rather the property of a female neighbour; it was accounted his because he failed to protest about it. The ensuing Talmudic discussion endorses the principle here suggested: that failure to protest when one is in a position to do so saddles one with responsibility for what one has failed to prevent. In this way one can acquire an unwelcome responsibility for the sins of one's household, of one's fellow townsmen, even of the world at large. Thus elders are liable to divine punishment for failing to protest against the misdeeds of princes. But what if protest would achieve nothing? The issue is raised in a discussion between God and Justice regarding certain righteous men among the sinners of Jerusalem. Justice alleges against them that 'it was in their power to protest, but they did not do so'; God's retort is that it was already known that, had they protested, the sinners would not have accepted it from them.

Finally, there is a duty to restrain others from forbidden actions (*le-afroshe me-issura*).[18] It is clear from the Talmudic passages in question that we have to do with a definite principle of law; it has a set phrasing, and in two instances is held to override other legal principles. Its performance, it emerges, may be by word (telling someone what to do, or shouting at them to restrain them from a violation), or by deed (stalking an unmarried couple with the intention of restraining them from performing a forbidden act). There is no reference to violence.

Here, then, we have the beginnings of a scholastic elaboration of a religious duty or duties similar in character to forbidding wrong, though relatively far less salient.

4 Medieval Catholicism

A duty strongly resembling forbidding wrong makes its appearance in Latin Christendom in the thirteenth century; it is known to the scholastics as 'fraternal

[17] 571f.
[18] 572.

correction' (*correctio fraterna*).[19] Rebuking others for their sins was, of course, a Christian habit of hoary antiquity and firm scriptural foundations. But to my knowledge, it was not the object of systematic doctrinal exposition in other branches of Christianity, or in the Latin West prior to the thirteenth century. The tradition then established has remained a part, though not perhaps a very prominent one, of Catholic Christianity ever since. The classic account is that of Thomas Aquinas (d. 1274), and it will give us most of what we need.

Much of the detailed argumentation of Aquinas's account is naturally peculiar to the Christian tradition, and more particularly to its Latin form.[20] Yet no reader who is familiar with the Islamic doctrine of forbidding wrong could fail to be struck by the broad similarities. Fraternal correction is a duty, but not an absolute one: it is not to be carried out without regard for place and time, and we are not to set ourselves up as investigators of the lives of others. Correcting a sinner for his own sake by simple admonition is the business of everyone who possesses charity, whether he be an inferior or a superior – though the duty presses more heavily on superiors. An inferior may thus correct a superior, provided this is done in private and in a gentle and respectful manner, without impudence and harshness; however, if there is imminent danger to the faith, it must be done in public (but not, it seems, harshly). Does a sinner have a duty to correct a wrongdoer? He at least commits no sin if he reproves him with humility. Do we have a duty to refrain from correction if we fear that it will merely make the sinner worse? In such a case, where it is judged probable that the offender will not accept the reproof, fraternal correction is not to be attempted. Does the duty require us to admonish the wrongdoer in secret before going on to public denunciation? The answer, in general, is that it does. What is more, we should continue to admonish him in private as long as there is hope that this will work. But when we judge that private admonition is unlikely to succeed, we go further; here Aquinas takes issue with unnamed authorities who are against such escalation.[21]

In later Catholic doctrine further resemblances appear.[22] The duty is held to be established by both reason and revelation, a point that Aquinas had not addressed. (This, of course, aligns Catholicism with an opinion held only by a minority of Muslim scholars.) The question whether it is obligatory to perform fraternal correction in the case of a venial sin is discussed. Aquinas's treatment of the conditions of obligation is by Islamic standards unsystematic; this is made good with the appearance of schemas of three, four or five conditions. One such schema sets out the conditions as follows: (1) the offender must definitely have committed the sin in question; (2) there must be good reason to expect success; (3) the performer of the duty must not thereby place himself in serious danger.[23]

19 573f.
20 574f.
21 575 n. 87.
22 575.
23 576 n. 91.

What then of the major differences between fraternal correction and forbidding wrong?[24] In the first place, two issues are treated at length that are alien to the Islamic doctrine of forbidding wrong. The first of the eight articles into which Aquinas divides his discussion is concerned with the question whether fraternal correction is an act of charity or of justice – the answer being that it is the former. The last of the eight articles likewise deals with an unfamiliar issue: whether witnesses should be brought in prior to public denunciation – the answer being that in general they should. This concern, which has no equivalent in Islam, is directly driven by Christian scripture (Matt. 18:16).

In the second place, there are a couple of points worth noting where the issues are the same, but the answers somewhat different.[25] First, Aquinas is by Islamic standards remarkably inflexible regarding the conditions that dispense one from performing the duty: it is a mortal sin to omit it out of fear. Thus fear would be no excuse in a case where one had reason to believe that one could persuade a sinner to pull back. Later Catholic doctrine, however, is much more cautious on this point, voiding the obligation where it would involve serious harm to oneself. Second, Aquinas, as we have seen, does not envisage situations in which it would be appropriate to speak harshly to a superior; Ghazzālī's espousal of harsh language directed at rulers has no place in Aquinas's scheme of things.

In the third place, there is a basic structural difference between the Christian and Islamic conceptions.[26] What I did not make clear above is that Aquinas repeatedly distinguishes two kinds of correction. The first is the fraternal correction with which we are now familiar. This kind is done in the interests of the offender (whence it is an act of charity); it is carried out by simple admonition, without any form of coercion; and it is the business of everyone. The other kind of correction is carried out for the common good (whence it is an act of justice); it is marked by coercive force, is reserved for superiors, and may involve punishment. Aquinas offers no term for this second type, but it passes under the name of 'juridical correction'. How does this compare with Islamic conceptions? Fraternal correction has its equivalent in the verbal rebuke that any believer should administer to an offender. Juridical correction is part of the exercise of superior authority against wrongdoers. What is missing on the Catholic side is thus the entire domain of forbidding wrong as performed by the individual believer 'with the hand', whether or not this includes recourse to arms.

Finally, it is significant that later Catholic doctrine, unlike that of Aquinas, tends to minimise the extent to which private persons are obligated to perform fraternal correction.[27] One authority concludes his account of the conditions of obligation with the observation that it is clear that little or no blame attaches to private persons who omit to perform the duty. Another stresses that it hardly ever extends

[24] 576.
[25] 576f.
[26] 577.
[27] 577f.

to correcting a stranger, the reason being lack of good grounds to expect success in such a case; hence it is rare for private persons to be obligated to perform the duty among themselves unless they know each other, and rarer still for an inferior to be obligated to correct a superior.

But what of the history of the scholastic doctrine of fraternal correction before Aquinas?[28] The earliest discussion I have come upon is that of William of Auxerre (d. 1231), which does not take us significantly further back. Much that is reminiscent of Islamic doctrine in Aquinas's account is missing here. In fact William deals only with three major questions. The first is whether all are obligated, to which he gives essentially the same answer as Aquinas. The second is about escalation; here to an extent he seems to side with the unnamed scholars with whom Aquinas takes issue. The third is concerned with rebukes administered by superiors; in other words, he does not yet distinguish this topic from fraternal correction proper.

5 Non-monotheist parallels?

Like the Islamic doctrine of forbidding wrong, both the scholastic parallels we have considered so far come from branches of the monotheist tradition. The question thus arises whether we can we find any worthwhile parallels outside the monotheist family. I know of none. By this I mean that, to the best of my knowledge, none of the major non-monotheist traditions gives our duty a name or lays much emphasis on it, let alone elaborates it in a scholastic fashion. A few words on the Zoroastrian, Buddhist and Confucian heritages will suffice to show this.

To represent Zoroastrianism, let us take a characteristic Middle Persian text containing several hundred moral sayings.[29] Here we find no set phrase identifying the value of preventing others from doing wrong, and little of its substance. We do learn that it is a duty to prevail on someone 'to turn away from a sin through which he might become wicked'. Likewise it is good to find a friend who will tell you your faults so that you can correct them. Yet in general it is a vice, not a virtue, to reproach a sinner for his sin; rather, it seems, one should correct one's own faults and learn from the goodness of others. In a couple of sayings the suggestive phrase 'the preservation of the good and the uprooting of the wicked' appears; but it seems to describe a function of rulers and magnates, not of individual believers.

Most Buddhist literature is for monks, but there are a few exceptions.[30] One is a text in the Pāli canon where, as we have seen, the phrase 'he restrains from wrong; he establishes in right' recurs three times. This has a formulaic ring. Yet the formula seems not to have achieved a wider currency in the canon. Nor does the

[28] 578 and n. 110.
[29] 581.
[30] 579f.

passage receive much attention in the exegetical literature, or even in the one post-canonical Pāli work that is devoted to a systematic exposition of the proper conduct of laymen. In short, the value failed to catch the eye of Buddhist scholasticism.

The Chinese record, so far as it is known to me, is no richer.[31] Confucius (d. 479 BC) has a saying to the effect that one should admonish friends, but give up if they fail to respond. Mencius (fourth century BC) describes the admonition of the ruler by his ministers in similar terms: 'If repeated remonstrations fell on deaf ears, they would leave him.' We have already met the Chinese phrase 'to encourage good and to reprove evil'. Such stray parallels could doubtless be multiplied. But here again, there seems to be no single central value corresponding to ours, and no scholastic elaboration of such a duty.

In short, if there are significant parallels to forbidding wrong outside the monotheist fold, I have not been lucky enough to find them.

6 Forbidding wrong and monotheism

What these soundings suggest is that there is a significant link between the monotheist religions and values comparable to forbidding wrong. This link could be genetic, and arise from the historical interactions between the monotheist faiths; or it could be structural, and reflect something about the character of monotheism.

Let us start with the idea that the linkage might be structural. It is not hard to improvise an explanation for why this should be so; several features of the monotheist faiths might be relevant. One is a sublimely ethical but personal conception of the divine – or to put it less respectfully, a supremely self-righteous deity. Another is a degree of active divine and human engagement in the affairs of this world, with much posting o'er land and ocean without rest. A third is a tight sense of religious community: believers are their brothers' keepers. One could certainly argue that this combination is alien or peripheral to the central messages of the religions and philosophies of India and China. But this approach seems to come to grief on Zoroastrianism.[32] Here we have a religion whose basic doctrines score quite well on the relevant features of the monotheist tradition. It is true that Ahura Mazdā is not an overbearingly personal god in the style of Israelite monotheism. But what better sanction for moral activism here and now than a conception of individual moral life as part and parcel of the cosmic struggle between good and evil? 'Every person ought to know: "Where have I come from? For what purpose am I here? Where do I return?" I, for my part, know that I came from Ohrmazd the Lord, that I am here so as to make the demons powerless, and that I shall return to Ohrmazd.' If it is something about monotheism that tends to

[31] 580.
[32] 581.

give rise to doctrines of forbidding wrong, we have yet to put our finger on just what it is.

If we prefer a genetic hypothesis, the chronology dictates the direction of influence in a very straightforward way: the Rabbinic conceptions would have to be the source of forbidding wrong, and forbidding wrong the source of fraternal correction. A Jewish background to the Islamic duty is historically quite plausible, particularly in the absence of a parallel in Syriac Christianity – though it is not, of course, proved by the general similarity of the conceptions found in the two religions. An Islamic source of the Latin Christian development is also in some ways historically plausible. Latin Christendom and Islam were neighbours, and Aquinas lived at a time when a considerable volume of material had been translated from Arabic into Latin and received with great excitement. The problem is that the process of translation from Arabic into Latin is reasonably well known, and the books translated were overwhelmingly works of science and philosophy; only a limited corpus of specifically religious texts was translated, under the patronage of Peter the Venerable (d. 1156), and this offered no coverage of the scholastic tradition of Islam.[33] We thus have no knowledge of a translation that would have included a systematic account of forbidding wrong, and the likelihood that there ever was such a translation is small. This is discouraging, inasmuch as the similarities between the Catholic and Islamic doctrines are in fact more striking than those between the Jewish and Islamic doctrines. In short, while we certainly should not rule out a monogenetic view of the incidence of the scholastic doctrines we have reviewed, the fact is that we have little chance of establishing such a hypothesis.

There are nevertheless two cases where a genetic approach cannot be challenged. Both involve non-Muslim communities living within the Islamic world.

One is Jews writing in Arabic.[34] Here we find that the Islamic terminology was readily adopted; it occurs as early as the tenth century in the writings of the Rabbanite Saᶜadya (d. 942) and the Karaite Qirqisānī. Ibn Paquda, the eleventh-century author of a pietistic work, has several passages in which he refers to forbidding wrong. He also makes mention of the three modes, and equates the duty with that of Leviticus 19:17. At the same time, some themes previously attested only on the Muslim side now make their appearance in the account of the duty of rebuke given by Maimonides (d. 1204) in his Hebrew law-book.[35]

As might be expected, the other case involves a Christian author. In general Christians seem to have been less receptive to the Islamic terminology of forbidding wrong than Jews. The exception is the Monophysite scholar Barhebraeus (d. 1286). In a work written in Syriac he gives an account of rebuke transparently derived

[33] 578.
[34] 572 and n. 68.
[35] 572f. and n. 69.

from Ghazzālī's treatment of forbidding wrong.[36] Of course Barhebraeus has stripped out all the Islamic elements in Ghazzālī's account and given it an appropriate Christian colouring. In place of Ghazzālī's examples of legitimate differences between law-schools, he cites the differing practice of Syrians and Greeks with regard to the day of the week on which they break their fast: each group inherits its practice from its teachers and fathers, neither is in sin, and neither may rebuke the other. In place of wrongs in mosques, we have sins committed in churches – though there is no lack of common ground. As to banquets, Barhebraeus has to limit his attack on liquor to excessive drinking, as opposed to the presence of wine as such. An argument of Ghazzālī's that is effortlessly adopted by Barhebraeus concerns the religious affiliation of the rebuker: he must be a believer, since rebuking is vindicating the faith, and how could one who is not a believer do that?[37] All that has changed here is the faith in which one has to believe. There are, of course, other significant differences; for example, Barhebraeus eliminates violence from Ghazzālī's account. But the deepest divergence relates to the question who is to perform the duty. Ghazzālī, like the Muslim scholars in general, is talking about a duty of believers as such. Barhebraeus, by contrast, limits the duty of admonition and rebuke to those who wield ecclesiastical authority. He is, in other words, a clericalist of a kind that we do not encounter even among the Imāmīs. Yet for all the revisions he makes, his dependence on Ghazzālī is unmistakable.

7 The distinctiveness of the Islamic case

Our Rabbinic and Catholic parallels put us in a position to conclude by asking what is distinctive about the Islamic conception of forbidding wrong.

In his commentary on Q3:110, the Shāfiᶜite Ashᶜarite Fakhr al-Dīn al-Rāzī (d. 1210) asks why the fact that the Muslims command right, forbid wrong and believe in God should have made them the best religious community, given that other communities have also shared these qualities.[38] (The Muslim scholars take it for granted that the duty of forbidding wrong was incumbent on the followers of earlier monotheist faiths.)[39] In answer, Rāzī quotes the Transoxanian Shāfiᶜite exegete Qaffāl (d. 976). According to this scholar, the difference between the Muslims and their predecessors is that the Muslims perform the duty in its most stringent form: fighting, which involves the risk of being killed. Though this view was not well received by Rashīd Riḍā, it is clear from the data on Judaism and Christianity presented above that Qaffāl cannot be faulted on his facts. Neither the Jewish nor the Christian accounts of the comparable duties provide any basis for

[36] 573; 600–3.
[37] See above, 13.
[38] 582.
[39] 47.

recourse to violence by individual believers. Nor, for that matter, do they incite them to confront unjust rulers; and the general tone of later Catholic doctrine is particularly tame.

All this is in marked contrast to the political salience and frequent abrasiveness of forbidding wrong in Islam. There are no Jewish or Christian parallels to the way in which Muslim rebels invoke forbidding wrong to grace insurrection.[40] Nor is there anything that compares with the frequency with which Muslim scholars link the duty to holy war.[41] Some make forbidding wrong a part of holy war, others invert the relationship; Ḥalīmī tells us that there is no fundamental difference between them, for both involve calling people to Islam, and if need be fighting them in this cause. There are even authors who elevate forbidding wrong above holy war: one remarks that it is the more binding duty, another that it earns the greater reward.

At the same time, the basic idea of the duty is antithetical to a hierarchic conception of society.[42] It is founded in the axiom that each and every legally competent Muslim possesses an executive power of the law of God. And as elaborated in scholastic doctrine, the duty usually takes no account of differences of social standing. It is true that there are some exceptions to this, such as the saying that sets out the tripartite division of labour;[43] but as we have seen, it is uncommon to find a major scholar who commits himself to such notions. Since hierarchic conceptions of society were commonplace in the thought of medieval Muslims, it is the relative absence of such notions in formal statements of the doctrine of forbidding wrong that is noteworthy. Thus while parents are regularly presented as a special case, this is not true of social superiors at large. It does not, of course, follow that the duty should be seen as actively subversive of all hierarchy. Indeed, it is remarkable that its implications for some of the most fundamental inequalities are rarely explored: those affecting slaves and women. Nevertheless, the egalitarian bias of the duty was by no means entirely neutralised in its exposure to a society that was in many ways saturated with hierarchic conceptions.

We have, then, a duty of an unusual character. It is an integral part of the mainstream scholastic tradition of Islamic societies; and yet it retains a marked potential for violence, subversion and egalitarianism. It is in this combination that the distinctive character of the Islamic conception of the duty lies.

Here the question of origins is arguably more straightforward.[44] The best part of a century ago a German scholar, who was much intrigued by what he called the 'democratic' character of the duty, was inclined to see its origin in a combination of two elements: on the one hand, the 'inclinations of a democratic Arabian ethos to a law of the jungle', and on the other, an 'idea of a religious community'. We

[40] See above, 108f.
[41] 490f.
[42] 583.
[43] See above, 17.
[44] 584.

have already touched on the relevance of a sense of religious community; what concerns us here is his invocation of the ethos of Jāhilī society.

Pre-Islamic Arabian society was tribal, and in considerable measure nomadic, inhabiting a land whose meagre resources favoured neither strong state authority nor elaborate social stratification. It was accordingly a society in which every man was an uncrowned king. Or to put it in more prosaic terms, political and military participation were very widely spread, far more so than in the mainstream of human societies – whether those of the steppe nomads, the later Islamic world or the modern West. It was the fusion of this egalitarian and activist tribal ethos with the monotheist tradition that gave Islam its distinctive political character. In no other civilisation was rebellion for conscience sake so widespread as it was in the early centuries of Islamic history; no other major religious tradition has lent itself to revival as a political ideology – and not just a political identity – in the modern world.

The uniqueness of the Islamic doctrine of forbidding wrong can be understood against this background. In Islam, of course, the sovereignty of God means that it is no longer admissible for every man to be a king. But as Ibn al-ᶜArabī put it, individuals act as God's deputies (*nuwwāb Allāh*) in forbidding wrong.[45] In arguing against the idea that forbidding wrong requires the ruler's permission, Ghazzālī spoke of the authority (*salṭana*) exercised by the individual Muslim in the performance of the duty.[46] Echoing him, we might almost speak of the sultanate of all believers.

[45] 365 n. 53; 584; cf. 38.
[46] 430; 431 n. 27.

References

[1] Snow, Theodore P., *The Dynamic Universe*, Second Edition. West Publishing Company, St. Paul, MN, 1985. pgs. 159-161.

[2] Ibid. p. 166.

[3] Ibid. pgs. 3-4.

[4] Department of Developmental Services, "Changes in the Population of Persons with Autism and Pervasive Developmental Disorders in California's Developmental Service System 1987 through 1998", A Report to the Legislature, March 1, 1999.

Pratt, Cathy, *The Reporter* (article on projected incidence rates for Autism, PDD and Asperger's Syndrome).

1998 National Autism Society of America Conference, Figures Provided by Dr. Marie Bristol-Powers from the National Institutes of Health.

[5] Freeman, John M., M.D., Kelly, Millicent T., R.D., L.D., Freeman, Jennifer B., *The Epilepsy Diet Treatment, An Introduction to The Ketogenic Diet*, Demos Publications, NY, NY, 1994.

[6] Guyton, Arthur C., M.D., Hall, John E., Ph.D., *Textbook of Medical Physiology*, Ninth Edition, W.B. Saunders Company, 1996. p. 826.

[7] Coulter, Harris L., Vaccination, Social Violence, and Criminality, North Atlantic Books, Berkeley, CA, 1990. p. 262.

[8-13] Confidential Personal Correspondence.

[14] Cohen, Donald J., M.D., Volkmar, Fred, M.D., Handbook of Autism and Pervasive Developmental Disorders, Second Edition, John Wiley and Sons, NY, NY, 1997. Chapter 21, pgs. 460-483.

[15] Secretin Outcome Surveys, The Autism Research Institute, San Diego, CA.

[16] Ehrlich, Eugene, Flexner, Stuart, Carruth, Gorton, Hawkins, Joyce M., *Oxford American Dictionary*, Avon Books, NY, NY, 1980.

[17] Gentz, William H., The Dictionary of Bible and Religion, Abingdon Press, Nashville, TN, 1986. p. 1112.

[18] Starling, Ernest H., The Wisdom of the Body – The Harveian Oration, H. K. Lewis and Co., Ltd., London, 1923. p. 7.

[19] Ibid. p. 8.

[20] Ibid. p. 9.

[21] Recommended with permission of the authors.

[22] The Autism Research Institute, newsletters and correspondence.

[23] Starling, Ernest H., The Wisdom of the Body – The Harveian Oration, H. K. Lewis and Co., Ltd., London, 1923. p. 6.

[24] Snow, Theodore P., *The Dynamic Universe*, Second Edition.. pgs. 3-4.

CHAPTER 13

Do we have a similar value?

One culture conspicuously absent from the comparisons made in the previous chapter is our own.[1] This culture may not have much standing *sub specie aeternitatis*, but here and now it has a certain call upon our attention, if only by virtue of being ours. What I have in mind here is Western culture in its prevailing modern form, which I would describe as broadly secular and liberal, though not necessarily irreligious. It seems to be readily compatible with a non-fundamentalist allegiance to a variety of traditional religions, including Judaism, Christianity and Islam. Does this culture possess a value similar to forbidding wrong?

1 Common ground

There is certainly no problem with the intelligibility – and indeed acceptability – of the basic idea of forbidding wrong in Western culture.[2] It is accordingly easy to apply the Islamic conception in a Western setting. A contemporary Muslim writing in Arabic tells a story about a Swede who told off a rich American tourist for speeding on a quiet Swedish country road; he comments aptly that this is an instance of forbidding wrong. (The American, of course, tells the Swede to mind his own business, but backs down in the face of the manifest solidarity of the Swedish bystanders with the author of the rebuke.)[3] But it is not just the basic idea that has this cross-cultural intelligibility. Almost everything of substance that Muslim scholasticism has to say about the doctrine can be understood by a Western reader who knows nothing about Islam; and a lot of it makes good sense. We can easily translate the doctrine of, say, the classical Imāmī scholars into plain English. It might go something like this: 'If you see someone doing something wrong, you ought to try to get them to stop. You should say something, or if that doesn't work, you should do something. Failing that, well, you can just wish them to stop. But

[1] 585.
[2] 585f.
[3] 585 n. 2.

don't get too violent – that's for the police. If somebody really ought to take a certain course of action, then you really ought to tell them to; but if it's just that it would be nice if they did, then maybe it's a nice idea to suggest it to them. If there's a lot of people there, and somebody else speaks out, you don't have to; but if nobody else does, it's up to you. But don't think you ought to jump in just like that. There may be several good reasons for keeping out of it, such as: "Come on, what's wrong with what he's doing?"; "Look, they've stopped anyway"; "Forget it – those people just don't listen"; "Forget it – he's bigger than you"; "Last time somebody told them to stop they smashed up his car"; "Try that and you'll just end up making matters worse."'

So far, the major respect in which the Muslim doctrine of forbidding wrong strikes us as alien is simply the scholastic manner of its presentation – whence my attempt to naturalise it by translating it into plain, rather than academic, English.[4] In part, this reflects a widespread feature of the moral thinking of Western populations today. Whatever people may say about us, we have our moral values, and we think, talk and argue about them. But we do not do so in a technical language characterised by formal definitions and rules. We might like to describe our moral language as more spontaneous, more nuanced, more sensitive to the uniqueness of each individual case. Others might call it subjective, arbitrary and inconsistent – a primitive and untutored colloquial. Whether our way of handling moral questions is a good thing or a bad thing is beside the point; what seems clear is that in this respect the Muslims have something we don't.

We do, of course, have moral philosophers in our universities. They are known to have a lot of sophisticated and inconclusive things to say about the foundations of morality, none of which they agree upon among themselves. But they have tended to provide us with relatively little direct assistance when it comes to thinking through the moral problems that most of us actually face. In any case, we are not in the habit of taking our moral dilemmas to moral philosophers, any more than a scientist would refer a research problem to a philosopher of science. Nor do they seem to expect us to consult them in this way.

This straightforward contrast between the scholastic moral thought of Islam and the vernacular thought of the modern West is not, however, quite right. For one thing, we can take it for granted that the overwhelming majority of Muslims down the ages did not think scholastically. For another, lawyers and philosophers in the West have in fact produced a body of systematic thought that is of some interest to us. This thought is not precisely concerned with our duty, but it does grapple with a theme sufficiently close to be relevant. The theme in question is the duty – assuming it is one – of rescue.

[4] 586f.

2 Rescue and forbidding wrong

The difference between rescue and forbidding wrong can be set out as follows.[5] The duty of rescue is by definition an obligation to come to the aid of people in trouble; whether or not the trouble is an intentional consequence of human wrongdoing is to this extent irrelevant. It is worth reconsidering here the case of the Chicago rape with which we began this book. If the woman had been the victim, not of rape, but of falling masonry in an earthquake, then – other things being equal – the bystanders would still have been under an obligation to try to assist her. Forbidding wrong, by contrast, is not a duty to help people in trouble, but rather to stop people doing wrong. In this case what is irrelevant is whether or not the wrongdoing has a human (or animal) victim. For example, if we assume for the sake of argument that consensual sex between an unmarried couple is wrong, then there would still have been a duty to stop the man having sex with the woman even if the two had been lovers. Each duty thus extends to an area that is foreign to the other. Where the woman is trapped by falling masonry, there is no wrong to be forbidden; where she is willingly having sex, there is no victim to be rescued.

But what of the intersection? When the man rapes the woman, we have both a wrongdoer and a victim. On this common ground, the two duties remain distinct in principle: one focuses on putting a stop to the wrongdoing, the other on coming to the aid of the victim. Yet in practice, things may not be so neatly compartmentalised. Real life is such that the two ideas are easily conflated, not to say confused, and the results are apparent both in our thinking and in that of the medieval Muslims.

On our side, the conflation is nicely illustrated by the disparity between the words and deeds of Randy Kyles, the hero of the events in Chicago. What he did was to ensure that a wrongdoer was brought to justice. Yet the reason he later gave for his conduct was that he 'had to do something to help that woman'. In other words, he presents himself as a good Samaritan; but what the Samaritan of the parable did was to attend to the needs of the victim, not to confront the long-departed robbers (Luke 10:29–37).[6] This confusion of roles may be conceptually infelicitous, but it articulates a basic psychological reality: when we see one person maltreating another, our anger against the perpetrator and our sympathy for the victim are two sides of the same emotional coin. It would be untrue to the emotions we characteristically feel in such cases to say, for example: 'I have every sympathy with rapists, it's just that unfortunately their actions are harmful to their victims.'

A similar conflation is latent on the Muslim side.[7] There is systematic thought in Islam about the duty of rescue, and in principle there should be no problem

[5] 587f.
[6] 588 n. 9.
[7] 588f.

distinguishing this from the doctrine of forbidding wrong. But in fact, most of what I have learnt of Muslim views on rescue derives from material incorporated into accounts of forbidding wrong. A particularly striking example is found in a major Ibāḍī account of the duty. Here at one point we encounter a statement of one's duty in a situation in which a boy is stuck up a palm-tree and shouting for help. This, clearly, is a case of rescue pure and simple: there is no question of any wrongdoing on the part of either the boy or the palm-tree, or of any right conduct that could be enjoined upon either. It is not, of course, that the Muslim scholars are unable to make the distinction between forbidding wrong and rescue when they want to, but rather that the border tends not to be well demarcated. Again, this corresponds to the way things are. In real life, it would surely go against the natural flow of emotion for a Muslim engaged in forbidding wrong to be a zealous antagonist of rapists and yet at the same time indifferent to the sufferings of their victims. In the reign of the caliph al-Muᶜtaḍid, the story goes, a tailor of Baghdad sought helpers to join him in confronting a high-ranking Turkish military officer who had abducted a beautiful young woman as she left the baths. He made his appeal in these terms: 'You know what this man has done. So come with me so that we can go and protest against him (*nunkir ᶜalayhi*) and save the woman from him.' In the circumstances, Randy Kyles might have said the same.

This close affinity between rescue and forbidding wrong is perhaps linked to a character trait shared by those who habitually practise them.[8] Modern Western study of rescuers suggests that, alongside their courage, they are marked by what might be described as the lack of a faculty of social discrimination found in normal human beings. A Silesian countess who helped Jews in the Second World War explained that she did so because they were persecuted, not because they were Jews; their ethnicity, she emphasised, 'was not important to me at all', though it was clearly very significant to many Jews and non-Jews at the time. But research suggests that it is not just ethnicity to which confirmed rescuers are blind: they do not discriminate, in the way that the rest of us do, between their kith and kin, on the one hand, and strangers, on the other. This trait would probably have been immediately recognisable to many medieval Muslims who made a practice of forbidding wrong. At a certain level we greatly admire such indifference, and we are sometimes ready to emulate it at the level of ethnicity – which for an educated Westerner today is usually not too difficult. But even such Westerners are much less likely to maintain this indifference where their friends and relations are concerned. In other words, habitual rescuers and inveterate forbidders of wrong may have something in common that separates them from humanity at large. The Silesian countess summed up her world-view in this way: 'You cannot just look at all this and do nothing. During my whole life, I've always been intervening in things I found unjust.' This is not how most of us think or act; if we intervene once

[8] 589f.

in a while, it is likely to be in reaction to something that touches us much more closely than 'all this'.[9] A pragmatic Yemeni ruler of the thirteenth century, refusing to take action against a pietist who had sabotaged plans for a party in Aden by pouring out large quantities of wine, remarked succinctly: 'Anyone who does that must be either a saint or a madman, and either way we have nothing to say to him.' He might perhaps have said the same about outstanding rescuers.

Be this as it may, we can conclude that rescue and forbidding wrong, though conceptually distinct, overlap in a sufficiently intimate way to make them broadly comparable. With that much established, we can go on to ask about the relative salience of systematic thought about the two duties in their respective cultures. My overwhelming impression is that the scholastic doctrine of forbidding wrong is far more salient in Islamic culture than the rather arcane discussion of rescue is in ours. The best evidence I can adduce for this is autobiographical: it was only as a by-product of my study of forbidding wrong in Islam that I became aware of the existence of a body of academic writing on the duty of rescue in my own culture.

3 Right and wrong

Muslim and Western notions of the duty to stop wrongdoing also differ in another important area: the understanding of right and wrong.[10] The differences are real, though not always as profound as they look.

Most obviously, there are significant differences as to which particular things are right and which are wrong. As we have seen repeatedly in this book, these differences are at their most colourful with regard to wine, women and song. Yet even here, Muslim norms are usually intelligible to us to the extent that they tend to be closely related to what we recognise as moral dangers. Mainstream Western culture has little use for an outright prohibition of alcohol; but we do not approve of drunken drivers or like to see people become alcoholics. Our ideas as to how women should be dressed and the degree to which they should be segregated, while puritanical by medieval West African standards, are a long way from traditional Islamic mores; yet we worry a great deal about the less desirable consequences of the interactions we permit between the sexes. It is perhaps only in the case of the stance of the Islamic scholars against music that cross-cultural intelligibility breaks down almost completely. It would be hard in the West to present the Saudi campaign against the mouth organs of the street urchins of Jedda as anything but comical. Yet even here, such attitudes to music can strike a chord in our past, not to mention the fringes of our present. There is, after all, nothing uniquely Islamic about puritans who do not like other people to have fun, and nothing exclusively

[9] 589 n. 13.
[10] 590–5.

Western or modern about disliking puritans. Nor should we forget one remarkable, if adventitious, convergence: middle-class America has come to regard smoking with an intolerance verging on that of unreconstructed Wahhābism. But whether we dwell on the similarities or the differences, the fact remains that questions about the rightness or wrongness of particular activities have only an indirect bearing on the way in which the duty itself is conceived. They are merely the circumstances that trigger it.

There is, however, a contrast between the Muslim and Western views of rights and wrongs that takes us somewhat closer to the core of the value. This has to do with conceptions of public and private. We can best approach this contrast by going back to the moral – or amoral – principle that is so often pitted against forbidding wrong: minding one's own business.

As we have seen, telling a busybody to mind his own business was a stock response to unwelcome attempts to forbid wrong in the traditional Islamic world.[11] The idea of minding one's own business is doubtless more complex than it looks in either Muslim or Western culture. Perhaps the main point to be made is that this value, though it may sound individualistic or parochial, is not necessarily so. What constitutes my business has as much to do with the social groups to which I belong as it does with the particular type of business in hand, and these groups may be large ones. For example, it was under the rubric of minding one's own business that, as a British child growing up in a Mediterranean country, I was counselled by fellow nationals not to interfere when the locals were cruel to animals. The corollary, I take it, was that within the British moral community cruelty to animals would indeed have been my business. A national group of this kind falls well short of embracing the entire human race, but it goes considerably beyond the social groups we usually encounter in everyday life.

In modern Western thought, the demarcation of our business tends to be dominated by a pair of strongly articulated principles. The first is that where wrongdoing inflicts harm on others, it is everybody's business. In accordance with this principle, we concern ourselves with violations of human rights in such culturally exotic regions as East Asia, the Middle East and Africa. Here our business is coterminous with that of the human race, and our censoriousness has no geographical or cultural bounds. As a black undergraduate at Princeton put it after being subjected to racial slurs, 'it's everyone's business when something like that happens'.[12] The second principle is that wrongdoing that affects only the wrongdoer is nobody's business but his own; indeed it may be argued that, for this very reason, there is no justification for calling it wrongdoing at all. In accordance with this second principle, we deny that moral puritans, social conservatives, missionaries and paternalists of all sorts have any business encroaching on our right to decide for ourselves how to live

[11] See above, ch. 8, section 5.
[12] 592 n. 21.

– and by extension, on the right of others to make the same decision for themselves. Here our business is transacted within the immunity of our castles, and would-be censors are contemptuously turned away. The two principles are in marked contrast to each other. But the combination is not illogical, and it makes very good sense – to us.

The situation in traditional Islamic thought is somewhat different, though once again not unrecognisably so. The distinction between wrongdoing that harms others and wrongdoing that affects only the wrongdoer is well established. The first is the business of a very large, though not in practice universal, group: the brotherhood of the Muslim community. If members of this community respond to fellow Muslims who reprove them for this kind of wrongdoing by telling them to mind their own business, this riposte will sound more like cynical irritation than moral outrage.

With regard to wrongdoing that does no harm to others, the situation in traditional Islamic thought is more complicated. It is beyond question that in Islamic terms such wrongdoing is indeed wrongdoing. This is related to the fact that it is necessarily the business of at least one other person, namely God; in other words, it is sin. But the most significant point for our purposes is perhaps that such wrongdoing, while not in itself the business of other members of the community, can nevertheless become so. As we have seen, while Islam has definite notions of privacy and gives them strong articulation, there seems to be a difference between Islamic and Western thinking along the following lines. In a Western perspective, certain kinds of behaviour tend to be thought of as an inherently private matter, whether or not they happen to become public knowledge. In Islamic thought, by contrast, such behaviour may be only contingently private. Wrongdoing that does not affect others will tend for that very reason to remain in the private domain; and by and large, it is urged, it should be allowed to remain there. But once it ceases to be private, the cat is out of the bag, and more drastic norms may properly come into play. Here the initial response to the censorious intruder that he should mind his own business does indeed bespeak a valid moral outrage; but the Muslim's home may in the event prove to be something less than his castle.

These differences between modern Western and traditional Islamic views have clear consequences in the modern Islamic world. As a consequence of the Western impact, the Muslim doctrine of forbidding wrong now confronts a conception of minding one's own business significantly different from its own. In the global setting in which we now live, there is a much stronger sense than before that the Muslim community is just one among others, and in consequence that it enjoys no monopoly of moral judgement. Its members are accordingly liable to be subjected to an unprecedented degree of moral scrutiny and condemnation from outside their own community. At the same time the focus of this scrutiny is often precisely on the attempts of zealous Muslims to impose their own standards of virtue on their co-religionists. Such zealots may be materially assisted in this by the power of the modern state, which has a way of turning castles into sandcastles. But in the long run such states seem not to be very successful in insulating the societies they rule against the global milieu, as the complaints of pietists about the responses they meet when forbidding wrong make clear. The prevalent Western values thus tell Muslims that it is *our* business how they treat other Muslims; and at the same time they tell them that it is not *their* business how other Muslims choose to live. Both messages involve sharp departures from the traditional – and modern – Islamic conception of forbidding wrong. It should not therefore be surprising that there has been considerable friction between Muslim and Western moral attitudes in such matters.

One example of this friction is a bruising exchange that took place between Āyatullāh Khumaynī and the Italian journalist Oriana Fallaci some months after the Iranian revolution.[13] With regard to the undemocratic direction in which the Islamic Republic was moving, Fallaci prompted Khumaynī to make these remarks: 'If you foreigners do not understand, too bad for you. It's none of your business, you have nothing to do with our choices. If some Iranians don't understand it, too bad for them. It means that they have not understood Islam.' Later Fallaci raised the even more contentious topic of the segregation of women. She made pointed reference to Islamic norms governing behaviour on the beach, and mischievously posed the question: 'By the way, how do you swim in a chador?' To this, Khumaynī responded tetchily: 'This is none of your business. Our customs are none of your business.' In claiming the standing to ask her impudent question, was Fallaci simply including herself in the brotherhood of all mankind? Or worse yet, was it her nefarious purpose to deny Khumaynī the standing to answer the question by virtue of his exclusion from the sisterhood of all womankind? It is striking that in the face of this provocation, Khumaynī should have been reduced to talking like the people of Ibn Tūmart's Dashr Qallāl; as one commentator indicates, an Āyatullāh might have been expected to appeal to a higher authority than local custom. Towards the end of the interview, Khumaynī's irritation increased perceptibly: 'And now that's enough. Go away. Go away.' Even at that point, however, Fallaci did not take her leave.

4 Concluding remarks

In conclusion, it is worth noting that the two major differences between Muslim and Western ideas discussed in this chapter are closely linked. The reason why Western thought concentrates on rescue and neglects forbidding wrong is bound up with the fact that in Western thought the category of victimless wrong – pure sin, so to speak – has been stripped of most of its practical moral significance, if not denied to exist altogether. 'They're not doing any harm' is regularly given as

[13] 595.

a sufficient reason for leaving them alone. If all wrongs must have victims, then what is left of the moral ground is covered by rescue. This, of course, takes us back to a fundamental point of tension between the two world-views: the standing, if any, of God in human affairs.

Index

ᶜAbbāsids, 65–7, 74, 109
ᶜAbd al-Ghanī al-Maqdisī (d. 1203), 102–3, 105
ᶜAbd al-Ghanī al-Nābulusī (d. 1731), 91–3, 95, 106
ᶜAbd al-Jabbār ibn Aḥmad al-Hamadhānī (d. 1025), 6, 45, 51
ᶜAbd al-Malik (r. 685–705), 67, 70
ᶜAbd al-Muᵓmin (r. 1130–63), 65
ᶜAbd al-Qādir al-Jazāᵓirī (d. 1883), 88
ᶜAbdallāh ibn al-Mubārak (d. 797), 78
ᶜAbdallāh ibn Farrūkh (d. 791), 81
ᶜAbdallāh ibn Muḥammad ibn ᶜAbd al-Wahhāb (d. 1826f.), 69, 125
ᶜAbdallāh ibn Shubruma (d. 761f.), 84
abduction, seizing of women, 30, 70, 73, 166
ᶜAbduh, Muḥammad (d. 1905), 113, 122–3, 131
Abū Bakr (r. 632–4), 86
Abū Ḥanīfa (d. 767f.), 6, 17, 34, 39, 81–2, 87
Abū ᵓl-ᶜAbbās al-Sarrāj (d. 925), 101
Abū ᵓl-Ḥusayn al-Baṣrī (d. 1044), 46–7, 51
Abū ᵓl-Layth al-Samarqandī (d. 983), 62, 90
Abū ᵓl-Qāsim al Balkhī (d. 931), 33
Abū Maḥallī (d. 1613), 108
Abū Muslim (d. 755), 74, 80
Abū Nuᶜaym al-Faḍl ibn Dukayn (d. 834), 67–8, 107
Abū Shuqqa, ᶜAbd al-Ḥalīm Muḥammad, 117
Abū Sulaymān al-Dārānī (d. 820f.), 90
Abū Yaᶜlā ibn al-Farrāᵓ (d. 1066), 40, 48–9, 56, 62, 76
Aden, 167
adultery, *see* sexual immorality
Afghanistan, 124
Africa, 168
Aghlabids, 108
Aḥmad ibn Naṣr (d. 846), 109
Aḥmad ibn Shabbawayh (d. 843), 76
Aḥsāᵓ, al-, 126
Ahura Mazdā, 157
Akhbārīs, 135
Āl al-Shaykh, Muḥammad ibn Ibrāhīm (d. 1969), 128–9
Albānī, Nāṣir al-Dīn al-, 117
alcoholism/alcoholics, 167
Alexandria, 109
Algeria, 122; French conquest of, 88
Algiers, 115
ᶜAlī (d. 661), 39, 66
ᶜAlī al-Qārī (d. 1606), 37, 88
ᶜAlī ibn Abī Ṭālib Foundation, 140
ᶜAlī Suᶜāvī (d. 1878), 113
ᶜAlids, 66
ᶜAllāma al-Ḥillī, al- (d. 1325), 42
Almohads, 65, 94
America, Americans, 163, 168

Āmidī (d. 1233), 38, 47
amphorae, *see* destruction of offending objects: wine vessels
ʿAmrī, Jalāl al-Dīn, 113, 116, 120
anarchy, 119–20
Anatolia, 59, 104–5
anger (in forbidding wrong), 36
animals, 165; cruelty to, 168; dogs, 99, 104–5; donkeys, 101; lizards (eating), 22–3; mules, 38–9; forbidding wrong, 104–5; slaughtering in street, 98; target of forbidding wrong, 21
Aquinas, Thomas (d. 1274), 154–6, 158
Arabia, 112, 147–52
Aristotle (d. 322 BC), 147
armed bands (in forbidding wrong), 30, 34–5, 70, 119–20, 123, 126
armed conflict (in forbidding wrong), 33, 41, 119–20; *see also* arms
Armenia, 109
arms (use of in forbidding wrong), 30, 33–4, 43, 119, 155; bow and arrow, 30, 33; knives, 39; sticks, 30, 33, 106, 129; swords, 33–4, 81–2, 107; whips, 33, 107
arson, 46, 52
Asfījāb, 60
Ashʿarism, Ashʿarites, 6, 8, 38, 46, 93, 111, 159
ʿAsīr, 110
Avicenna (d. 1037), 105
avoiding scene of wrongdoing, 39–41
ʿAwda, ʿAbd al-Qādir (d. 1954), 120, 129
Ayyūbids, 106
Azhar, 116, 119

Babylonia, 152
Babylonian Talmud, 153
Badr, Battle of, 81
Baghdad, 8, 33, 59, 67–8, 74, 76, 103–4, 109, 166
Bahāʾ al-Dīn al-ʿĀmilī (d. 1621), 20, 43
Baḥrayn, 135; *see also* Akhbārīs
Bājī (d. 1081), 46
Banū Sahm, 150
Banū Zubayd, 150
Barbahārī (d. 941), 33, 103
Barhebraeus (d. 1286), 158–9
baths, bath-houses, 25, 31, 73–4, 98–9, 105–6, 166
Bayānūnī, 116
Bāzargān, Mahdī (d. 1995), 132
beards, 138; *see also* shaving (beards)
beduin, xi
Beirut, 122
Belhadj, Ali, *see* Ibn Ḥājj, ʿAlī
belief, *see* enjoining belief
Bible, 152; Lev. 19:17, 152, 158; Luke 10:29–37, 165; Matt. 18:16, 155
Birgili (d. 1573), 71, 91–2
Bishr al-Ḥāfī (d. 841f.), 39, 83
Blackstone, William (d. 1780), 147
bonfires, *see* destruction of offending objects
Boumedienne, 115
bow and arrow, *see* arms
boys, 98; forbidding wrong, 13–14; targets of forbidding wrong, 21
Brahmins, 89
British, 128, 168
brothels, 74; *see also* sexual immorality/impropriety
B'rrāqī, 115
Buddha (*c.* fifth century BC), 148
Buddhism, 156–7
Byzantines, 151

cafés, 116
Cana, miracle of, *see* water (turning wine into)
cards (playing), *see* games
carnivals, 100
Catholicism (medieval), 153–6, 158–60

censor (*muḥtasib*), censorship (*ḥisba*), 5, 41, 63, 67–8, 71, 91–2, 98, 106, 128, 131, 142, 149–50, 152
Chaudry, Muhammad Sharif, 116
cheating (customers), 100
chess, chessboards, *see* games
Chicago, 1–2, 165
Chicago Tribune, 1
children: forbidding wrong, 13–14, 16; leading prayers, 117; target of forbidding wrong, 21
China, 148, 152, 157
chivalry (European), 103
Christians, Christianity: Catholic, *see* Catholicism (medieval); Copts, 74, 101; Greek, 159; Monophysite, 8, 158–9; Syriac, 158
Chrysippus (d. 207 BC), 147
churches, 67, 87, 159
cinema, 116
civility (when forbidding wrong), 29, 78
clothing, 138, 167; forbidden, 74, 98, 129; Islamic, 128; second-hand clothing, 98; washing clothing, 108
coffee, 125
collective obligation (forbidding wrong as), 19–21
Cologne, eau de, 128
colonialism, 136, 138
Committee for Commanding Right and Forbidding Wrong, 126–7
common people (forbidding wrong), 17, 47, 124
Companions of the Prophet, 4, 75, 78, 83, 86–7
compensation for damage in destroying offending objects, 31; *see also* liabilities
Confucianism, 156–7
Confucius (d. 479 BC), 157
Constitutional Revolution (1906, Iran), 133
constitutionalism, constitutional government, 113, 123
Copts, *see* Christians, Christianity
corpses (washing), 40
craftsmen, 104

Damascus, 87, 90, 94, 100
dancing, 115; war-dance, 127
danger condition in forbidding wrong, 46–7, 51, 53–6, 76–8, 135, 140
Dārayyā, 90
Darwaza, Muḥammad ʿIzzat (d. 1984), 116, 120
Dashr Qallāl, 94–5, 170
Dawānī (d. 1502), 24
Dāwūd ibn Nuṣayr al-Ṭāʾī (d. 781f.), 78, 90
decorative images, 31, 98–9, 104
decorators, 104
democracy, 115
Denizli, 105; *see also* Laodicea
destruction of offending objects, 29–32, 39–40, 58–9, 119; bonfires (used to destroy offending objects), 125; chessboards, *see* games; decorative images, 31; illustrations, 104; musical instruments, 29–32, 40, 101, 104–5, 125, 143; sacred trees, 31, 93; tobacco pipes, 31, 125; wine, 29–32, 38–9, 103, 167; wine vessels, 30, 39, 59, 100, 106, 115
deterrence, *see* future wrongdoing
devil, the, 80, 93
dignity of the faith (Islam), 55; *see also* elevation of the faith
Dilāʾ, 108
disagreement of scholars/law-schools on forbidding wrong, 22–3
drinking, 24, 45–6, 51, 57, 60–1, 70–1, 73, 99–100, 105, 115–16, 159; setting out wine glasses, 25; *see also* wine

drugs, dealing, 141; *see also* medicine
drunken drivers, 167
drunkenness, drunkards, 53, 62, 70, 98, 128
dung, use in spoiling wine, 31

East Asia, 168
eating, 40; forbidden things, 74, 99; with the left hand, 24
eavesdropping, *see* spying
efficacy condition for forbidding wrong, 46–51, 140
Egypt, 61, 66, 74, 87, 93, 119–20, 123
Elᶜazar ben ᶜAzariah, Rabbi, 153
elevation of the faith (Islam), 56; *see also* dignity of the faith
emigration (from land where wrongdoing prevails), 39–40
enjoining belief, 3
escalation, 42–3
eulogies (of kings), 125
Europe, 113, 116, 120–1, 133
exception to duty (to advocate good and denounce evil), xi
exhortation (in correcting wrong), 28
exile, 126

facial expression (in forbidding wrong), 36–7, 39
Fakhr al-Dīn al-Rāzī (d. 1210), 159
Fallaci, Oriana, 170
fasting, 68
fathers as targets of forbidding wrong, 29
Fatimah Jinnah Medical College, 116
female infanticide, 61
Fez, 94, 103–4
Filipinos, 128
flogging, 79, 100, 103–4, 106, 126
flutes, *see* musical instruments
food, *see* eating
fornication, 136, 165
foul language, 126
France, 116
freedom of association, 114
freedom of opinion and expression, 114, 132
freedom of the press, 113
frowning, *see* facial expression
Fuḍayl ibn ᶜIyāḍ (d. 803), 78, 88
fundamentalism/fundamentalists, Islamic, 115–22, 125, 129
future, 86–88
future wrongdoing, preventing, 24–5, 47–8

Gabriel, 3
gambling, 141
games: chess, chessboards, 14, 22, 30, 59, 74; playing cards, 116
Gardet, Louis, 115
Ghazzālī (d. 1111), xi, 4, 6, 8–9, 13–16, 18, 21–5, 27–9, 31–8, 40–1, 47–55, 59, 61, 70, 73–9, 82–3, 90–1, 98–9, 102, 105, 116–20, 122–3, 129, 131, 143, 155, 159, 161
Gīlān, 100
gnostics, 37, 88
goldsmiths, 74, 79–80
Goldziher, Ignaz, 152
gossip, 61, 139
gramophone, *see* musical instruments
Greeks, 105, 159

Hādī, al- (d. 911), 66–7, 80
ḥadīth, 3, 5
Ḥāfiẓ (d. 1389), 89, 94
hair, 138; cutting, 124; improperly covered, 74
Ḥakīm, Muḥammad Bāqir al-, 133
Ḥākim al-Jishumī, al- (d. 1101), 80
Ḥakīm ibn Umayya, 149
Ḥalīmī (d. 1012), 18, 62, 70
Hamadānī, Ḥusayn al-Nūrī al-, 136–8

Ḥanafīs, 5–6, 8, 17, 22–3, 32–3, 37, 40, 42, 46, 50, 62, 69, 75, 77, 81–2, 84, 86–7, 89, 91, 93, 111, 118–19
Ḥanbalites, 5–6, 8, 14, 17, 24, 31–4, 40, 46–50, 56, 59, 75–7, 82, 84–5, 101–4, 112, 127
hand (forbidding wrong with), 15, 17, 27, 29–36, 39, 45, 81, 119–20, 123, 144, 155
Ḥarrān, 103
harsh language (in forbidding wrong), 28–9, 52, 76–7, 118, 155
Hārūn al-Rashīd (r. 786–809), 106
Ḥasan al-Bannā (d. 1949), 119
Ḥasan al-Baṣrī (d. 728), 78, 82, 84
Ḥasan ibn Ṣāliḥ ibn Ḥayy (d. 783f.), 81–2
Ḥashwiyya, 84–5
Ḥawwā, Saᶜīd (d. 1989), 115, 118, 120, 123
Ḥaydarīzāde Ibrāhīm Efendi (Ottoman Shaykh al-Islām, d. 1931), 118
heart (forbidding wrong with/in), 15, 17, 27, 35–9, 43, 45, 83, 88, 118, 124
Herat, 103–4
heresy, heretics, 89, 98–9
Ḥijāz, 125–6
Ḥīra, 82
Hishām ibn Ḥakīm ibn Ḥizām (d. 656?), 79, 103
holy war, 19, 75, 79–80, 89, 91, 95, 136, 160
home (committing wrong in), 73; illegal occupation of, 99; sanctity of, 57–8, 129, 142
honey, turning wine into, 38
hospitality, 98–9
human rights, 114, 133, 168
humiliation of the faith (Islam), 56
humour (improper), 99
Ḥusayn (d. 680), 134, 136
Ḥusayn, Aḥmad, 120
hypocrites, 70
Ibāḍīs, 5, 7–8, 14–15, 17, 21, 23, 27, 32–5, 38, 47, 50, 52, 60, 63, 66–9, 71, 75, 77, 80, 85, 100, 108, 112, 166
Ibn ᶜAbbād al-Rundī (d. 1390), 89
Ibn Abī Dhiᵓb (d. 775f.), 108
Ibn al-ᶜAbbās, ᶜAbdallāh (d. 687f.), 78–9
Ibn al-ᶜArabī, Abū Bakr (d. 1148), 33, 161
Ibn al-ᶜArīf (d. 1141), 78
Ibn al-Ḥājj (d. 1336f.), 71
Ibn al-Jawzī (d. 1201), 34, 76–9
Ibn al-Naḥḥās (d. 1411), 93
Ibn al-Qiṭṭ (tenth century), 108
Ibn al-Rabīᶜ al-Khashshāb (d. 956f.), 57, 62
Ibn Baraka (tenth century), 15, 77
Ibn Baṭṭūṭa (d. 1368f.), 103, 105
Ibn Ḥajar al-ᶜAsqalānī (d. 1449), 82
Ibn Ḥājj, ᶜAlī, 115–16, 120–3
Ibn Ḥanbal (d. 855), 6, 8, 14, 29, 31, 33, 40, 50, 58–9, 71–2, 76–7, 85, 88, 93, 109
Ibn Ḥazm (d. 1064), 6, 14–15, 34, 81, 113
Ibn Hubayra (d. 1165), 102
Ibn Karrām (d. 869), 100; *see also* Karrāmiyya
Ibn Khaldūn (d. 1406), 82
Ibn Masᶜūd, ᶜAbdallāh (d. 652f.), 83, 86, 93
Ibn Paquda (eleventh century), 158
Ibn Qayyim al-Jawziyya (d. 1350), 82
Ibn Qudāma (d. 1223), 40
Ibn Rajab (d. 1393), 77–8
Ibn Rushd (the elder, d. 1126), 19, 46–7, 87
Ibn Saᶜūd (r. 1902–52), 127
Ibn Shuᶜba (tenth century), 134
Ibn Ṭāwūs (d. 1266), 40
Ibn Taymiyya (d. 1328), 52–3, 57, 69, 82, 100, 119
Ibn Tūmart (d. 1130), 94–5, 170

Ibrāhīm al-Matbūlī (d. 1472), 37, 88
ignorance (wrong resulting from), 28
imam, 66, 69, 80; permission of in forbidding wrong, 24, 134, 137
Imāmīs, 5–8, 12–13, 16, 18–20, 23–4, 27, 29, 34–7, 39–43, 46–51, 53–6, 66, 69, 71, 75, 77, 80, 85, 112, 131–45, 159, 163
imperialism, 138
India, 35, 157
individual obligation, forbidding wrong as, 19–21
individualism, 115
inheritance rights, 101
injustice, 84
Iran, 5, 7–8, 71, 85, 94, 100, 132–44; *see also* Constitutional Revolution, Islamic Republic, Islamic revolution, Khumaynī, Shah, Supreme Guide
Iranian revolution, *see* Islamic revolution
Islāmī Ardakānī, Sayyid Ḥasan, 142–4
Islamic Republic, 131, 137, 140, 142–3; *see also* Iran, Islamic revolution
Islamic revolution (1979), 132, 141, 143, 170
Ismāᶜīl (khedive of Egypt, r. 1863–79), 116
ᶜIṣmat Allāh ibn Aᶜẓam (d. 1720f.), 35, 89
Istanbul, 92
ᶜIyāḍ ibn Ghanm (d. 640f.), 79

Jaᶜfar al-Ṣādiq (d. 765), 16, 77
Jāhilī poetry, 149, 151
Jāhiliyya, 149–50, 161
Jahm ibn Ṣafwān (d. 746), 108
Jamāl al-Dīn al-Qāsimī (d. 1914), 118
Jaṣṣāṣ (d. 981), 42, 84
Jayṭālī (d. 1349f.), 35, 52–3
Jedda, 125, 127–8, 167
Jenne, 101
Jeroboam, 152
Jerusalem, 152–3
Jews, 89, 158, 166; *see also* Rabbinic Judaism
journalists, 114, 170
Jubayr ibn Nufayr (d. 699f.), 87
Jubbāʾī, Abū ᶜAlī al- (d. 916), 12
Jubbāʾī, Abū Hāshim al- (d. 933), 12
Judaism, *see* Rabbinic Judaism; *see also* Jews
Jurhum, 150
Justice, 153
Juwaynī (d. 1085), 22, 33, 38, 81, 113

Kaᶜb al-Aḥbār (d. 654f.), 87
Karaites, 158
Karrāmiyya, 100
Kātib Chelebi (d. 1657), 93
Khālid al-Daryūsh (ninth century), 109
Khalīlī (d. 1871), 14, 16
Khāminaʾī, 137
Khārijites, 5, 80, 82, 106, 108
Kharrāzī, Muḥsin al-, 136–7, 140
Khaṭṭābī (d. 998), 78
Khayr al-Dīn Pāshā (d. 1890), 113
Khubūshānī (d. 1191), 106
Khūʾī, Abū ʾl-Qāsim al- (d. 1992), 135
Khumaynī (Ayatullāh, d. 1989), 8, 132, 134–7, 139–41, 170
Khurāsān, 108
Khwānsārī (d. 1985), 135
killing (in forbidding wrong), 33–4, 42–3, 51, 137
kinship (in forbidding wrong), 141, 166
kissing in public, 115
knives, *see* arms
Koran, 3, 6–7, 9, 12, 54, 61, 69, 104, 109, 117, 131, 134, 136, 151; *see also* Koranic verses

Koranic verses, 114, 121, 133, 152; (Q2:189), 58; (Q2:195), 77; (Q2:228), 14; (Q2:256), 91; (Q3:102), 11; (Q3:104), 3, 11, 17, 19, 113–14, 121–2, 132, 138; (Q3:110), 3, 66, 159; (Q4:34), 14; (Q5:79), 121; (Q5:105), 85–7, 94; (Q9:67), 70; (Q9:71), 3, 14, 16, 116–17, 134; (Q9:112), 121; (Q16:125), 119; (Q24:27), 58; (Q31:17), 54; (Q33:33), 14; (Q49:9), 42; (Q49:12), 58, 129; (Q51:55), 50
Kudamī (tenth century), 15
Kūfa (in Iraq), 4, 67, 81–2, 104
Kurds, xi
Kyles, Randy, 1–2, 165–6

Laodicea, 105; *see also* Denizli
laymen, *see* common people
leaving scene of wrongdoing, 39; *see also* emigration
Lebanon, 119
legal competence of those being forbidden, 21; of those forbidding, 20
liabilities, 99; *see also* compensation
libertinism, 115
liquor, *see* wine
liquor stores, 120
littering, 98
lizards, *see* animals
lunatics, 98; exclusion from duty to forbid wrong, 13; target of forbidding wrong, 21
Luqmān, 54
lutes, *see* musical instruments
luxurious living, 74, 101

madmen, *see* lunatics
Madrid (newspaper), 124
Maghīlī (d. 1503f.), 101
Maḥammad ibn Abī Bakr al-Dilāʾī (d. 1636), 108
Mahdī, al- (r. 775–85), 71
Maḥmūd al-Naᶜᶜāl (d. 1212), 103
Maimonides (d. 1204), 158
Mālik (d. 795), 6, 39–40, 48–9, 53, 70, 73, 75, 77, 79, 107–8
Malik al-ᶜĀdil, al- (r. 1196–1218), 106
Mālikīs, 6, 8, 17, 19–20, 31, 33, 46–7, 49, 51, 56–7, 59, 71, 77, 87, 103, 107–8
Malkum Khān, Mīrzā (d. 1908), 133
Mamlūks, 74
Maʾmūn, al- (r. 813–33), 59, 67, 74, 79, 95, 106–7, 109
mandolins, *see* musical instruments
Mānkdīm (d. 1034), 42, 45–8, 51, 55, 68
Manṣūr, al- (r. 754–75), 65
Manṣūr al-Qāsim ibn Muḥammad, al- (d. 1620), 43
markets, market-place, 40–1, 67, 73, 98, 125, 129
Martin, Daisy, 1–2
martyrdom, 55, 74, 76, 91, 136
Marw, 74, 79–80
Marwān (governor of Medina, d. 685), 4
Mashhad, 136
Masᶜūd, ᶜAbd al-ᶜAzīz al-, 117–18, 119
Masᶜūd, Muḥammad ᶜAlī, 124
Maṭᶜanī, ᶜAbd al-ᶜAẓīm Ibrāhīm al-, 119–20, 144
Māturīdism, Māturīdites, 6, 8
Māwardī (d. 1058), 4, 6, 41, 63
Mawlawī, Shaykh Fayṣal, 116, 120–1
Maymūn ibn Mihrān al-Raqqī (d. 735f.), 78
Māzandarān, 71
Mazātī (d. 1078f.), 50
Mecca, 31, 74, 117, 122, 125–8, 149–50; *see also* Sharīf of Mecca
medicine, 98; pills (forbidden), 128
Medina, 4, 29, 40, 74, 106–7, 122, 125, 127
Mencius (fourth century BC), 157

Mesopotamia, 79
Middle East, 168
missionaries, 123
modernism, Islamic, 112–15
Moghul India, 89
Mongols, 53
monotheism, 157–9, 161
Morocco, 102
mosques, 30–1, 73, 87, 92, 98, 101, 115, 125–6, 159
mothers as targets of forbidding wrong, 29
motorcycles, 128
mouth organs, *see* musical instruments
Mubarqa^{c} (ninth century), 108
muezzins, 98
Muḥammad, *see* Prophet Muḥammad
Muḥammad al-Bāqir (d. *c.* 736), 54, 134
Muḥammad ibn ^{c}Abd al-Wahhāb (d. 1792), 112, 125
Muḥammad ibn ^{c}Alī al-Idrīsī (r. 1908f.–1923), 110
Muḥammad ibn Ismā^{c}īl (d. 1536), 107
Muḥammad ibn al-Munkadir (d. 747f.), 106
Muḥammad ibn Muṣ^{c}ab (d. 843), 104
Muḥaqqiq al-Ḥillī (d. 1277), 49
Muḥsin al-Fayḍ (d. 1680), 37, 71, 77
Muhtadī, al- (r. 869–70), 65
Mujbira (predestinationists), 84, 86
mules, *see* animals
Munshi Ihsanullah, 127
Muntaẓirī, Ḥusayn-^{c}Alī, 133, 136, 138
Muqaddas al-Ardabīlī (d. 1585), 43
Muraqqish al-Akbar, 151
murder, 84
Murtaḍā, al-Sharīf al- (d. 1044), 46, 49, 56
music, 31–2, 40, 45, 58, 60–1, 63, 65–7, 73, 94, 99–101, 104–5, 116, 126; martial music, 32; singing, 31, 71, 100, 167; *see also* musical instruments, singing-girls
musical instruments, 29–32, 58–60, 98–9, 123, 125; drums, 40; flutes, 30, 70; gramophone, 127; lutes, 58, 61, 71, 101; mandolins, 105; mournful pipe, 32; mouth organs, 127, 167; tambourines, 32, 125; war-drums, 125; *see also* destruction of offending objects
Muslim (d. 875), 7, 12
Muslim Brotherhood/Brothers, 119–20
Muslims: forbidding wrong, 11–13; non-Wahhābī, 39; target of forbidding wrong, 13, 21
Mu^{c}taḍid, al- (r. 892–902), 91, 166
Muṭahharī, Murtaḍā (d. 1979), 131, 136–7, 139–40, 142–3
Mutawakkil, al- (r. 847–61), 77
Mu^{c}tazilites, 6, 8, 12, 19, 21, 23–5, 27, 33–4, 38, 41–2, 45–6, 48, 50–1, 55–6, 69, 80, 84–5, 109, 114, 131
Muwayliḥī (d. 1930), 114

Najd, 112, 127
Nawawī (d. 1277), 36, 49–50
Nawrūz (celebration of), 74
New York Times, 1–2
Nīshāpūr, 101
non-Muslims, 74, 79, 123; forbidding wrong, 13
normative practice, 4, 107, 109
nudity, 99, 101, 107, 115, 123, 148
Nūrī, Abū ʾl-Ḥusayn al- (d. 907f.), 91, 93–4
nurse, 134

offending objects, 29–32, 58, 98; alternative licit use for, 30–1; concealment of, 58–9; *see also* destruction of offending objects, musical instruments, precious metals
Ohrmazd, 157
Oman, 67, 107, 109

ostracism (in forbidding wrong), 37, 39
Ottomans, 71, 83, 92, 109–10, 113, 118

pagan societies, 115, 121
paint (sipping), 128
Palestine, 102, 108, 123
Palgrave, W. G., 126
Pāli canon, 148, 156–7
pantheists, 89
parents as targets of forbidding wrong, 21, 40
Paris, 133
past wrongs, 47–8
pen (forbidding wrong with), 124
perfume, *see* Cologne, eau de
persistence of wrongdoing, 24, 48
persons obligated to forbid wrong, 13–21; *see also* children, common people, legal competence, Muslims, non-Muslims, political authorities, scholars, sinners, slaves, women
Peshawar, 114
Peter the Venerable (d. 1156), 158
Pharaoh, 66, 106–7; *see also* tyrants
photographs, 116
pilgrimage, 126
pills, 128; *see also* medicine
plunder, 87
poetry (love), 125
police, 164
political authorities, 170; forbidding wrong by, 17, 32–5, 65–72, 118–29, 137; permission of in forbidding wrong, 30, 34–5, 123; as targets of forbidding wrong, 22, 28, 53, 73–82, 102, 105–8
polytheists/polytheism, 39, 125; *see also* Muslims: non-Wahhābī
posters, 116
prayer, 40, 68, 98, 101, 108, 115, 125–7, 139; failure to wash before, 25; improper performance of, 28, 98–9; non-attendance, non-performance, 24, 126, 129, 134, 141; roll-calls, 126
precious metals, 98–9
press, *see* freedom of the press
Princeton (University), 168
privacy, 168–9; in forbidding wrong, 29, 57–63, 78–9, 129, 141–4
Prophet Muḥammad, 3–5, 12, 14, 22, 36, 81, 86, 94, 122, 150
prostitution, 100, 105
proximity of wrong, 25
public, concept of, 168; forbidding wrong in, 29; public affirmation of the norms of Islam, 50
public disorder, 30, 52
purity of intention (in forbidding wrong), 78

Qāḍīzādelis, 92–3, 104
Qaffāl (d. 976), 159
Qāhir, al- (r. 932–4), 65
Qāᶜida, al-, xi
Qarᶜāwī, ᶜAbdallāh al- (d. 1969), 129
Qirqisānī, 158
Qumm, 142
Quranī, ᶜAlī ibn Ḥasan al-, 128
Quraysh, 81, 149–50
Quṭb, Sayyid (d. 1966), 115, 121–2, 124

Rabbanites, 158
Rabbinic Judaism, 153–4, 158–60
racial slurs, 168
radio, 116
Rāfiḍa, 85
rape, rapists, 1–2, 38, 165–6
Rāshid, Muḥammad Aḥmad al-, 121, 123
reason as source of obligation to forbid wrong, 12–13, 42
rebellion against unjust rulers, 52–3, 79–82, 87, 108–10, 160; *see also* public disorder

religious police/policing, 124–8, 140, 143
removal of wrongdoer, 29
rescue, 165–7, 170–1
Resurrection, 141
revelation as source of obligation to forbid wrong, 12, 42
revolution, 113; *see also* Islamic revolution
Riḍā, Rashīd (d. 1935), 113, 122–3, 131, 159
righting wrong, 4, 12; in Shīᶜite tradition, 4; in Sunnī tradition, 4
Riyāḍ, 126, 128
Rome, 152
rudeness, *see* harsh language
rulers, *see* political authorities

Saᶜadya (d. 942), 158
Sabbath, 152
Sabt, Khālid al-, 117, 119, 121, 129
Saᶜdī (d. 1292), 143
Sahāranpūr, 35, 89
Sahl ibn Salāma (ninth century), 109
Saḥnūn (d. 854), 71, 77
Saᶜīd ibn al-Musayyab (d. 712f.), 62, 71
Saᶜīd Muḥammad Aḥmad Bā Nāja, 114
saints (forbidding wrong), 17, 88
Saladin (r. 1169–93), 74, 105–6
Ṣāliḥī, Zayn al-Dīn al- (d. 1452), 8, 35, 38–9, 71, 85
Sālimī (d. 1914), 14
salt used in spoiling wine, 31, 59
Samaritan, good, 165
Sāmarrāʾī, Fārūq al-, 124
sandals, 33, 101
Saudis, Saudi Arabia, 31–2, 39, 65, 67, 69, 110, 112, 120, 125–9, 140, 167
Sayyid, Riḍwān al-, 122
scholars, forbidding wrong, 17–18, 47, 102–3, 124; targets of forbidding wrong, 22
scowling, *see* facial expression
Seconal, 128
Second World War, 119, 166
sectarian allegiances, 5–7
Seljūqs, 74
sexual immorality/impropriety, 13, 59–60, 67–8, 83, 99–101, 107, 115, 128; *see also* prostitution
Shabistarī, Aḥmad Ṭayyibī (d. 1971), 134, 136–40, 144
Shāfiᶜī (d. 820), 6
Shāfiᶜites, 5–6, 17–18, 22–4, 27, 33, 36, 47, 49, 51, 62, 75, 77, 81–2, 87, 93, 101, 106, 111, 159
Shah (of Iran), 132, 135
Shahīd al-Awwal (d. 1384), 42
Shahīd al-Thānī, al- (d. 1557f.), 36
Shāhnāma, 104
Sharīᶜatī, ᶜAlī (d. 1977), 132, 138
Sharīᶜatmadārī, Kāẓim (d. 1986), 135, 139–40
Sharif, Nasreen, 116
Sharīf of Mecca, 125
Shaukat Hussain, 114
shaving (beards), 116
Shaykhīs, 85
Shīᶜites, Shīᶜite tradition, 5–6, 12, 40, 56, 81, 85, 108, 112, 142; righting wrong, 4
Shīrāzī, Muḥammad Ḥusaynī, 135, 137, 139
Shuᶜayb ibn Ḥarb (d. 811f.), 107
side-effects condition of forbidding wrong, 30, 33, 45–6, 51–3, 81–2, 135–6
Silesian countess, 166
silk, 98–9
sin, 169
singing, *see* music, singing-girls
singing-girls, 65–6, 99, 100
sinners, exclusion from duty to forbid wrong, 18
slaves, 74, 101, 105, 160; forbidding wrong, 13–14, 16, 28
smoking, 125–6, 168; *see also* tobacco, tobacco pipes

social avoidance (in forbidding wrong), 37; *see also* ostracism
sodomy, 128
soldiers, officers, 67–8, 73, 101, 107, 166
solitary life, 41, 83
Solomon, 152
Songhay, 101
sons forbidding wrong, 28, 62
Spain, 89, 108
spiritual energy (*himma*) (in forbidding wrong), 37–9; *see also* supernatural intervention
spying (on neighbours), 58, 61–3, 129, 142–3
Sri Lankans, 128
staring at women, 25
state, *see* political authorities
sticks, *see* arms
Stoics, 147, 151
street (committing wrong in), 73, 98, 129; *see also* public disorder
Successors, 75, 77
Ṣūfīs, Ṣūfism, 7, 93–4, 102, 104–6, 109; forbidding wrong, 15, 36–7, 38–9, 61, 78, 88–93
Sufyān al-Thawrī (d. 778), 40, 61, 71, 77, 106–7
suicide, 56, 77, 136
Sulaym, 149
Sulaymān ibn Mihrān al-Aᶜmash (d. 765), 104–5
Suleymān (Ottoman sultan, r. 1520–66), 113
Sunāmī (fourteenth century), 90
sunna, *see* normative practice
Sunnīs, Sunnī tradition, 5–7, 11–12, 22–3, 27, 33–5, 38, 40, 42, 56, 58, 65–6, 77, 80–1, 84, 100, 108, 111–29, 131–4, 137–8, 141–5; righting wrong, 4
supernatural intervention, 38–9; *see also* spiritual energy (*himma*)
Supreme Guide, 137, 141
Swedes, 163
swords, *see* arms
Syria, 53, 87–8
Syriac Christianity, 158–9

Ṭabarī (d. 923), 22, 81, 86
tact (use in correcting wrong), 28; *see also* civility
Ṭāghūtī regime, 141
tailors, 104, 166
Ṭālibān, 124–5
Talmud, *see* Babylonian Talmud
Tᶜang dynasty (China, 618–907), 148
Ṭanṭāwī, Muḥammad Sayyid, 119
targets of forbidding wrong, 21–2; *see also* animals, children, legal competence, lunatics, Muslims, non-Muslims, parents, political authorities, teachers
Ṭāshköprīzāde (d. 1561), 33–4
taxes, tax collection, 67; illegal collection of, 42–3, 51, 74, 101, 106
teachers as targets of forbidding wrong, 22
tear-gas, 115
television, 116
temporary marriage, 23
temptation, 99
terminology of forbidding wrong, 3–5, 17
terrorism, xi, 120
theft, 101
thorns (transport of), 98
Tihrānī, ᶜAlī, 136
tobacco, 125; *see also* smoking, tobacco pipes
tobacco pipes, 32; *see also* destruction of offending objects, smoking, tobacco
Toledo, 102
tongue (forbidding wrong with), 15, 17, 27–9, 36, 39, 43, 45, 50, 80, 91, 124, 129

torture, 74, 79
tourists, 163
toy animals, *see* decorative images
traditionalists, 111
traditions, 3–4
Transoxania, 60, 108
trees: destruction of sacred trees, 31, 90, 93; rescue from palm-tree, 166
Tunisia, 108
Turks, 101
Turkī ibn ᶜAbdallāh (r. 1823–34), 65
Turkish dynasties, 17
Ṭūsī, Abū Jaᶜfar al- (d. 1067), 20, 77, 133
tyrants, 66; *see also* Pharaoh

ᶜUmar ibn al-Khaṭṭāb (r. 634–44), 58, 129, 142
ᶜUmāra, Muḥammad, 113–14
Umayyad clan, 149
Umayyads, 67, 108
ᶜUnayza, 129
unbelief (forbidding unbelief/unbelievers), 36
Universal Declaration of Human Rights, 114; *see also* human rights
ᶜUqba ibn ᶜĀmir (d. 677f.), 61, 71
ᶜUqbānī (d. 1467), 87
usury, 98, 116
ᶜUthmān (r. 644–56), 67
ᶜUthmān, Fatḥī, 116–17

vandalism, 104
videos, 140
vinegar, 38, 59; turning wine into, 38
vines (growing for wine), 40
violence in forbidding wrong, 30, 32–4, 43, 69, 71, 82, 85, 118–20, 124, 134, 137, 153, 159, 164; *see also* armed bands, arms, flogging, killing, whipping, wounding

Wahhābīs, Wahhābism, 67, 112, 126–7, 168
Walīd (r. 705–15), 87
war-drums, *see* musical instruments
water, improper discharge of, 98–9; turning wine into, 38
watermelons, pelting with rind, 127; scattering rind, 98
ways of forbidding wrong, 27–43; *see also* anger, arms, avoiding scene of wrongdoing, civility, destruction of offending objects, exhortation, facial expression, hand, harsh language, heart, leaving scene of wrongdoing, ostracism, privacy, public, rape, removal of wrongdoer, social avoidance, spiritual energy, sticks, tact, tongue, violence
weddings, 32, 125, 143
West, culture/thought, 163–71; influence, 111–15, 132–3; Latin West, 154, 158
whipping, 106
whips, *see* arms
William of Auxerre (d. 1231), 156
wine, 29–32, 38–40, 58–9, 61, 65, 67, 74, 83, 91, 93, 99–100, 103, 105, 115, 123, 126, 128, 167; licit, 32; *see also* destruction of offending objects, drinking, drunkenness, dung, honey, salt, vinegar, vines, water
wives forbidding wrong, 28, 62
women, 71, 98–100, 107, 116, 123, 129, 139–40, 160, 167; forbidding wrong, 13–16, 104, 116–18, 134; segregation of women, 126, 167, 170; *see also* abduction/seizing, staring at women, wives
wounding in forbidding wrong, 34, 137

wrongs to be forbidden, 22–5; *see also* animals, drinking, eating, future wrongdoing, games, music, persistence of wrongdoing, polytheists/polytheism, prayer, proximity of wrong, staring at women, temporary marriage, unbelief

Yaḥyā Ḥamīd al-Dīn (r. 1904–48), 109
Yaḥyā ibn Ḥamza (d. 1348f.), 14, 116
Yemen, 5, 66–7, 109, 167
Yūsuf al-Barm (eighth century), 108
Yūsuf Khān Mustashār al-Dawla, Mīrzā (d. 1895f.), 133

Zamakhsharī (d. 1144), 51
Zaydān, ᶜAbd al-Karīm, 117, 123
Zaydīs, 5–8, 14, 23–5, 27, 31, 33–4, 38, 42–3, 45–6, 49–50, 52, 55, 59–60, 66–7, 71, 80, 108, 112, 114, 116
Zayn al-Dīn, Muḥammad Amīn (d. 1998), 135
Zelators, 126
Zilfī, 128
Zindīqs, 89
Zionism, 138
Zoroastrianism, Zoroastrians, 84, 156–7